The Gaucho Genre

DATE DUE

The Gaucho Genre

A Treatise on the Motherland

Josefina Ludmer

TRANSLATED BY MOLLY WEIGEL

Duke University Press   Durham and London 2002

© Duke University Press   All rights reserved
Printed in the United States of America on acid-free paper ∞
Typeset in Adobe Minion by G&S Typesetters, Inc.
Library of Congress Cataloging-in-Publication Data
appear on the last printed page of this book.

In memory of my father.

For my son.

Contents

Prologue to the second Spanish edition

This book was written out of the absolutist idea that the critical imagination is purely verbal. Therefore it is deployed in a series of words that are set in motion through contact with another, sonorous, verbal universe, that of the gaucho genre, whose substance is the relation between heard voices and written words. The writers of the genre used the positions and tones of the gaucho's voice in order to write the genre, and in that same moment gave the gaucho his voice. "Use" and "gift"—the words that organize *The Gaucho Genre.*

In this book written in two voices, words turn into concepts, make contact with each other, refer to each other, split each other, and trace chains, bands, rings, montages, goings, and returnings. The net of words in motion constitutes something like a verbal apparatus for reading what wants to be read in the gaucho genre: the forms taken by the relations between the oral and the written, and the space of the alliance or the ring, the place where they unite. "Use" and "gift" therefore appear as notions with two sides or two meanings and are subject to a perpetual splitting. The two sides of the use of the gaucho: the literary use of the voice and the economic or military use of bodies. And the two sides of the gift or master: the writer who gives the gaucho his voice and the boss or superior.[1] The dual logic of language (which dominates the verbal matter of this book and which functions on two levels of "reality": the literary reality of the genre and "the other reality") seeks to represent the relation between popular and learned culture in the gaucho genre.

In a certain sense, in the perpetual splitting of this book, another genre, or gender, may also be read: the feminine. One of the formulas of the genre's verbal world is: "in the voice of the gaucho the word 'gaucho' is defined."

In New Haven, years after the publication of *The Gaucho Genre*, wanting to insert myself somehow in a Latin American critical tradition, I imagined that the verbal apparatus for reading the gaucho genre could also function in other regions where texts had been written that placed

---

1. [*Don* in Spanish can mean either gift or master; see chap. 1, n. 58. *Trans.*]

oral and written culture in relation to each other and used the voice of the Other: the indigenist literature of the Andean region in Perú and Ecuador and the antislavery literature of the Caribbean. I would write a book in three parts: the first would consist of an abstract fiction about the verbal (and political, economic, military, didactic, literary, sexual) devices with which *The Gaucho Genre* was read and written. The second part would be an analysis of the indigenist literature of the Andean region and the Caribbean antislavery literature using this reading apparatus based on the notion of the use of bodies in correlation with the use of voices. And the third part would be a theory about these three Latin American literatures, which would allow the voice of a body used by war, economy, and sex to be heard. The future book would also seek to be a history of the problems of modern, progressive subjects, who wrote these fictions within the frame of the nation-state. (It would analyze the writer's dramas of representation: generating subalterities or subalternities, speaking for or through the Other, speaking of the Other, speaking the Other: using his voice, giving him his voice.)

These three literatures were written or culminated in moments in which regional economies entered the world market and thus in the moment in which gauchos, Indians, and blacks were the producers of national wealth (the future book would have to contain precise economic data for the three regions). It would therefore place these genres of distribution and administration of voices within specific territories: the ranch, the hacienda, the mine, the sugar plantation. These would be the book's scenarios; one chapter would follow the trajectories of foreigners and runaway slaves—two subjects who persist in all three genres—through these territories.

I imagined the title of this book ("Gauchos, Indians, and Blacks: An Alliance of Voices in Latin American Cultures") in order to be able to verbally consider the three regions that made these literatures (these "genres" of two cultures) a central element of their cultural and national identity. Gaucho genre, indigenist genre, antislavery genre accompanied the history of the idea of the "national-popular" (there would be a chapter on the history of this state idea). These genres also accompanied the history of the constitution of Latin American identities in the relation between region and nation (another chapter would be dedicated to this relation).

And since there is no postulation of identity without work with the tones of the voice, without affect-music in the voice, it would pay attention in the literature of José María Arguedas to what the characters say in Quechua and what they say in Spanish, in order to examine the exact relations between the two languages-cultures: the relations of translation, transcription, publication. The key would be the positions and tones of the voices of Indians and blacks in conjunction with writing; the key would be, again, what kind of alliance was constructed. The book would also be a history of alliances—dreamed, desired, postulated—among these modern, progressive (in relation to the state and the law) writers, Others, and their cultures (with their voices and languages) against the political or economic enemy. A chapter dedicated to Arguedas's *Diamantes y pedernales* [Diamonds and flints] (1954) would show the possible limits of the alliance.

These specifically Latin American textualities suggest that literature, when it works with two voices and their respective cultures, is immediately politicized by them. It fuses the political and the cultural because it fuses languages with social relations of power. And because there is no relation between cultures without politics because between cultures there is only war or alliance, I wanted, again in an absolutist way, the imagined book to be purely politicocultural. I wanted it to be a reflection on certain Latin American literature founded in the differential uses of the voices and words of gauchos, Indians, and blacks, which define the meanings of the uses of bodies. I imagined that in the tortured, marked, abject bodies of these literatures I would find the secret of the perpetual splitting of language. I thought that in Clorinda Matto de Turner's *Aves sin nido* (1889) and Gertrudis Gómez de Avellaneda's *Saab* (1841) the feminine gender/genre could also be read, which, like the gaucho genre, forms an allegory with indigenism and abolitionism and also with the genre of testimony.

Throughout these years in New Haven this book was always the future book because there is no relation between cultures without the dimension of the future: the gaucho, indigenist, and antislavery genres would form series with various lines of descent and would open onto other literary genres such as the Bildungsroman, autobiography, and testimony.

The desire to continue and pluralize the *Treatise on the Motherland* only generated a spectral and excessive book, which dissolved into thin air when I immersed myself in the bibliography of this Latin American critical tradition and realized that what I had imagined was all already said and written, and that I would never write this book.[2] It is to fill this void that

2. The history of the relation between two cultures is identified with the now classic history of a Latin American critical tradition that begins with Fernando Ortiz's concept of transculturation (*Contrapunteo cubano del tabaco y el azúcar*, 1940) and concludes perhaps with the concept of subalternity. The two histories coincide.

For Fernando Ortiz, transculturation is a sociocultural process in which different cultures merge in daily life and culture. This concept was adapted to literature by Angel Rama (*Transculturación narrativa en América Latina* [Mexico: Siglo XXI, 1982]), who also wrote *Los gauchipolíticos rioplatenses: Literatura y sociedad* (Buenos Aires: Calicanto, 1976). For Rama, transculturation is manifested as cultural mixing; it takes place between high and subaltern cultures, it is under the charge of a vanguard of writers and critics, and it is related to national identity and the establishment and consolidation of the state. According to Rama, the literature of José María Arguedas demonstrated that the fusion of cultures was possible, because these operations are situated not only at the level of themes or explanatory programs but function also within the text itself.

Antonio Cornejo Polar situated the problem within the category of heterogeneity. In heterogeneous literatures, he writes, one or more of the constitutive elements correspond to a sociocultural system different from that which presides over the composition of the other elements deployed in a concrete process of literary production. The way the heterogeneity that defines indigenism takes shape in the indigenist novel is a case in point. This novel must be understood not in exclusive relationship with the indigenous world but rather as a cultural exercise that is located in the conflicting intersection of two sociocultural systems, attempting a dialogue that is often polemical and expressing, at the level to which it corresponds, one of the medullary problems of nationality: its dismembered and conflicting constitution (*Literatura y sociedad en el Perú: La novela indigenista* [Lima: Lasontay, 1980], 88).

In *Escribir en el aire: Ensayo sobre la heterogeneidad cultural en las literaturas andinas* (Lima: Horizonte, 1994), Cornejo Polar reelaborated and pluralized the concept of heterogeneity. And in one of his most recent works ("Una heterogeneidad no dialéctica: Sujeto y discurso migrante en el Perú moderno," *Revista Iberoamericana* (1996): 176–77, 837–44), he analyzed the migration from the high Andean plateau to the coastal cities in Perú. Cornejo Polar writes that this "diasporic phenomenon" weakens the essentialist Andean basis of Arguedas's utopian nationalism, which imagined a "new city" that would synthesize the best elements of the creole–half-breed coast and the indigenous Andes. Arguedas produced this "national allegory," but immigration weakened the authority of the indigenist model.

Alejandro Losada (*La literatura en la sociedad de América Latina: Perú y el Río de la Plata, 1837–1880* [Frankfurt: Vervuert, 1983]) also belongs within this critical tradition, as does Martín Lienhard (*La voz y su huella: Escritura y conflicto étnico-social en América*

The Gaucho Genre is now reissued. And in order to let the critical imagination manifest its purely verbal substance, I have tried to remove from this edition the numbers, letters, and graphics of which there were so many in the first edition in Spanish.

New Haven, March 2000

Latina, 1492–1988 [Hanover: Ediciones del Norte, 1991]), as well as Carlos Pacheco, with "Trastierra y oralidad en la ficción de los transculturadores" (*Revista de crítical literaria latinoamericana* 15, no. 29 [1989]: 25–38), and with his book *La comarca oral: La ficcionalización de la oralidad cultural en la narrativa latinoamericana contemporánea* (Caracas: La Casa de Bello, 1992).

The following essay collections are also important: *La voz del otro: Testimonio, subalternidad y verdad narrativa,* edited by John Beverley and Hugo Achugar (Lima: Latinoamericana Editores, 1992); *Asedios a la heterogeneidad cultural: Libro de homenaje a Antonio Cornejo Polar,* coordinated by José Antonio Mazzotti and U. Juan Zevallos Aguilar, and published by the Asociación Internacional de Peruanistas in 1996 (this includes Martín Lienhard's article "Mestizajes, heterogeneidades, hibridismos y otras quimeras," in which the relation between the two cultures is conceived of as diglossia).

The history of the relation between two cultures in Latin American criticism could be said to culminate in "Declaración Fundadora del Grupo Latinoamericano de Estudios Subalternos" ("Founding Statement, Latin American Subaltern Studies Group," published in *The Postmodern Debate in Latin America,* edited by John Beverley, José Oviedo, and Michael Aronna (Durham, N.C.: Duke University Press, 1995). This group based itself in part on the historiographic deconstruction performed by Ranajit Guha (founder of subaltern studies) in his essay "La prosa de la contra-insurgencia" (published in *Debates postcoloniales: Una introducción a los estudios de la subalternidad,* ed. Silvia Rivera Cusicanqui and Rossana Barragán [La Paz: Historias/SEPHIS/Aruwiyiri, 1997], 33–72). For Guha, as for the Latin American Subaltern Studies Group, subalternity is a problem of representation. Guha critiques teleological constructions (the explaining of a past event as an antecedent of future events) and "master narratives."

John Beverley (in "Los límites de la ciudad letrada: Subalternidad, literatura y transculturación," *Historia y Grafía* [Mexico City: Universidad Iberoamericana], no. 12 [1999]: 149–76) relates Angel Rama's idea of transculturation to the theory of dependence (the need to produce a national culture and literature), arguing that what is important for subaltern studies today (faced with the changes produced by the mass media who do not consider the idea of a literary culture as a model or practice for citizenship) is to register the moments in which a counterrationality appears in opposition to the rationality of the colonial or bourgeois-national state. Moreover, he argues the need for a multicultural or culturally heterogeneous nationalism that is not based in the logic of transculturation or hybridization.

Acknowledgments: On the Side of the Gift

This book was conceived during the military dictatorship (1976–1983) in Argentina and written during the return to democracy.

The following made it possible: Gerardo L. Maeso; the support and friendship of my teaching and research group from the University of Buenos Aires; a fellowship from the Council of Humanities at Princeton University (1981); grants from the Social Science Research Council (1982–1983) and from the Guggenheim Foundation (1984–1985).

The translation of this book was carried out with the help of a grant from the Fundación Antorchas, and was published with the assistance of the Frederick W. Hilles Publications Fund of Yale University.

To all of you, many thanks.

Chapter One

The Body of the Genre and Its Borders

Essay toward the Construction of a Context and a System of Objects

I. On the Side of Use

In this first moment only two categories are of interest, that of use and that of emergence. The first is that which perhaps defines and allows us to think about the gaucho genre:[1] a learned use of popular culture.[2] It con-

1. [The Spanish *género* is translatable as either "genre" or "gender." Ludmer's study engages both meanings; hence, the term "genre" in the English text should be understood to include the meaning of "gender." *Género* may also refer to a kind of fabric, and this additional meaning sometimes resonates in Ludmer's spatial metaphors. *Trans.*]

2. This is opposed to the popular use of "high" or hegemonic culture (for example, the popular use of religion in the form of superstitions or miracles or various popular tricks like the trap, the lie, or dissimulation, which are always inscribed in a space of confrontations, resistance, and conflicts). When we say "popular" in gaucho literature, we are referring to the rural folk culture of subaltern and marginal sectors like the gaucho; this culture must be rigorously distinguished from urban popular culture or from "popular culture" as mass culture. The popular culture of the gaucho includes not only the folklore that it inherited from the Spaniards and transformed, but also its customs, beliefs, rites, rules, and common laws. The gaucho genre used this culture to constitute itself: verses, refrains, sayings, fables; it used the voice, the verbal modes of this culture. This voice is part of a multileveled system that doesn't distinguish among art, education, and law, between practical life and political life. Or between public and private life.

This treatise is not concerned with idyllically exalting traditional oral culture or falling into the empiricist illusion of a "natural" and immediate object independent of any conceptual system of classification and categorization. The writers of the genre were the first to construct, with that object, an epistemology: a mode of knowing it while using it.

Moreover, we conceive of popularity as a phenomenon of use and not of origin, as a position and a relation and not a substance (see Alberto M. Cirese, *Cultura egemonica e culture subalterne: Rassegna degli studi sul mondo popolare tradizionale,* 2d ed. [Palermo: Palumbo editore, 1973], and in the Latin American arena, the journal *Comunicación y cultura* [Mexico City] 10 [*Interrogantes sobre lo popular* (Interrogating the popular) [August 1983]). Certain texts (originating from anywhere or in any way) are adopted by certain groups according to specific modalities: in this case oral transmission, shared elaboration and reelaboration. Further, popularity is defined by its difference from nonpopular phenomena: as something that is present in a certain social sphere and not in others. Defining gaucho poetry as a learned use of popular culture does not mean denying it popularity; many texts returned to their partial source and one privileged text became a part of folk culture: *Martín Fierro* was adopted by oral diffusion and left its mark on the language and national culture. The popular and educated strata are connected by

cerns the use of the voice, of a voice (and with it an accumulation of meanings: a world) that's not the voice of the one who writes. The category of use derives above all from the instrumental condition of the gauchos: it's the category of meaning for those who lack something that the one who writes and uses their meanings has.

The second category has precise meanings: emergence is a coming into being and also an urgent need of use.[3] The moment of the emergence of the genre is the moment before the repetition, variation, and convention that precisely constitute a literary genre; it's the illusion of the first time, when the ideas of the genre are not yet received ideas. Hence the written is entirely transparent; it seems to say everything and allow everything to be read simultaneously. Verbal categories form an irreducible link among referentiation, action, and formalization. The use of the genre scatters and autonomizes this link. The reading of the genre changes according to the way the categories of use and emergence are set up.

But the moment of transparency is doubly paradoxical. First, because what is not yet genre is read here as genre. Second, because that transparency (which is, in part, a product of the theft of the past and of the convergence of multiple forces on one point) is also an effect of perspective: it can only be read from within the already constituted genre, from the perspective of the future and its convention. It can only be read from the completed deployment of the meaning of the genre. These are the two

---

a web of exchanges, loans, and reciprocal relations. (For this point and for the levels of antagonism and conformity in oral culture, see Luigi M. Lombardi Satriani, *Antropologia culturale ed analisi della cultura subalterna* [Florence: Guaraldi, 1974], and, by the same author, *Apropiación y destrucción de la cultura de las clases subalternas* [Mexico City: Nueva Imagen, 1978]. For a critique of a naive realism toward popular culture and a systematic approach linked to Russian formalism, see Pëtr Bogatyrev, *Semiotica della cultura popolare* [Verona: Bertani Editores, 1982]. With Roman Jakobson, Bogatyrev wrote the "Program for the Study of Popular Theater" [1919] and "Folklore as a Specific Form of Creation" [1929]. In the same tradition and also in Russian, see Juri M. Lotman, *Testo e contesto: Semiotica dell'arte e della culture* [Rome: Bari, 1980]. In the Italian arena, from which the majority of these studies and translations clearly come, in the wake of Antonio Gramsci, see Giovanni B. Bronzini, *Cultura popolare: Dialettica e contestualitá* [Bari: Dedalo, 1980].)

3. [The Spanish *emergencia* is translatable as both "emergence" and "emergency." Ludmer's category of emergence suggests an originary moment as a kind of crisis. *Trans.*]

characteristic paradoxes of the use of meaning that arise when we attempt to read the meaning of the category of use.

Use and emergence and their paradoxes are defined here within temporal mobility and the diversity of literary objects. Mobility: each moment, stage, length, border is read from the perspective of others (Hidalgo from Castañeda, from Hernández; *La vuelta* [The return] from *La ida* [The departure], from Borges, from Hidalgo; *La ida* from Luis Pérez's *Biografía de Rosas* and Pérez's work from de Angelis's biography; the entire genre from the perspective of *Fausto* and *Fausto* from current Argentine literature).[4] Diversity: we move among tones, voices, enunciations, actions, narratives, names, places, words as we postulate the founding character of the literary differentiation of objects and fields.

The Two Chains

Two interlaced chains of use may delimit the gaucho genre.

Laws

The first border of the genre is popular lawlessness. On one hand the so-called rural delinquency (the "vagrant" gaucho, unlanded and without fixed work or domicile; the well-known equation dispossessed = delinquent), and on the other, by correlation, the existence of a double system of justice that distinguishes city from country: the law of vagrants and its corollary, the law of conscription, reign above all in the countryside. This

---

4. [*La ida* and *La vuelta* are common Argentine designations for the two separate volumes that comprise the long gauchesque poem *Martín Fierro* by José Hernández (1834 – 1886). Their official titles are *El gaucho Martín Fierro* (1872) and *La vuelta de Martín Fierro* (1879). These unofficial titles are mentioned frequently in the text and they engage with other departures, turns, and returns of the genre.

The other writers mentioned here, all of whom wrote within or engaged with the gaucho genre, include, besides Borges, the Uruguayan poet Bartolomé Hidalgo (1788 – 1823), the Franciscan friar, educator, and journalist Francisco de Paula Castañeda (1776 – 1832), the writer Luis Pérez (d.1841), and the historian Pedro de Angelis (1789 – 1860), who emigrated from Italy to Argentina. *Fausto*, or the "Argentine *Faust*," is a long gauchesque poem by Estanislao del Campo (1834 – 1880). These writers (with the exception of de Angelis) are discussed at length later in the text. *Trans.*]

duality is in turn linked to the existence of a central, written law that in the country is confronted by the oral, traditional code of custom: the juridical regulating of rules and prescriptions that forms the basis of the rural community. The "delinquency" of the gaucho is nothing more than *the effect of difference* between the two juridical regulating systems and between the differential applications of one of them, and it matches *the necessity of use:* of field hands for the ranchers and of soldiers for the army.[5]

Wars

The second border of the genre is the revolution and the war of independence, which begin the practice of the military use of the gaucho and his demarginalization.[6] With laws and wars the first chain of use may be established, articulating the totality of the genre and giving it meaning:

5. See C. O. Bunge, "El derecho en la literatura gauchesca," in his *Estudios jurídicos* (Madrid: Espasa-Calpe, 1926); A. Cali, *Martín Fierro ante el derecho penal,* 2d ed. (Buenos Aires: Abeledo-Perrot, 1979); G. Gori, *Vagos y malentretenidos,* 2d ed. (Santa Fe, Argentina: Colmegna, 1965); R. Rodríguez Molas, *Historia social del gaucho* (Buenos Aires: Marú, 1968); J. Lynch, *Argentine Dictator: Juan Manuel de Rosas 1829–1852* (Oxford: Clarendon Press, 1981).

Lynch writes: "The ruling class in the countryside had traditionally imposed a system of coercion upon people whom they regarded as *mozos vagos y mal entretenidos,* vagabonds without employer or occupation, idlers who sat in groups singing to a guitar, drinking maté, gambling, but apparently not working. This class was seen as a potential labour force and was therefore subject to all kinds of constraints and controls by the landed proprietors—punitive expeditions, imprisonment, conscription to the Indian frontier, corporal punishment, and other penalties" (104).

See also Michel Foucault, "Sobre la justicia popular" [On Popular Justice] in his *Microfísica del poder* [Anatomy of Power], (Madrid: La piqueta, 1979), and especially *Discipline and Punish: The Birth of the Prison* (New York: Pantheon, 1977). On the relation between states and nomadic and itinerant bodies, the attempts to settle the workforce, to assign it channels and transport, and to interpellate the forced laborer, see Gilles Deleuze and Felix Guattari, *A Thousand Plateaus: Capitalism and Schizophrenia* (Minneapolis: University of Minnesota Press, 1987).

6. [In their *Historical Dictionary of Argentina* (Metuchen, N.J.: Scarecrow Press, 1978), Ione Wright and Lisa Nekhom write "On July 9th, 1816, the Congress of Tucumán formally declared the independence of the United Provinces from Spain and the anniversary of that date is annually celebrated as independence day in Argentina; most Argen-

tines, however, consider their national independence to have begun more than six years earlier with the May Revolution when, on May 25, 1810, the cabildo abierto of Buenos Aires deposed the Spanish viceroy and established a patriot government; it attempted to bring all the provinces of the former viceroyalty of the Provincias Unidas de la Plata under its authority but eventually Paraguay (1811), Bolivia (1825), and Uruguay (1828) became independent republics. . . . Much of the Argentine long war for independence (1810–1824) was fought outside Argentine territory, except for the vicious fighting in the northwestern area, and formed part of the South American fight for independence from Spain, under the command of an Argentine general, José de San Martín, from 1813 to 1822" (411–12).

Between the May Revolution of 1810 and the federalization of Buenos Aires as the national capital in 1880, Argentina was deeply divided by a bitter, violent struggle between federalists and unitarists for control of economic resources and national political organization. While federalists envisioned "a united nation . . . made up of semi-autonomous provinces with rights clearly defined and protected," unitarists "desired a progressive, modern, centralized [republican] government, with Buenos Aires as capital, patterned somewhat along [the] lines of such Western European nations as England and France." The struggle between federalists and unitarists was also a cultural struggle; according to Wright and Nekhom, "federalists rejected [the] alien European culture admired by unitarists, who, in turn, viewed federalist criollo culture as barbarism" (304). The unitarist Constitution of 1826 was rejected by the provinces, who feared that Buenos Aires would attempt to monopolize economic resources and political power, and "the nation disintegrated into various kinds of autonomous groups, anarchy, *caudillismo* [provincial leadership], [and] interprovincial alliances of short duration" (303). Formally governor of the province of Buenos Aires, the federalist Juan Manuel de Rosas was the repressive dictator of Argentina from 1829 to 1832 and from 1835 to 1852. According to David Rock, "Contemporary opponents reviled Rosas as a bloody tyrant and a symbol of barbarism, while a later generation canonized him as a nationalist hero, but he is more accurately depicted as the embodiment of the Federalist *caudillo,* a conservative autocrat dedicated to the aggrandizement of his own province and to its ranchers and *saladeristas.* For Rosas all other concerns were secondary, to be ignored, circumvented, or obliterated" (Rock, *Argentina, 1516–1982* [Berkeley: University of California Press, 1985], 104).

Rosas's government was overthrown by Justo José Urquiza in 1852; a federalist and governor of the province of Entre Ríos, Urquiza supported a stronger national organization. Concerned that Urquiza might become another dictator and desirous of safeguarding its own political power and economic resources, the province of Buenos Aires withdrew from the newly formed Argentine Confederation; "while open hostilities continued to break out, the representatives of the other Argentine provinces met in Congress at Santa Fe and drew up the federal Constitution of 1853; it was accepted by most of the provinces and in 1854 Urquiza began a six-year term as first constitutional president of [the] Argentine Republic, with its capital in Paraná, Entre Ríos" (Wright and Nekhom, *Historical Dictionary,* 988). After continuing conflict over the incorporation of Buenos

a) use of the "delinquent" gaucho by the patriotic army;
b) use of his oral register (his voice) by the learned culture: the gaucho genre.[7] And thenceforth:
c) use of the genre to integrate the gauchos into the "civilized" (liberal and civic) law.

The chain, almost circular (the logic of uses seems to take that form), begins with the texts of Hidalgo and concludes with *The Return of Martín Fierro*. Voice and law are modulated from within the army and the war to

---

Aires into the confederation, Bartolomé Mitre, then governor of Buenos Aires, defeated Urquiza in 1861 and became the first elected president of Argentina in 1862, with Buenos Aires as the capital. Struggles over political organization continued, however, until 1880, when "the city of Buenos Aires was detached from the province of Buenos Aires and named the federal capital of the republic; standing armies in the provinces were [also] abolished" (Rock, *Argentina*, 131).

According to Rock, the last of the great federalist *caudillos* was "Ricardo López Jordán in Entre Ríos, who took control of the province after his followers assassinated Urquiza in 1870. For several years, López Jordán resisted attempts from Buenos Aires to eliminate him, but in 1874 he was defeated. . . . Formal politics, however, remained a narrow preserve of the mercantile and landed elites. The electoral law of 1863, which purported to allow popular participation in the political process, from the beginning proved itself a sham. Elections were invariably ritualistic parodies, stage-managed by lackeys of the powerful, with only a minute fraction of the electorate participating. By 1880 the term *caudillo* was losing its earlier connotation of regional or provincial leader and now referred to the local political bosses who controlled elections on behalf of their elite patrons" (129). *Trans.*]

7. [Here and throughout *The Gaucho Genre*, the Spanish word *letrado* describes the culture that through the written word has set itself apart from popular oral culture. Thus I have translated *letrado* throughout the book as "learned," a term that more closely matches the Spanish word's range of implications here than "literate" or "lettered." While "literate" merely implies the ability to read, and "lettered" suggests one well-schooled in literate culture, "learned" has the broader sense of one characterized by learning. At certain points in the text, the use of the word "learned" produces tension, as in the phrase "learned gaucho," to describe a gaucho who has learned to read and write. While the more expected word in such a case would be "literate," the use of "learned" maintains the connection to the larger meaning of Ludmer's concept of "learned" or *letrado:* the gaucho who has learned to read and write has, in a symbolic sense, crossed the border into the other cultural territory, with all the implications of that act in terms of voice, identity, and power relations between the two cultures. *Trans.*]

the national state: this passage and this modulation are the history of the forms of the genre.

The chain not only marks the time of the genre and gives it a meaning; it also narrates the passage from "delinquency" to "civilization" and situates the genre as one of the producers of this passage. Moreover it postulates in the center a parallelism between the use of the gaucho's body by the army and the use of his voice by the learned culture, which defines the genre. Through this use of the body, which separates the gauchos from one field in order to carry them to another, that of the battle, the voice arises: the first fictitious locutor of gaucho literature is the gaucho as singer and patriot. The voice, the register, appears written, hypercodified and subject to a series of formal, metrical, and rhythmic conventions; it also passes through a disciplinary institution—written poetry—like the gaucho who passes through the army and is transformed into a literary sign. The two institutions, army and poetry, embrace and complement each other. The gaucho can "sing" or "speak" for all, in verse, because he fights in the armies of the motherland: his right to the voice settles and remains in weapons. Because he has weapons he must have a voice or because he has weapons he takes another voice. That which defines the gaucho genre from the beginning thus arises: language as weapon. Voice law and voice weapon interlace in the chains of the genre.

Sarmiento and the Words of Exterior Space
The Heart of the Historic Space of the Genre

Facundo afterward reappears in Buenos Aires, where in 1810 he was enrolled as a recruit in the Arribeños regiment, which was commanded by General Ocampo, a native of Facundo's own province, and afterward president of Charcas. With the first rays of the May sun, the glorious career of arms opened before him; and doubtless Facundo, with the temple of the soul with which he was gifted, and with his instincts for destruction and carnage, could he have been moralized by discipline to submit to civil authority and ennobled by the sublimity of the purpose of the struggle, might some day have returned from Peru, Chile, or Bolivia as a general of the Argentine Republic, like so many other brave gauchos who began their careers in the humble position of a private soldier. But Quiroga's rebel soul could not endure the yoke of discipline, the order of the barracks, or the time required to rise within the ranks. He felt called to command, to rise at a single leap, to create for himself, alone, in spite of civilized society and in emnity with it, a career in his own style, combining bravery and crime, government and disorganization. He was later recruited into the army of the Andes, and enrolled in the Mounted Grenadiers. A lieutenant García took him for an assistant, and very soon desertion left a vacancy in those glorious ranks. Afterward Quiroga, like Rosas, like all the vipers that have prospered in the shade of the motherland's laurels, became notorious for his hatred of the soldiers of Independence, among whom both of the above-named men caused horrible slaughter. (Domingo Sarmiento, *Facundo,* chap. 5, "Life of Juan Facundo Quiroga: Infancy and Youth")[8]

This is the exact reverse of the genre and marks the border of its external space. Sarmiento defines the outside of the genre by making a leap in that which defines it: the voice (in this case Facundo's voice: this is a biography and not an autobiography). In the chain of uses, Sarmiento passes from *a* to *c:* the army partially substitutes for the law in the definition of the "gaucho"; to serve in the army is to accept discipline and "the glorious career of arms": it is to be "moralized" and "ennobled." To subtract oneself from use is to fall back into illegality and also into the definition of the law: to direct one's "instincts for destruction and carnage"[9] elsewhere. The

8. [Translated by Molly Weigel; unless otherwise noted, all translations are Weigel's. A new translation of *Facundo* by Kathy Ross is forthcoming from University of California Press. It will be a welcome replacement to the sometimes inaccurate translation by Mary Peabody Mann (1868; reprint, New York: Hafner Press, 1974).

Domingo Faustino Sarmiento (1811–1888), politician, writer, and educator, was exiled in Chile for his unitarist beliefs during much of Rosas's dictatorship (1829–1832, 1835–1852). In 1845, in protest of Rosas's regime, he wrote *Facundo,* whose subject is Juan Facundo Quiroga (1793–1835), a gaucho who became a commander of the federalist army. Sarmiento was president of the Argentine republic from 1868 to 1874. *Trans.*]

9. There are numerous records of escapes and desertions from the army. In 1811 the country people complained because the recruiters removed laborers from their work and drove them, "tied, to the frontier" (see Rodríguez Molas, *Historia social* 185, 197, 217, 222, and, by the same author, *El servicio militar obligatorio* [Buenos Aires: CEAL, 1983]). Tulio Halperin-Donghi, whose works are essential reading on this subject, writes that in order

gaucho genre situates itself in choice itself, and that is its point of contact with the exterior space, its border. It constructs the ennobled voice of the patriot gaucho in order to produce patriotism (in order to give meaning, with the voice, to the struggle) and in order to ward off the subtraction of bodies. The written construction of the voice of the gaucho has a multiple meaning: it refers to the patriotic body of the soldier, the subtracted body of the deserter, and the body of the "delinquent." Or to his "soul" or "instincts," as Sarmiento writes from the other side of the genre, from the learned, written word.

Sarmiento speaks of the genre in a way in which the genre couldn't speak as it was emerging because it would have to have been written precisely with the voice of Facundo and not through the word of Sarmiento. Or with Facundo's soul, which for Sarmiento is a terrifying shade. Twice Sarmiento uses the word "soul": "with the temple of the soul with which he was gifted, with his instincts for destruction and carnage," and "but Facundo's rebel soul could not endure the yoke of discipline." The word "soul" belongs precisely to the external space of the genre; within, it would be "spirit" = voice.[10] When Sarmiento's word "soul" becomes central and occupies the heart of a text of the genre, in *Fausto,* it will be possible to make a cut in its history—in the history of the genre. It may also be said that that word marks the first turn of the genre, another, internal border.

---

to constitute their military organization, the revolutionaries of 1810 continued to use "the old authoritarian style," since "the marginals' enthusiasm for the army was not universal"; one of the proofs of this would be "the diffusion of banditry after the Revolution" (*Revolución y guerra* [Buenos Aires: Siglo XXI, 1972], 186). In 1810 the revolutionary powers limited the obligation for armed service to the marginal population and *ordered a rigorous conscription of vagrants;* they did not solicit the free, economically active population (214). Even [José Gervasio] Artigas agreed that the peasants should be obligated to fight (329). In General Paz's *Memorias póstumas* we can read the obsession with desertions in almost every line covering the period from 1815 to 1842 (2 vols. [Buenos Aires: Almanueva, 1954]). Already in 1811 Paz refers to the disbandments of the armies of Belgrano (1:23); later he tells how Rivera recruited in the Banda Oriental [Uruguay before the republics were established—*trans.*], carrying off laborers from the ranches; desertion armed the squadrons and disarmed them (2:243).

10. [I am translating *alma* as "soul" and *ánima* as "spirit." *Anima* or "spirit" is the archaic term still in use in the nineteenth century among gauchos. Etymologically, *ánima* is related to "breath," "air," and "voice." "Spirit" here, besides "soul," might also mean "ghost." *Trans.*]

In any case, in *Fausto,* the word "soul" will create a play with the word "wool,"[11] and with the sale of wool, in order to occupy a space that until then was exterior to the genre: the Colón Theater.[12] When the Colón Theater enters the genre, Sarmiento's word "soul" enters with it. But the one to sell his soul won't be the gaucho but rather Doctor Faust.

For Sarmiento, Facundo's "soul" is a terrifying shade, an enigma, because he has taken its voice away. It is not like the shade of Hamlet's father, whose death came through his ears, who is all voice. The enigma that interrogates Sarmiento is none other than the spoken language, the exact rhythm and tone of the voice, its intensity, its modulations and registers: the way in which a voice becomes volume and in that volume becomes a world. It is not that Sarmiento had never heard that voice. Because he was hearing it constantly, because it was the voice of his madness, of his dream, because it was inside him, and because it was the voice of the motherland when he wrote *Facundo*—he wrote *Facundo.* Sarmiento's role is to try to seize the emergence of the genre, because he writes during Rosas's regime, when the entire space of the motherland is almost coterminous with the genre. The motherland and the genre touch, and Sarmiento writes in exile from Chile, which extends the length of the motherland and travels along it in its entirety. He is separated by the Andes from San Martín's grenadiers, from whom Facundo deserted. And thus he occupies the exact reverse of the genre and is in complete contact with it, except at the precise point at which they could become the same, could become only genre: in the voice of the gaucho.

Sarmiento introduces one of the fundamental theoretical problems of

11. [It was the gauchos who typically sold wool in Buenos Aires. *Trans.*]

12. [See the discussion of Hilario Ascasubi's involvement in building the great Buenos Aires theater, p. 95. Ascasubi (1807–1875), an active fighter against Rosas, spent twenty years in exile in Montevideo (1832–1852) because of his strong unitarist principles. He was the author of the gauchesque epic poem *Santos Vega* (1872), which narrates the life of the pampa in brief descriptive vignettes, and of the gauchesque romance *Paulino Lucero* (1872), and the editor of *Aniceto el Gallo* (Aniceto the rooster), a periodical in prose and verse. He also adopted the name of the latter as a nickname. In Estanislao del Campo's *Fausto* (1866), a gaucho, Laguna, recounts his experience of a performance of Gounod's opera at the Colón Theater to his companions. Del Campo also refers humorously to Ascasubi's involvement with the theater and includes a character named El Pollo (The chicken), a reference to Ascasubi's nickname. *Trans.*]

this Essay. Is Sarmiento summoned to the genre so that it may be read in its emergence, or is it the genre that allows the reading of what Sarmiento writes in exile, and afterward, with the other, written word, the learned word, that of the nonvoice of the gaucho? The question is, What is it that allows the reading of that which wants to be read? Sarmiento is on one side of the frontier of the motherland, the genre is on the other side, and they are the same except in the voice of the gaucho. Sarmiento is the fiction of the genre in its moment of emergence because he says what the genre, with the voice of the gaucho, cannot say as it constitutes itself against another exterior space in order to constitute the motherland. (He says that there are desertions, that being delinquent or not depends on the army, that the gauchos are brave but rebellious, that they associate bravery with crime, that they are hostile to civilization.) And he says it afterward—a moment afterward, when the genre occupies the entire space of the motherland. And he has lost the motherland and therefore raises his literary writing against the voice that is the monument to Facundo, the first cathedral of Argentine culture.

In other words, *the historical space* differs from one side of the genre to the other, at its border. There is an afterward that says the before without the voice of the gaucho, and there is a before that may be read in the afterward or in another space and register. Interior and exterior spaces, before and after, frontiers, borders, heard voices, written words, written voices. These are the words that can transport us along this first stretch of the treatise on the motherland.

Sarmiento will return at the very center of the treatise, at its heart, when the penultimate moment of the turn and return of the genre appears with *La ida* of Martín Fierro, when the moment arrives in which the gaucho tells his life with his voice: when the singer sings. Once again, there will be a problem with the exterior and interior borders and again Sarmiento will allow this moment to be read by his gaucho singer without a voice.[13] And this moment may be read with Sarmiento's words from *Facundo:* he names the gauchos of the army "brave gauchos" and not "patriotic gauchos," which the genre names them when it emerges. Or rather, Sarmiento names the gauchos *as they name themselves* in *La ida,* when Fierro and

---

13. [That is, Sarmiento's gaucho is without a voice because in *Facundo* Sarmiento himself narrates his life, while in Hernández's *La ida,* the gaucho narrates his own life. *Trans.*]

Cruz unite against the army and the judge and leave for another exile and another language.[14] Each time Sarmiento's words enter a text of the genre, a turn of the genre in its historical space is produced. But in *La ida* there is another word of Sarmiento's, of his present and *La ida*'s: *the name of his minister of war:* "a ministry or something like that . . . / they called Don Gander" (ll. 953–954), the gaucho Fierro says before deserting.[15] *La ida* is the text of the gaucho who has lost everything, written when Sarmiento was the father of the motherland, its president, and *Facundo* is written when Sarmiento was the one who had lost everything.

Facundo's words, "moralized" and "ennobled," will appear again at the end of this treatise with the final return of Martín Fierro, when the genre is in such complete contact with the exterior space that they are again only differentiated by the voice. But now Sarmiento's Other will be there, his enemy and true interlocutor, the only one who really read him: Juan Bautista Alberdi. A poster of the founding fathers separates them.[16] And another kind of exile, of voices and of writings (in between Sarmiento and Alberdi are the sea, the other language, and the posthumous writings). In the circle of *La vuelta* the two enemies, both founding fathers, one the father of law and the other of education, come together: in the voice of the gaucho, education and law are the same. *La vuelta*'s perfect sphere united them forever.

14. [At the end of *La ida*, Fierro and Cruz set off for Indian territory and the Indian language. Fierro tells Cruz, "Indian country is out of reach / from the arm of the law" (ll. 2189–90). *Trans.*]

15. [All quotations from *La ida*, unless otherwise indicated, are from the translation by Frank Carrino, Alberto Carlos, and Norman Mangouni (José Hernández, *The Gaucho Martín Fierro* [Albany: State University of New York Press, 1974]). The translators explain that "Don Gander" refers to "Colonel Martín de Gaínza, Secretary of War under President . . . Sarmiento (1868–1874). In the Spanish version the narrator calls him 'Ganza' from *gansa*, goose" (73). *Trans.*]

16. [This refers to large posters of important Argentine historical figures displayed in elementary school classrooms. Juan Bautista Alberdi (1810–1884), judge, writer, and politician, was one of several intellectuals who came to power after Urquiza's victory over Rosas; his tract *Las bases* was instrumental in the development of the Constitution of 1853, which consolidated the aims of the unitarists after the fall of Rosas's federalist dictatorship. According to David Rock, the constitution "enunciated commitments to increasing population through immigration, the development of communications, and the promotion of new industry" (*Argentina*, 124); Alberdi's dictum was *gobernar es poblar*, to govern is to populate. *Trans.*]

Sarmiento, *Facundo,* is the historical guide to the genre *through his written words and through the space from which they are written.* Each time Sarmiento's words—the exact reverse of the genre and their maximum point of contact—enter a text of the genre there is a turn, and Sarmiento becomes present at its heart, to such an extent that it might be said that he *is* the genre; he marks its frontiers and traces its history. He traces the form of its history: at its heart, a white and sky blue ribbon with three turns.[17]

Literature begins in the treatise with this paragraph from *Facundo,* perhaps the most literary anthologized fragment of nineteenth-century Argentine literature. It has everything: heights, tensions, attacks, intensities; it is a volume with time and with a verbal texture that produces vertigo. It is also a political fragment, perhaps the founding political text of Argentina. And it is a fragment of history. Urquiza's text, his classic, was written by Alberdi, the father of politics and law; Mitre's text is a classic of history; only the text of Sarmiento, the other father of the motherland, is a classic of all three: literature, politics, and history.[18]

The fragment is organized around the word "motherland." It draws the Argentine national coat of arms (it is a blazon, a frequent figure in literature or in what is still taught as literature) and all of *Facundo* is defined therein. It is also organized around the word "vacancy" and has a vacancy at its core. In the fragment, the first motherland occupies the upper space, with the name "Facundo" enrolled therein, the date 1810, and the regiment "commanded by General Ocampo, a native of Facundo's own province, and afterward president of Charcas." This space is Facundo's first motherland, the small motherland, the province of La Rioja, Facundo and

17. [The blue-and-white-striped Argentine flag as a Moebius strip. *Trans.*]
18. [Urquiza (1801–1870), governor of the province of Entre Rios under Rosas, later opposed the dictator and led the forces that defeated him in the battle of Caseros in 1852. Proclaimed provisional director of the new Argentine Confederation, Urquiza assumed the presidency in 1854. Mitre (1821–1906) commanded the Argentine artillery in the battle of Caseros and, after serving in various posts, was proclaimed the constitutional president of the Republic of Argentina upon the defeat of the Confederation in 1862. In 1868 Mitre delegated his power to Sarmiento, and in 1874 he was defeated in elections by Nicolás Avellaneda. Mitre wrote a number of histories, including *Historia de Belgrano y de la independencia argentina* and *Historia de San Martín y de la emancipación americana;* translated Dante's *Divine Comedy* into Spanish; and founded the great Buenos Aires newspaper, *La Nación. Trans.*]

Ocampo's common origin. The first motherland passes again through the name "Facundo," "moralized" and "ennobled," and ends with "soldier": "like so many other brave gauchos, who began their careers in the humble position of a private soldier." This first space is condensed around the May sun, "the glorious career of arms," and the sublimation of the soldier's "instincts of destruction and carnage." The countryman Ocampo has an "afterward" that Facundo doesn't have, but Facundo nonetheless also possesses the word "afterward": "Facundo afterward reappears," "General Ocampo, a native of Facundo's own province, and afterward president of Charcas." Ocampo's afterward is that of power, above.

If we go down in the text to the other "afterward," to the other power (there are three powers in the fragment, Facundo's, Ocampo's, and Quiroga and Rosas's), the motherland is the other motherland, of shadow and death, from which Sarmiento is once more excluded. When in the upper part of the fragment the motherland is the sun, glory, the birth of the motherland (and, paradoxically, the motherland is the province), Sarmiento is excluded from that solidarity. While below: "Afterward Quiroga, like Rosas, like all the vipers that have prospered in the shade of the motherland's laurels, became notorious. . . ." Above, with the sun, and as a soldier, Facundo is Facundo: the title of the book, the first name; below are Quiroga and Rosas, *the vipers of the land* and the shade of the laurels on the motherland's coat of arms. The motherland is death for Sarmiento; for the others, motherland or death.[19] Each "afterward" of the three who mark names and moments and powers has a verb in a different tense and mood: the present in "Facundo afterward reappears"; the imperfect with Ocampo, "which was commanded by General Ocampo, a native of Facundo's own province, and afterward president of Charcas" (and here the verb goes before the afterward; they are "afterward" opposed). Below the verb follows the afterward and is past perfect: "have prospered," "became notorious," "caused."

Between the two motherlands from which Sarmiento is excluded, that of the sun and glory and that of shadow, earth, and death, there are two events: one that begins with "But Quiroga's rebel soul could not endure the yoke of discipline," and one that begins with "He was later recruited

19. [*"Patria o muerte,"* an expression used by Rosists, is still used by extreme nationalists. *Trans.*]

into the army of the Andes." One event defines *Facundo,* the text itself; the other defines vacancy and exclusion. In the first event, the double contradiction emerges: without discipline, order, or patience Facundo wants to command and to set himself apart by combining bravery and crime, government and disorganization. It is the moment of the division of the text and of the gauchos; the possibility of choosing between discipline and desertion. The gaucho genre inserts itself into this division. Here Facundo disappears and Quiroga is born: "alone, in spite of civilized society and in enmity with it." In this confrontation, bravery and crime, government and disorganization *form a partnership* in Quiroga's own style. This second, internal tension sustains the text and demonstrates it; it is the *and* that connects "Civilization and barbarism" with "Life of Juan Facundo Quiroga." Barbarism dramatizes not only the confrontation with "civilization" but also a second, interior, confrontation with itself. This is the tense and dual position of barbarism in *Facundo:* it is hostile to civilized society and hostile to itself. Barbarism contains a part of civilization, bravery, and government that is associated with crime and disorganization. This double tension, toward the outside, and within itself, is the best definition of *Facundo,* Sarmiento's text.

That space and that event end precisely with the tension between government and disorganization. "Later," the space and event that follow, end with desertion and a vacancy: "desertion left a vacancy in those glorious ranks." Here is glory again, but joined to a vacancy. And the word "glorious" names another vacancy or absence, that of the name of San Martín, the patriot of the army of the Andes. A nobody substitutes for San Martín, "a lieutenant García." This is a fragment of exclusions and vacancies: Sarmiento's exclusion from the motherland, the absence of the name of San Martín, who represents the motherland, and the vacancy that represents this vacancy, namely Facundo's desertion. (And the vacancy or absence of the word "afterward," for which the word "later" substitutes, playing with and tensing itself against "very soon.") Desertion and a vacancy in Sarmiento's text end the process of independence and bring us to the land and to the shade of the motherland. (And to the death that is the dead Facundo.)

The vacancy of the name of San Martín is filled by the first text of the gaucho genre, Hidalgo's first cielito, which carries the mark of what will afterward be the defining feature of the texts of the genre: it is the *first in which it is written that a gaucho composed it and sings it.* Or the first in which the voice of the patriot gaucho emerges: "Patriotic cielito. Composed by a gaucho to sing of the Battle of Maipú," 1818. There is San Martín, the motherland, freedom, independence. In 1818 and in the voice of the gaucho, Hidalgo speaks Sarmiento's vacancy in 1845. And Sarmiento doesn't cease narrating Hidalgo's silences in the space and time of his own text.

The Word "Gaucho" in the Voice of the Gaucho: the Interior Space[20]
An Exercise with the Dictionary

The militarization of the rural sector during the wars of independence and the concomitant rise of a new social sign, *the patriotic gaucho,* may be postulated as bases of the genre to the extent that they allow access to the verbal register of the gauchos through its sole written representation, the statute of literary language. The war is not only the foundation of the gaucho genre but also its material and logic. And a material and a logic are a genre. It might also be said that the change in the meaning of the word "gaucho" inaugurates and is the genre.[21] As if the words faced each other in war.

20. [The Spanish word *voz* means not only "voice" but also "word." The following section plays with the overlap of these two meanings. *Trans.*]

21. The revaluation of the gaucho was due above all to Artigas, Martín Miguel de Güemes, and San Martín. As the *Gazeta de Buenos Aires* of March 22, 1817, states: "Until now, the title 'gaucho' conveyed an unfavorable idea of the subject to whom it was applied, but the honored farmers and ranchers of Salta have now managed to make it illustrious and glorious through countless acts of prowess that make them worthy of eternal recognition." See Bonifacio del Carril, *El gaucho a través de la iconografía* (Buenos Aires: Emecé, 1979). This work contains a testimonial by Teodorico Bland of the Rodney Mission, who was sent by the United States government to collect information about the political and social situation in Argentina. Bland's note of November 2, 1818, reads: "This is what the cowboys of the pampas and plains are like. They are generally called gauchos, an epithet, like *yanqui,* that was originally pejorative, but has now been transformed into a common term of definition that is no longer offensive." See also Emilio A. Coni, *El gaucho,* 2d ed. (Buenos Aires: Solar-Hachette, 1969), which contains many testimonials on the "delinquency" of the gaucho.

　　Lynch writes: "Even the use of the word 'gaucho' was ambiguous in Rosist terminology. It had two meanings, depending on the situation. In public it was used as a term of esteem, and perpetuated the idea that the gaucho, like the rancher, was a model of native virtues and that the interests of the two groups were identical. . . . In private, however, es-

These new words, "patriotic" and "courageous," create a scandal (the same scandal that produced the revolution). They add themselves to "gaucho," connecting with its earlier, legal meaning; *they connect with "delinquent" and do not cancel it out altogether.* The meaning continues to oscillate and is the same as the indeterminacy between accepting discipline and deserting. This dislocation between the new and the prior produces the first confrontation that constitutes the genre: "patriotic gaucho." This is the first confrontation because within it different universes of meaning collide (universes of meaning, and of uses of bodies, and of spatial fields): the meaning of "vagrant" is economic and juridical; for the gaucho, that of "patriot" is at this moment military. The respective opposites are worker (one who has working papers or servant's papers, who lives in one place, who has a wife) and deserter. The genre intervenes in this indeterminacy and dramatizes it. The genre attempts to undifferentiate this indeterminacy through definitions and assumes the voice of the patriot not simply to define him but also to define the Other: *in the voice of the gaucho the genre defines the word "gaucho."*

---

pecially in police use, 'gaucho' meant vagrant, ill-kempt, delinquent. The first usage represented political propaganda. The pejorative sense expressed class distinction, social prejudices and economic attitudes; the land-owner, in need of workers, used it to confront the man of the country who wanted to remain free" (*Rosas*, 112).

It may be that in Uruguay, with Artigas, the process was different from Argentina's, or even its opposite. Artigas's political agenda benefited the rural masses with the Rule of Lands, an attempt at agrarian reform, and incorporated the gauchos, and also the Indians, in the revolutionary process. According to various historians there were no desertions from Artigas's army but only from Rondeau's. See León Pomer, *El soldado criollo*, La Historia Popular 22 (Buenos Aires: CEAL, 1971); Alfonso Fernández Cabrelli, *Los orientales* (Montevideo: Grito de Asencio, 1974), vol. 2; Washington Reyes Abadie, *Artigas y federalismo en el Río de la Plata* (Buenos Aires: Hispamérica, 1986).

From this point of view, only an Artigist Uruguayan like Hidalgo, who participated in the first siege and in the exodus, could have founded the genre.

Lucio V. Mansilla (1831–1913), in *Una excursión a los indios Ranqueles* (1870; reprint, Buenos Aires: Estrada, 1959), 2:263, still writes of the two meanings of "gaucho" or of the two types of gaucho: the "peasant gaucho" (who has a home, work, and respect for authority), and the "pure gaucho," gambler, fighter, and enemy of discipline, who flees military service and hides among the Indians when he's stabbed someone. The first is a farm hand and soldier; the second only allows himself to be employed in seasonal branding and is a deserter.

This oscillation of meaning between the use of the body and of the voice, between the war and the war of words, constitutes the fundamental literary material of the genre. It constitutes this material because there is literature and because what matters for literature is an indeterminacy and discrepancy (between laws, between being or not being in the army) in words: in the words "patriotic" and "gaucho." The verbal scandal serves as the birth and the closure of the genre: because there are two meanings of the word "gaucho," a new one and another that continues to resonate, because for the gaucho there is a differential and dislocated system of laws and of military and economic universes, because he could accept discipline or desert, *there is a use of the differential voice of the gaucho.*

The second chain of uses thus inserts itself in the center of the first, between the army's use of the body and the culture of the written word's use of the voice (and thus, between the two chains, a volume is already constructed). This second chain is the chain of the voice and of the meanings of the voice:

a) the army's use of the gaucho adds a different meaning to the word "gaucho";

b) the meanings of the word "gaucho" are defined by the use of the differential voice of the gaucho: the gaucho genre; and henceforth:

c) the genre defines the meaning of the differential uses of the gaucho.

And here is another, alternative chain for this essay:

a) the use of the gaucho for the war turns the meaning of the word "gaucho" upside down;

b) the meanings of the word "gaucho" are defined, making turns, in the use of the differential voice of the gaucho: the gaucho genre; and henceforth:

c) the genre is a series of turns in the meanings of the differential uses of the gaucho.

Let us thus abbreviate the use of the gaucho's voice to define the word "gaucho" as the word/voice (of the) "gaucho." The problem of the word/voice (of the) "gaucho" is not lexicological or etymological but rather political and literary. (The linguistic problem is political, the politics of language are political, and the languages of politics are politics. The genre is politicoliterary in a nondifferential way.) The use of the word "gaucho" in the voice of the gaucho implies a definite mode of construction of that voice. The genre explores the meaning of the word "gaucho," submitting it to precise rules: marks, borders, interlocutions, tones, distortions, and silences. The meaning of that word is its construction and at the same time its interpretation. The genre, like the army and the law, now serves to define the word "gaucho" or the "gaucho" voice; the genre may substitute for the law (which defines the gaucho as "delinquent") and for the army (which defines him as "patriotic") because it defines the conditions and meanings of both law and army in the construction of its voice. It defines the possible uses of the word and with the word the uses of bodies; it says what a gaucho is and how he may be divided into legal and illegal, "good" and "bad," what he is for, what places he occupies, and all this in the voice of the gaucho himself. Once again there is a circularity in the uses of bodies and in the meanings of words. If the gauchos can be used, the word/voice has a possible meaning and use in literature; if they are not usable, if they subtract themselves like Facundo, the word "gaucho" has a negative meaning. The genre is situated between the two meanings in order to contemplate its difference in the differential uses of words. And the logic of uses makes another turn: the genre explores the meaning of the word "gaucho" in and by the use of the voice of the gaucho, and that use is at the same time the use of the gaucho, the Other of the genre's meanings or definitions. The genre is a treatise on the differential uses of voices and words that define the meanings of the uses of bodies.

The second chain has, therefore, a meaning transversal to that of the first, as of escape and volume: from the use of voices it refers to the use of bodies. It is the chain between the exterior space and the interior of the genre. The form of the two chains is the form that *La ida* and *La vuelta* trace, and that circularity is desire, dream, logic, and the other border of the genre.[22]

22. **An Exercise with the Dictionary**
It cost me a lot of trouble to come up with the formula of the genre: "in the voice of the gaucho the word 'gaucho' is defined: the word/voice (of the) 'gaucho.'" This took years of work with the challenge and the lament. And when I discovered the formula, it seemed to me that I had found THE FORMULA of the gaucho genre and at the same time the formula of all literature. A single formula for both: just what I had always been looking for without knowing it. *This formula seems to say everything* in such a synthetic way *and at the same time it says nothing*: it says that a word is defined through a voice or that a voice

defines itself or that a voice defines the same word in two different ways that are really the same or that a word defines itself.

This is a literary definition of the genre; it is the way in which the genre defines itself literarily in the minimal space between the synonym and the homonym, in the field of minimum difference. If we think that the "signified" of a word, of the word "gaucho," implies the maximum possibility of the synonym and that the absolute synonym questions the set of language in the field of signifieds (there would then be no difference between two words), we arrive at one of the basic problems of the genre, that of the difference between the gaucho voice and the word "gaucho." And if we imagine that the homonym of "voice" implies no difference between the fields of sound and writing, we arrive at the two extremes of the spectrum of minimum differences by which the genre is literarily defined; by which literature is defined. And this places all language—unlimited semiosis—in the narrow space of minimum difference.

At the same time, this definition opens up the fields of tautology (the impossible world of the absolute synonym) and contradiction, because tautology would imply a verbal scandal capable of placing the very foundation of language, minimum difference, in question or in contradiction. This seemed to me so disquieting and strange (or sinister) that I felt obliged to resort to the full spectrum of dictionaries. [Because there is no English equivalent of the coincidence in meaning between the Spanish words *voz* and *palabra*, I have omitted a part of the original footnote that quotes dictionary definitions of the two Spanish words. *Trans.*]

The "Dictionary" of the Academy
If we now take Angelo Marchese and Joaquín Forradellas's *Diccionario de retórica, crítica y terminología literaria* (Barcelona: Editorial Ariel, 1986) and look up the terms "voice," "word," and "tautology," we arrive once again at troubling results:

> VOICE: Genette (*Figures III*) uses "voice" to refer to the narrative instance, that is to say, to the process of enunciation (q.v.) or of narration in which the narrator is located. The narrator may be absent from the related story (Homer or Flaubert) or present as a character in the story (the so-called I-narrator); in the first case he may intervene (for example, through formulas of this type: *let us see how our hero responds; let us leave in the first part of this story the courageous Biscayan and the famous Don Quijote . . .*); in the second case we would have a homodiegetic narration (the "I" can be a protagonist, like Dante in the *Divine Comedy*, or a witness). The status of the narrator is defined by the narrative level (extradiegetic: the narrator outside the story; intradiegetic: the narrator inside the story) and by means of his relation to the story (heterodiegetic and homodiegetic). [The authors go on to reproduce and explain Genette's graphic paradigm of the narrator. They continue:] By analogy with Jakobson's functions of language, Genette postulates several functions of the narrator: the narrative function proper, centered in the story; the function of management, when the narrator refers to the text, and to its internal organization; the function of communication, when the orientation is toward the reader; the function of witness, when

the narrator directs the story toward himself, toward the part that he has played in the story; the ideological function, when the narrator's intervention in the story takes the form of a commentary on the action (q.v. STYLE, 1; evaluative discourse). The ideological function may also be realized by means of a kind of transference, when the writer makes use of a kind of "spokesperson" character to express his personal convictions. (421)

WORD: The traditional, merely empirical, definition of the word as a linguistic element has been questioned and rejected by students of structuralist tendency, who distinguish, ordinarily, between the word as discursive or textual unit and the vocable as lexical unit (s.v.). Beyond the word, minimal units of meaning are morphemes (q.v.) or monemes (q.v.). Lexical units are called lexemes (q.v.). (305)

TAUTOLOGY: A logical figure that consists of presenting a proposition whose predicate adds nothing new to the subject: *Mario, believe me, courtship is courtship* (Delibes). Considered a logical vice, tautology may at times acquire an extreme expressive value, as in the famous passage from Gertrude Stein: *A rose is a rose is a rose.* Or it may be accompanied by a diaphoric (q.v.) use of terms: *And through the streets the blood of the children / ran simply, like the blood of children* (Neruda). This diaphora may lead to the admission of the contradictory proposition with equal terms: *But I am no longer I / nor is my house still my house* (García Lorca). (396)

The Other "Dictionary"
Gerd Brand, *The Central Texts of Ludwig Wittgenstein,* trans. and with an introduction by Robert E. Innis (Oxford: Basil Blackwell, 1979): it was Wittgenstein who gave me the category of use, among other things. The volume is ordered alphabetically from A to O. In D, "The Doubling of Reality," part XI, sections 57 and 58, pp. 37–38, read:

> 57. If I construct a system of propositions with which I want to determine and grasp reality, then I follow rules, rules governing the manner of representation. The boundary-stakes of these rules are tautology and contradiction. Tautology and contradiction have the external form of propositions. While the proposition shows what it says, tautology and contradiction show nothing at all. Tautology represents nothing and a contradiction can represent nothing (see NB [*Notebooks, 1914–16*], p. 24). Tautology and contradiction are senseless, because through them I cannot bring the proposition up to the point where its truth or falsity can be decided (see T [*Tractatus Logico-Philosophicus*] 4.461). In the one case it is already true unconditionally and in the other case it cannot be true. "Tautologies and contradictions are not, however, nonsensical. They are part of the symbolism, just as '0' is part of the symbolism of arithmetic" (T 4.4611). That is, every time I arrive at "0" I have to begin anew in a certain way.
>
> Tautology and contradiction are not, however, two null-points in the scale of propositions. They are opposed poles. In this sense they do not say nothing but say where a proposition is located: namely between them (see NB, p. 45).

58. A tautology is no rule and we do not let a contradiction function as a rule. If we want to represent reality why do we fear a contradiction more than a tautology (see z [*Zettel*] 689)? Because we do not get entangled in a tautology, and if we did in fact do so, it would be without meaning, since it is true unconditionally. Besides, we can use a tautology in a certain sense. "What characterizes the application of a tautology is that we never use a tautology itself in order to express something with this propositional form but that we avail ourselves of it only as a method in order by means of it to make visible logical relations between other statements.

"If we were blind the telescope would not be able to make us see; should language not already show everything logical, then tautology would also not be able to teach us anything.

"*To the method of tautology there corresponds in mathematics the proof of an equation.* The same factor used in the case of tautologies—namely, the making visible of the agreement of two structures—is also utilized in the proof of an equation. If we prove a numerical calculation we transform the two sides until their equality is *shown.* That is, in fact, the same procedure on which the use of tautologies rests.

"*Something* in this conception is therefore correct. *The equation is no tautology.* Rather the *proof of the equation* rests on the same principle on which the application of a tautology rests.

"It is common to mathematics and to logic that the proof is no proposition but that the proof *demonstrates* something" (w [Waismann, *Wittgenstein und der Wiener Kreis*], p. 219).

After having briefly touched upon the one boundary-mark of rules, tautology, let us turn to the other one, contradiction. I do not allow a contradiction to function as a rule. Now what happens if I discover a contradiction amidst my rules? With this I discover that they are no rules at all and look for new ones. "What is a rule? If I, for example, say: 'do that and don't do it!' the other person does not know what he is to do: that is, we do not allow a contradiction to function as a rule. We call precisely a contradiction not a rule—or more simply: the grammar of the word 'rule' is such that a contradiction is not characterized as a rule. If, now, a contradiction appears among my rules, I would say: those are not rules in the sense in which I otherwise speak of rules. What do we do in such a case? Nothing is simpler: we give a new rule and thereby the matter is settled" (pr [*Philosophical Remarks*], pp. 344f; see pr, p. 322; w, pp. 124–25). (Emphasis in original.)

In Part n. "Will, Religion, Ethics," part VI, sect. 287, p. 163:

"But it is nonsense to say that I wonder at the existence of the world, because I cannot imagine it not existing. I would of course wonder at the world round me not being as it is. If for instance I had this experience while looking into the blue sky, I could wonder at the sky being blue as opposed to the case when it's clouded. But that's not what I mean. I am wondering at the sky being *whatever it is.*" (e ["Lecture on Ethics"], p. 9).

First Outline of the Genre

The two chains and their links (which form an escape, a return, a volume) define the logical space of the genre, the space shared by the totality of the genre and its external frontier or its opposite: the margin where the use of the voice and the use of the gaucho relay back and forth, in a circle. As if they were self-referential. On one side of the boundary and on the other. And also, the place where on one hand learned words of laws and armies that define the uses of bodies are on the other hand the "gaucho" voice and may be spoken by something like a weapon-voice and a law-voice and a motherland-voice and even a state-voice. Because it's about a written voice. The margin where laws and the differential uses of bodies *are* the differential written voice of gaucho texts. The chains of use bind the two margins that constitute the logical space of the genre because their links (their rings) are on one side and on the other; they form not a linear sequence but rather different levels: each ring designates a leap from one register of the language to another, a passage from one universe to another. Bodies, voices, written voices, written words. The Treatise is not about determinism, functionalism, or moralism; it's not about vertical causalities or horizontal implications. To cross by way of the written law from the body to the written voice (genre), and from the genre back to the use of the body, implies leaping from one universe of meaning to another. Those leaps are welded to the links of the two chains, *which are rings or alliances.*

Another approximate version for the essay: the tracing of the genre's boundaries performed by the two chains of use has the form of points of circularity (alliances), of different levels, between the uses of the gaucho's voice and the uses of the gaucho in the other language, in the no-voice of the genre that is the learned word. Each time the gaucho is defined and used differentially in the universe of the learned word (because different laws apply to it and because through those laws its body is used differently in war and work than other bodies) one encounters the external frontier, or the reverse of the genre. This is the universe of the learned word in the written register. The other side of the frontier, that of the genre, follows

---

One could perhaps want to say that in this case we are astonished at a tautology. But it would be nonsense to say this because it is impossible to be astonished at a tautology, because everything lies open. (Emphasis in original.)

the same contour but in the differential voice, in the difference of register: in the written voice that is the specific language produced by the genre. On one side, *Facundo,* Echeverría's *El matadero,* Pedro de Angelis's *Biografia de Rosas,* Alberdi's *Bases* and the *Póstumos,* the *Excursión a los indios Ranqueles* and even the National Hymn, which everyone sings. And the armies, the dispositions, practices, and laws pertaining to vagrants. On the other, the genre. (The genre condemns the external to undifferentiation, to indefinition: to the unclassifiable genres of *Facundo,* the *Excursión, El matadero,* and even the hymn. And it also condemned criticism to argue for decades over *those* "genres" or to read *that* object as no genre in order to delimit it.) The region where one margin touches the other is inhabited by circles or mutual systems of reference (rings, alliances) between the uses of the voice (the written voice of the gaucho) and the learned word. And, outside, the uses of bodies. Those alliances also designate the fiction of the genre in its relation to the other side of logical space (and also contaminate that other side with fiction). Because there the written voice of the gaucho collides with "the real" (*and reality is the other word, the learned word and not the voice*), and returns on itself, again, to follow a route that in its turn makes a series of turns, almost a circle. In those remissions and mutual references, in those alliances, collisions, circles, comings, and goings, the genre may be recognized as genre. And it may be reproduced each time a written word appears calling itself the voice of a gaucho and defining him. And each time that that written voice is weapon-law-motherland-state.

The logical space of the genre, the interior space of the chains of use and the alliances, has one more dimension: the historical space (*time*) between independence and the definitive national Constitution of 1880. It's in the historical space that the turns of the links and rings of the chains of the logical space of the genre unfold. When we travel the two chains of use we travel the entire historical space and thus return almost to the starting point, but in reverse, on the opposite margin. *Martín Fierro,* after the first turn of *Fausto,* returns to trace the entire genre but in the opposite direction, in the opposite direction from Hidalgo, in *a Departure that turns* on the emergence of the genre to allow it to be read because it positions itself below, at its bottom margin, and in *a Return that turns on the Departure and* nearly touches the other margin of the chain, its top and outside, at its furthest point.[23] Almost at the boundary of the external frontier. *La ida* thus appears as the foundation of the genre, its place of self-reference, and *La vuelta* sets the chain in motion again, to open and close it at the same time at its point of departure and, this time, almost at the top margin of the external space (this is where Sarmiento and Alberdi unite and revolve forever). Because *Martín Fierro* exists at the two extremes, the bottom (*ida*) and top (*vuelta*) margins of the outline of the genre, and *in its final part,* which contains the entire design and form of the genre but in another direction. In the other direction of the Return. It inhabits the extreme of the logical space, whose other extreme is inhabited by Hidalgo, because he inhabits the end of historical space when it turns on itself to give the final rotation. This happens because the two chains with their rings have been traveled in their entirety and they are found at their final point, at the extreme of the circle and, on another level and in reverse, at the starting point.

La vuelta returns to recuperate the legal meaning of the "delinquent gaucho" and returns to the law in the written voice. At this point the chain of uses and the law of definitions are closed: 1879. It's the end of the voice of the gaucho (who in the counsels of *La vuelta* is already "the man")[24] and at the same time the point of maximum contact with what is not genre. *La vuelta* is the institution of the "gaucho" voice in definitive opposition to the "delinquent" and to the soldier of the differential law: as worker. But *La vuelta* also returns to Hidalgo and his enemies and the entire system at the moment of its emergence, and it even cites *La ida.* It includes everything that it once opposed as an enemy because now there are no longer enemies that must be opposed with and by gauchos. The black man of the minstrel contest closes the circle: he challenges Martín Fierro with song, with his voice, and loses. He is below Martín Fierro and is *his Other,* and says that from now on he is going *to sing for consolation,* which returns to the prelude of *La ida.* Borges was able to read this (because of his present, because of his own history) and in writing it he definitively closed the classic because *he brought down its margin:* to begin afresh the eternal turns of infamy would require moving on to another, lower, color. But when *La*

23. [This refers again to the two parts of Hernandez's *Martín Fierro,* commonly referred to as *La ida* (The departure) and *La vuelta* (The return). See n. 4, above. *Trans.*]
24. [This refers to Martín Fierro's advice to his sons and Cruz's son Picardía at the end of *La vuelta. Trans.*]

vuelta closes the genre there is no Other black genre (later there will be Vicente Rossi's *Cosas de negros,* which Borges was so fond of), but rather something else that opens, another chain of uses: the use of the genre for passage to another literary genre. To burlesque, to grotesque, or straight to the song from which it emerged, to the tango and the milonga. And also to the novel where the voices of the gaucho and the learned words are strictly delimited, *separated,* in *Juan Moreira* and *Don Segundo Sombra.*[25] Or to the story. Here Borges marks the end (in "The End") of that other chain of uses born in *La vuelta:* the use of the genre to produce literature. And he closes it in 1940, because that is the end of another historical space, which closes the logical space of the chains of use of the genre that begins with *Martín Fierro.* The blacks are Others. The last chain of the genre that opens with *Martín Fierro,* that of the use of the genre to produce literature in another genre, seems thus to close itself with the closing of the historical space that opened when the historical space of the genre closed.

When the blacks are the Other blacks, the chain of production of literature of the genre opens again, incredibly, and with a leap backward.[26] Borges and Bioy Casares hear them during Peronism (its voice seems to occupy the entire space of the motherland), and hence, from within, they give a leap back and return to Ascasubi, who was exiled for writing "La fiesta del monstruo." They write Ascasubi's "La refalosa," but the victim of the savages with their impossible voices is not the gaucho Jacinto Cielo (Ascasubi's gaucho Jesus) but rather the other Jesus, the Jew.[27] The monsters and written voices of Borges-Bioy kill a Jew.

As may be seen, the turns and returns below and back, to the lower and upper margins, and also to various heavens and places of exile, seem to define the body of the genre. And starting from the leap of Borges and Bioy, or starting from Peronism, the genre undergoes a structural transformation: it is read and written in twos, and from a different calling, to

25. [*Juan Moreira* (1879) is a gauchesque novel by Eduardo Gutiérrez (1851–1889); *Don Segundo Sombra* (1926) is a novel by Ricardo Güiraldes (1886–1927) evoking gaucho life. *Trans.*]

26. [The reference is to *cabecitas negras,* a disparaging and racist term for the white proletariat from the interior brought by Juan Domingo Perón to work in Buenos Aires. *Trans.*]

27. [The *refalosa,* that is *resbalosa,* or "slippery one," is a dance in which the slipperiness is created by the blood of someone whose throat has been cut. Ascasubi's poem appears in full on pp. 138–41. *Trans.*]

call it something. Borges and Bioy, the sons of *El caudillo* and of *Antes del 900:* one a poet, short-story writer, essayist, and the other, above all, a novelist. And soon, also in twos, in 1966–67 and 1969, Osvaldo Lamborghini and Leopoldo Fernández, a writer and a critic, will return to writing the *refalosa* of the motherland or the death of the end of the 1960s that is *El fiord.* Thus the logic of the alliance of the genre is brought to its authors. As if *Fausto's* Pollo and Laguna reappeared in the future as writers of the genre, permitting it to be read and writing it with a heard voice and a written word (as if "El Fausto Criollo" of *El tamaño de mi esperanza* became reality).[28] The time of the genre is always the future, the literature of the future, the future book.

The Top and Bottom Margins of the Genre
Literary Revolutions and Two Definitions of the Gaucho
as Argentine Man

The first border of the genre, the margin with what is not itself, with its exterior space, places it in contact with all the works written between independence and the establishment of the state in 1880. It is in contact with everything: poems, journalism, political pamphlets, theater, narratives of all kinds, descriptions of battles, war bulletins, peace treaties, laws, letters, petitions, wills, notices, card games, threats, jokes, farewells, insults, dances, parties, and even birthday greetings (see the indexes of Ascasubi's *Paulino Lucero* and some of Luis Pérez's *Toritos*). Evidently, this does not have to do only with written words: everything is here. The literature of the epoch is here (this may be found on the other side, dispersed and divided into unclassifiable genres: it is the nongenre), and also something else: music, the murmuring of voices, laughter, shouts, and fears: *certain things that had never been written.* It could thus be said that the genre contains the entire epoch and not merely the literature of the epoch. Or that only the genre allows the epoch to be read. And everything is contained in

28. [In "El Fausto Criollo" (The creole Faust), a brief essay about del Campo's *Fausto* from Borges's book of essays, *El tamaño de mi esperanza* (Buenos Aires: Editorial Proa, 1926), Borges wonders what happens to Anastasio el Pollo after the end of del Campo's *Fausto* and imagines himself encountering, at the end of a long journey, an old gaucho or an old china (gaucho woman) "who will tell me of the death and miracles of such an immortal man" (13). *Trans.*]

the genre because it is written in the voice, in the writing of the voice of the Other, in another, lower register. It is written from a lower border *and therefore can say everything.* On the side of use, the genre is defined from below, and therefore can say everything.

When Hidalgo writes the voice of the patriotic gaucho for the first time, he creates another, literary scandal. He widens the definition of "literature" because he places within it the not-yet-written, the sung music of his present. A literary revolution is no more than a leap or the widening of a frontier. It occurs when what is below the margin that defined the literary (the literary of the epoch: odes, the National Hymn, the *Marcha Oriental* of Hidalgo himself and his monologues) *turns* and by this revolution takes up a position above the margin. Thus the space is reorganized—not merely that space that is above ("literature") but also that which is below ("nonliterature"). The space below: the multiple, nearly infinite scale of heard voices that exist below the written, below the written word (I am speaking of the music of language and of music, of sound), in which we do not want to or cannot get lost because then we would lose our voice. And also that which is above the written, another scandal of geographies and stories that is lost in space and time and that turns the literary space of written voices.

But the genre is always about margins and about the alliance between the voice and that which is written. And Hidalgo's literary revolution requires a double movement. On the lower side, it requires a raising of never-written voices. This is an ascent of songs, passwords, choruses, guitars, shouts, hurrahs, and curses: the voices of the people in revolution and in the army. The volume grows to such a point that the sound opens a door and *occupies the entire space.* This is the scandalous recreation of the revolution. On the upper side, it requires a lowering of written words that come from other written words in other languages and are translated (this is a lowering of the written word to the exterior space) and *take up exactly the same space,* at the same border, that the unwritten voices occupied: these words are the universals of the motherland, the universals placed in the whole space of the motherland. They are equality, freedom, independence, which come from above, from other words written in other languages and translated, and which, through the revolution, lower themselves and touch the voices that come from below and may thus translate them, reproduce them, in written form. The alliance between gaucho literature's universals of the motherland and the songs that occupy the space of the motherland founds the genre. That is to say, when *man* and his universals (when the universal rights of man) lower themselves and delimit themselves in voices. There the patriotic gaucho, the Argentine gaucho, is born. The voice that sings has crossed a border and enters written literature. The genre erased a division and transgressed the frontier that separated literature and nonliterature according to the categories of the oral and the written. It wrote the never-written and thus sang the never-sung in the space of the motherland.

This is not just a literary definition of the genre. It is another attempt at construction of a context (an apparatus to permit the reading of what one wants to read), and, as such, it proposes another story. This story of voices and words moves up from below and down from above. It does this in the complete field of heard and never-before-written voices, which are rising up to writing in the word/voice (of the) "gaucho"; and also of translated, never-before-said-or-sung words, which lower themselves to occupy the space of the word/voice (of the) "gaucho." From universal abstractions downward to the heard and never-written voice of the gauchos. The genre tells this movement in its history, and it ought to be possible to construct another specific apparatus that would measure, with mathematical precision, this system of movements of high and low margins, written universals, and heard voices, both written and not written, that wed each other each time to create the alliance of the genre and deploy its history. For the moment we cannot construct this apparatus to measure the passions. We propose several facts, a schema, and a turn. The facts would be several points in space through which voices and written words pass. First the writing in other alphabets, passing through its own alphabet, and, from there, through the multitude of languages that draw maps and even degrees of nearness and distance. This is the earthly sphere. When they enter their own written word (translated or not from other languages), they may pass the voice on their way down: noises, sounds, shouts, sung words, heard words, words distorted, heard poorly, words heard from other, foreign, languages. And in spaces such as the motherland, the province, the estate, one's own land, the ranch, the *pulpería*,[29] the frontier, the body of the voice that sings, and the land of the Indians.

29. [*Pulperías* began as rural trading posts where gauchos sold hides of cattle "to procure essential goods: yerba mate, clothing, hunting implements, alcohol, and wine" (Rock,

The turn that we propose is to measure the furthest points (the lowest point, the bottom margin of the genre, which is *La ida,* and the highest, the top margin of the genre, which is *La vuelta*), and to see there how *the Argentine man* is defined in the written voice of the gaucho.

To do this the following is needed:

First, the logical space and historical space of the genre: the chains with the alliances and the departures, turns, and returns of *La ida* and *La vuelta:* their furthest points;

Second, the ascending and descending ladders of written voices in the heavenly sphere;

Third, the inside and outside of the space of the motherland and its de-limitation;

And *finally,* literature: the universe of words. Their distortions, mean-ings, references, literal meanings. The writing of language's creativity.

The World of Accepted Meanings
Two Critics of Martín Fierro

La ida. Here are the genre's first borders: that of laws, the law of con-scription (*the differential law*), and that of the use of bodies by the army. The moment of conscription in the pulpería and the moment in which the army, at the frontier with the Indians, is about to tie Fierro's limbs to stakes in the ground. When he is already on his way to the point where he will define himself as *the one who has lost everything.* The moment of the army occurs when they have already taken away his horse and clothes, and he has not received payment for the use of his body (his name did not ap-pear on the written list). Following his staking is the moment of desertion.

First, the differential law. The officers of conscription enter the pulpería where, besides Fierro, there is a stranger, or rather one not subject to con-

---

Argentina, 48). Wright and Nekhom write that the *pulpería* "combined [the] functions of [a] country store selling sugar, tobacco, liquors, a post office or message center, saloon, social gathering place, etc." The origin of the name may come from "the lean meat, known as *pulpa,* often sold there; or from the Mexican *pulquería,* where pulque was sold, as alcoholic beverages were sold in the *pulpería;* for various reasons Spanish and early Ar-gentine national governments attempted to regulate the sales, privileges, racial status of [the] *pulperías* but had little success" (*Historical Dictionary,* 738). *Trans.*]

scription. Fierro quotes this stranger strangely in indirect discourse: "Even an English ditch-digger / who said, in the last war, / that he was from Inca-la-perra / and so shouldn't have to serve" (ll. 325–328).[30]

Second, the frontier, the army. Where there is a *gringo recruit* (this one gets paid for his service): "He was a gringo with a bad accent / and no one could understand him. / Who knows where he came from! / Maybe he warn't even a Christian, / since the only thing he said / was that he was a *Papolitano*" (ll. 847–852).[31]

Inca-la-perra and *papolitano:* words never written in the genre. They are an oral translation—written—of foreign words in the voice of the Argentine gaucho. They are not words that toss out challenges to their subjects, such as we will later see, but rather descriptions, to call them something. They are descriptions with a specific intonation.

In *La lengua de Martín Fierro* (Buenos Aires: Instituto de Filología, Universidad de Buenos Aires, 1930), Eleuterio Tiscornia writes about these two phrases:

> The basis of this decomposition, marked thus with intent in the text, is "Ingalaterra" with an epenthetic vowel, common in *Old Spanish*. The peasant *hears this word* and converts it *with mischievous intent* into the phrase *hinca a la perra* whose natural subject is 'el perro' [the dog]. The figurative meaning of the verb *hincar*, "to fornicate," illuminates the meaning of the whole. (Emphases mine and Tiscornia's: different emphases) (Chap. 6, p. 87)

As for *papo*-litano, which is discussed in the note that follows:

> Although there are *other words* that peasants more commonly use to refer to the vulva, the noun "papo," *which does not appear in dic-*

---

30. [In a note to their translation, Carrino, Carlos, and Mangouni explain, "*Inca-la-perra* approximates a broken Spanish pronunciation of 'England': *Inglaterra*. The gaucho was prone to converting unfamiliar words into off-color phrases; thus, *Inglaterra* (England) becomes *Inca-la-perra* (Inca-the-bitch)" (Hernández, *Gaucho*, 94). *Trans.*]

31. [*Papolitano:* Neapolitan. "Besides imitating the broken speech and bad pronunciation of the gringo, the prefix 'papo' had a derogatory meaning for the gaucho." Catherine Ward, trans. *The Gaucho Martín Fierro* (Albany: State University of New York Press, 1967: 65). *Trans.*]

tionaries of Argentine expressions, is also used. This metaphoric meaning is itself *scrupulously avoided* in the official lexicon, but the accepted meaning of "mount of Venus" for *papo* is *current in Spain and America,* as Lenz has already affirmed in *Dic.,* 1015, and as Wagner has just repeated. (Once again my emphases and Tiscornia's differ)

Tiscornia titles this chapter "Phonetic Modifications of Humorous Intent." We don't agree with his emphases (with his humor) but we believe in his quotation marks (his accepted meanings).

Ezequiel Martínez Estrada writes on page 24 of the first volume of *Muerte y transfiguración de* Martín Fierro, 2d ed. (México/Buenos Aires: Fondo de Cultura Economica, 1958):

> The forbidden language—it is not a secret but a censored language—of sex has its own vocabulary within the *language of the rural countryside,* as it does in *cities* and in *all parts of the world,* with its own genuine characteristics, as those languages always respond to forms *of infantile origin that are preserved through the years.* The register of these voices would be of great interest if they offered *a universal common denominator,* or showed the *typical features of different regions within a country.* One would want to investigate how nouns and verbs without any formal or functional analogy have fallen into this most severe of taboos. *The Martín Fierro provides absolutely and categorically no element for this kind of investigation.*
>
> When we consider the Poem in this light, as a piece free from words and even ideas related directly or indirectly to sex, we find ourselves before a specimen of rare beauty, *hard to equal in other literatures,* much less in the picaresque novel, to which it must be related. If this genre served as the basis of comparison *between one country and another, Argentina would exist at a much higher level than Spain* with respect to sexual modesty and rejection of the cynicism that infiltrates genius. But one must precisely warn that this cleanness of speech, this censorship of everything sexual, requires as a condition a contempt for women, *the Catholic prejudice that women are inferior and unclean.* (Emphasis mine)

Evidently, in this case, only the critics' humor differs. When the heard and never-before-written words appear (when the genre moves in history), they speak of Argentina and other countries, of Spain and religion, of high and low levels, and of infancy. They use the terrestrial sphere and universals. They compare, they relate evasions and censorship and even produce absolute negations.

Only their humor differs: their world or earthly sphere. Both of them use one. Tiscornia says that those "words" do not appear in the dictionaries of Argentine expressions (that they are not in reality Argentine), but that they do appear in dictionaries from Spain and from other parts of America. Tiscornia's earthly sphere is composed of dictionaries. Martínez Estrada says that these censored voices of sexuality (which exist everywhere and which constitute a universal) do not figure in any way in *Martín Fierro*. And that this demonstrates Argentina's superiority over Spain. His earthly sphere (*the figure of his world*) is the censored, the unsaid: prejudices. The man of the dictionary defines the accepted meaning and the thing, and provides the signified; the man of the unsaid speaks the meaning when he defines the Catholic prejudice: that the woman (vulva) is an inferior animal (bitch) and a dirty animal.

In *La ida* a "translation" *of the names of other countries to the female sex* appears in the voice of the gaucho. Here a crucial border has been crossed: *precisely that of the gender/genre,* which is at its lowest point. The written voice of the gaucho defines itself as a "man" facing the foreign "woman," and, moreover, "bitch"; his country is no more than the masculine member. And immediately afterward, the voice repeats this definition when it describes the gringo recruits: "And these high-class gents spend the day / jabberin' away all at the same time / till a recruit comes / to serve them their roast . . . / They're so hoity-toity / they act like sons of the rich" (ll. 901–906). Everything is turned around, several times: the Argentine soldiers serve the gringos, and, moreover, those who are served get paid. Therefore: "hell! They're only fit / to live with sissies" (ll. 915–916).

From below, from the incessant rising of unwritten voices that the genre incorporates in its history, the lowest margin of the genre is reached: to define the gaucho as an Argentine man, the sex, the gender, of the foreigner must be changed. The gringo recruits are women and carry this identity inscribed in the names of their countries, which are differential parts of the female sex. Only the gaucho's motherland belongs to the masculine gender.[32] And the foreign voices the gaucho never heard exist outside the genre and perhaps even outside of God (or Christ). The genre of the gaucho has definitively defined itself by what is low in order to define itself as Argentine, as existing in the Argentine army and under the Argentine law of conscription. The universal rights of man that Hidalgo instituted in the motherland are now the corporeal universals of each sex.

(Perhaps this is precisely the point at which Lugones and his impossible hearing of immigrant voices—which for him occupied the entire space of the motherland—were installed when he wrote *El payador,* or when he spoke it.[33] And, since these voices were Christian, he had to go to Greece and to another alphabet and another genre, the heroic epic, to find the emergence of the virile voice of the gaucho as Argentine man.)

The World of References

In *La vuelta,* where the voices proliferate with the sons of Fierro and Cruz, what has so often been heard can be read:

> Brothers should stand by each other
> because this is the first law;
> keep a true bond between you
> at each and every time—
> because if you fight among yourselves
> you'll fall prey to those outside. (Ll. 4691–4696)[34]

This is the highest point of the genre in the definition of the gaucho as Argentine man and is one of the counsels Martín Fierro gives to his sons.

Here the written voice of the gaucho descends from other written voices. Hernández himself says so in the prologue, "Four Words of Conversation with the Readers"—that is to say, he says it *at the initial margin of the book,* which follows the title, where there is no voice of the gaucho.

---

32. [In the play on words, only the gaucho's motherland is masculine because *papo-litano* (*Napolitano*) and *Inca-la-perra* (*Inglaterra*) are connoted by "vulva" and "bitch," that is, by feminine signs. *Trans.*]

33. [Leopoldo Lugones (1874–1938), the great Argentine modernist poet. *Trans.*]

34. [All quotations from *La vuelta,* unless otherwise noted, are from Ward's translation. *Trans.*]

Or where the gaucho is the Other. Hernández reproduces the alliance between the oral and the written (the logic of the genre) in his learned word: it is a conversation (oral, written) with the reader (oral, of the written).

At the first margin of the book, the four learned words of Hernández have four references:

> I deliver to the benevolent public, under the title *The Return of Martín Fierro,* the second part of a work that has had such a generous welcome that in six years it has gone through eleven editions with a total of forty-eight thousand copies.
>
> This is not an author's vanity, since I do not pay tribute to that false god; nor a publisher's inflated praise, since I have never acted as such to my humble productions.
>
> It is rather a timely and necessary reminder, to explain why the first printing of the present book consists of 20,000 copies divided into five sections or editions, each one of 4,000 numbers, and I would add that I am confident that the esteemed typographical Establishment of Señor Coni will produce a painstaking printing, which all the books that come from their workshops possess.
>
> This edition also includes ten illustrations incorporated into the body of the text, and I believe that in the realm of literature this is the first time that a work from our national presses comes with this advantage. Thus it begins.
>
> . . . In short, to create a publication in the most advantageous artistic conditions, no sacrifice has been omitted.

Hernández refers to his own book as a work of art. He makes numbers of all kinds: second part, first printing, first time; 6, 11, 48,000, 20,000, 5, 4,000, 1, 10. Perhaps he himself conceived of it as a work of art of numbers. And he says that the book is made in Argentina, the first literary work that is, at the same time, an art book printed in Argentina. (He might also think of the edition of Ascasubi's *Paulino Lucero* and *Santos Vega* in Paris: Paul Dupont, 1872.)

This prologue differs radically from *La ida*'s earlier two.[35] "Four Words

---

35. In "Letter to Don José Zoilo Miguens," dated "Buenos Aires, December 1872," which opens the first edition of *La ida* and remains in subsequent editions, beginning "Dear Friend," Hernández refers to his text as "my poor Martín Fierro" and as "that type of com-

position" when he compares it with *Fausto*. This has to do with the genre and the name (after Hidalgo the texts of the genre carry the name of the gaucho, or, in *Fausto,* the name of the doctor). He asks his friend, the rancher Zoilo Miguens, not "[to]deny [the work] his protection" when the poor Martín Fierro "sets out to discover the world with the aid of his name," and to pass over its defects and judge it "with benevolence" when he compares it to *Fausto*. Zoilo Miguens, father and patron of Martín Fierro-Hernández.

(In the same way Ascasubi named Varela as his patron: "Gaucho supplication addressed to the illustrious editor of *Comercio del Plata,* Doctor Don Florencio Varela, asking him to announce the forthcoming publication of the poem 'Paulino Lucero.'" This is a letter addressed to "Señor Narrator of the Commercio del Plata, Montevideo, November 14, 1846," which contains two stanzas of ten lines each. The last one reads, "And if by grace / my verses please you, / in your *noted gazette* / tell the city / in the right and proper way / that the gaucho will soon come forth / since you are the first / to whom I extend this *offer,* / so that you may recommend me, / if that is your pleasure, patron. PAULINO LUCERO." Hilario Ascasubi. *Paulino Lucero.* Buenos Aires, Estrada, 1945: 434.)

In the "Letter to the publishers of the eighth edition" of *La ida,* dated "Montevideo, August 1874," which begins "Dear Sirs the Publishers," Hernández refers again to his text as "my humble work": "Its appearance was as humble as the man it represents, and as the author's pretensions." But the "Argentine press" honored it by quoting from it, and so did the writers "whose honorable judgments you collect at the front of the new edition": he calls the latter "protectors." He defines his text as a *pamphlet:* "To plead for the relief of the evils — created by a defective regime — that oppress this social class, that weigh on it and bring it down, there are the parliamentary tribune, the newspapers, clubs, books, and lastly the pamphlet, which, rather than the degeneration of the book, is one of its chief assistants. I have made use of this last medium, and the judgment of the form employed belongs only to the domain of literature."

He now asks the public to offer protection to the publishers: "May the public repay with generous protection, not the merit of the work that you offer, which is certainly quite meager, but rather your efforts and the sacrifices you have made to produce a handsome and painstaking edition!"

And already the movement of expansion that reaches its highest point in "Four words" in *La vuelta* has begun: "Allow me now to show you the confidence with which I await your shrewd attention, who reserve for this letter a small space between the pages of the pamphlet, because I long to satisfy therein a debt of gratitude that I have with the public, with the Argentine press and with much of the Uruguayan press; with several publications not from the Americas, and with the writers who, deigning to give their attention to my humble work, have ennobled it with their judgments, thereby offering me, without themselves procuring it, the most complete recompense and the most intimate satisfaction."

In each prologue Hernández defines his own text in different ways, asks a different kind of protection, and expands his space accordingly as literature enters it. The insis-

of Conversation with the Readers" changes the destinator and the meaning; it does not provide a date and does not ask for protection but rather requests the indulgence of the public, to whom the book is dedicated: "accept this humble product that we dedicate to you, since you are our best and oldest friend!" And the conclusion states, "We close this prologue by saying that this book is called *The Return of Martín Fierro,* because the public has already given it this title, long before I had thought of writing it; and it goes forth with my paternal blessing." Hernández, who continues to refer to his writing as "humble," is now the father of its return.

The second reference from "Four Words of Conversation with the Readers" is *to the gaucho:* therein appear Sarmiento's words, to "ennoble" and "moralize" while "exalting the moral virtues." And Alberdi's: "teaching that honest work is the principal source of all improvement and well-being." For the gauchos, work (= economy) and education (= law).

Morality and the law exist already in the *heard voice* of the gauchos, which contains an ecumenical proverbial knowledge.

> How singular, and how worthy of observation, it is to *hear* our most uncultivated peasants express in two clear, simple lines *maxims and moral ideas that the most ancient of countries,* India and Persia, *preserved* as the inestimable treasure of their proverbial *wisdom:* that the Greeks *listened to* with veneration *from the mouths of their most profound wise men,* from Socrates, the founder of morality, and from Plato and Aristotle; that the renowned Seneca spread among the Romans; to which the men of the North accorded a privileged

---

tence on *Fausto* (Hernández's obsession) is notable: it is direct in the letter to Zoilo Miguens and indirect in the letter of 1874. In the latter he quotes a letter (another letter within a letter) from Ricardo Gutiérrez, which appeared in a newspaper and is dated Paris the "twelfth of last July"; he transcribes paragraphs asserting that the gauchos are not savage but Christian, noble, and intelligent. It is worth remembering that del Campo dedicated the manuscript of *Fausto* to Ricardo Gutiérrez, and submitted the poem for his judgment five days after the performance of the opera. And that the first edition of *Fausto* was preceded by the *letters* of its first three readers and critics, Ricardo Gutiérrez, Juan Carlos Gómez, and Carlos Guido y Spano. Gutiérrez says in his letter that it was he who tempted del Campo to write in gaucho style about his impressions of the spectacle.

place in their robust and energetic literature; that *modern civilization* repeats through the writings of its most distinguished moralists, and that have been fundamentally consecrated in the *religious codes* of all the great *reformers* of humanity. (Emphasis mine)

The art book, of Argentine manufacture, for the gauchos' education, labor, and enjoyment, is written with their very own heard voice, which is a *universal wisdom* that covers the entire space and history of humanity, of philosophy, and of the religions, in different places, times, and alphabets. The earthly sphere and the history of civilization in *the voice that is both preserved by and reforming of* the voice of the Argentine gaucho. The wisdom of the Argentine gaucho is universalized for the first and only time in the genre.

The fourth word refers to *the difference* between the wisdom of the gaucho—that is, popular wisdom—and that of learned people and European professors. And that, according to what *Argentine doctors* write in *other prologues,* refers to the neuroses.

> The human heart and morality *are the same* throughout the centuries. Civilizations essentially *differ.* "A professor, says *Doctor Don* V.F. López *in his prologue* to *Las Neurosis,* will never be made from a Brahmin"; it must be so: but making a wise Brahmin out of a gaucho would not offer the same difficulty; if it is true that all the Brahmins' learning is contained in their proverbial wisdom, as *the erudite conservator* of the Library of Paris depicts them in *La sabiduría popular de todas las naciones,* distributed in the New World by the American Pazos Kanki.

Only in the world of the popular is there a universal grammar of knowledge. And that is *the difference* between sages on the one hand and professors or prologues by doctors of neurosis on the other: from the latter it is impossible to make a universal Brahmin. The Argentine gaucho is a Brahmin heard and read in a book written by the erudite conservator of the Library of Paris, and distributed by an American. Doctors write prologues to *Las neurosis,* and sages and artists (like myself: Hernández) write prologues (this very one) to the popular wisdom of the universal Brahmin of *The Return of Martín Fierro.*

To summarize: reading the references in the four words of Hernández's prologue to *La vuelta,* an enunciation like this may be constructed: this work of art—*illustrated,* of national manufacture, destined to inculcate the law and morality necessary to make the gaucho a modern worker—is written by me in the heard voice of popular proverbial wisdom of the Argentine gauchos, which is *the same as the popular wisdom of all* nations throughout the history of civilization, as may be read in the written compilation of the *erudite conservator* of the Library of Paris, which in our language was distributed by an American, like me.

The World of the Literal: Names and Numbers
The Text and Its Voices

This is how the written and translated voice of the gaucho installs itself in Martín Fierro's voice in *sextina* 17 (= 8 or two 4s) of Fierro's counsels to his sons and Picardía, in order to define the Argentine man.[36] Here the motherland is a family with a father, sons, and brothers. The father says to the sons that the brothers are united because it's *the first law:* fraternity is *the universal value of the rights of man* that defines the motherland (equality and freedom exist in other parts of the text and define other types of universals). But the sons to whom he directs this word are not all brothers; Picardía is somebody else's son, and he has no brothers. The brothers, moreover, are ordered in the text in a strange way, using two different kinds of classification: Older Son and Second Son. Rather than names, they have numbers (and "the first," the number of the order that the older son lacks, appears in sextina 17 with the first law: the only first is the law).

The universal voice that came down from the earthly sphere (to link itself with another voice that also occupies the entire space, namely God's) is located within a family that excludes one member. If foreigners ("the outsiders") are the enumerated nonbrothers, then Picardía is a foreigner. Notice his position at another point in Fierro's counsels, in sextina 14 of

---

36. [The Spanish *sextina* appears to differ somewhat from the sestina—both consist of six six-line stanzas followed by a three-line stanza, but in the former the focus is on the number of syllables per line (they are hendecasyllabic), while in the latter the focus is on the complex recurrent pattern of end words. *Martín Fierro* does not strictly follow the sextina form, but adapts it for use in an epic, using six-line stanzas and between seven and twelve syllables per line. *Trans.*]

the 31 that comprise the counsels (number 4 is the number of reason, truth, and writing that Hernández uses in his prologue: the four words of conversation with the readers). *Here the voice of Martín Fierro speaks of man:*

> A man is born with the astuteness
> that has to serve him as a guide.
> Without it he'd go under;
> but in my experience,
> in some people it turns to discretion
> and in others, dirty tricks [*picardía*]. (Ll. 4673–4678)[37]

Picardía is included in only half of the astuteness with which a man is born; he is excluded from the other half for not being prudent. *His position is differential and divided,* both as "brother" and as "astute, prudent man."

Finally, *another voice, the narrator's,* in the first two sextinas (12 lines) of the 33rd canto (two times 3: sextina), the end (and two times two sextinas is 24 lines), *gives everyone a space:*

> After this, the four of them
> turned towards the four winds.
> They made a promise amongst them
> which they were all to keep—
> but as they swore it a secret
> I can't tell you what it was.
>
> The only thing I can tell you—
> and don't anyone be surprised,
> because a man is often obliged
> to do things in this way—
> they made an agreement amongst them
> to change their names from then on. (Ll. 4781–4792)

---

37. [The noun *picardía,* which Ward translates here as "dirty tricks," and which I will generally translate as "trickery," expresses the double-edged quality of mischievous, cunning, playful, or malicious intelligence, and it also refers to the genre of the picaresque novel developed in Spain in the sixteenth and seventeenth centuries. In *La vuelta,* picardía is both the proper name of a character, Picardía, Cruz's son, and the abstract noun expressing this ambiguous quality. *Trans.*]

The four, including Picardía, occupy the entire space of the mother-land, with a promise (the secret) and a change of name. They have promised to keep the new name secret. But Picardía cannot change his name because he is "a man [who] is often obliged to do things in this way," and Picardía is half astute or half man.

In the *last two* sextinas of canto XXVI (26 = 8), before the *two* cantos in quatrains (= 8), the old cantos with the quotations from *La ida,* Picardía himself speaks, in his own voice:

> By making efforts constantly
> I learned how to mend my faults;
> I managed to forget them all—
> except that, for my sins,
> I wasn't able to get rid of Picardía—
> the name they'd given me.
>
> A man who has a good name is spared
> from a lot of unpleasantness;
> so out of all this meandering
> don't you forget this warning—
> it was by experience I learned
> that a bad name can't be rubbed out. (Ll. 3577–3588)

If this is read literally and in all the voices, it can be clearly seen that Picardía's place in the beginnings, endings, counsels—in all the divisions of space of the motherland—is differential and divided, exactly like the gaucho in *La ida:* it is always about inclusions and exclusions, insides and outsides, halves or quarters (fatalities, condemnations, disgraces, impossibilities). He is included in half the astuteness of man and excluded from the other because of imprudence; he is included in a quarter of the entire space of the motherland but with a name: *Because he has bad in his name, and that can't be rubbed out.* He is not a brother and not an outsider. He is always a no-yes or a yes-no; half-stranger, half-brother, half-son. He is the fourth member, or a fourth of the Argentine man. He is *the Other:* the gaucho genre of *La ida.* His parents are in *La ida.* He also belongs to another genre: "*la* Picardía" (the Picaresque).[38] As in *La ida,* the text has

---

38. [See note 37. *La picardía* is a feminine noun, and the picaresque is a genre that originated in Spain; thus Picardía contains the feminine and the foreign. *Trans.*]

again leapt a crucial border to define the gaucho as Argentine man. In *La ida*, the foreigner is a woman (while the motherland is the masculine member); in *La vuelta*, the "trickery" is half female foreigner (while the motherland is the family of father and brothers). Picardía is the only one of the sons who has a name, but it is a half-name, a nickname that cannot be erased. And the nickname is a *generic quality* of man, as it is inscribed in the world of Fierro's counsels. Picardía is a name, a nickname, and a generic quality: *he is the son of the female Other.* In the third quatrain from the end of canto XXVII (one canto short of the 28) Picardía says in his own voice:

> And I'll say, though it's not my place to say
> what nobody else has said,
> that our Province is a mother
> who does not look after her sons. (Ll. 3713–3716)

And in the last quatrain of canto XXVII:

> And while I'm at it, I'll say also,
> because it springs from my heart—
> that if you don't take care of your countrymen
> you're not a true patriot. (Ll. 3721–3724)

Not only do the top and bottom margins of the gaucho genre include the other genre, the difference from the genre, in order to define the gaucho as Argentine man; something else also happens. *The words of Sarmiento*, of *Facundo*, reappear: the fellow countryman is the native of the same province, like Facundo and Ocampo—the patriot of the small motherland rather than of the entire space of the motherland.

Hidalgo's Transparency Is the Distribution of Voices

The words/voices (of the) "gaucho" are delimited and distributed in the interior space of the genre and in the interior of the genre's texts. Hidalgo founded the genre because he mapped the first distribution of the written voice of the gaucho. He erected a cosmos in the middle of silence. He couldn't simultaneously represent the fighting body—the soldier's body (or the deserter's, as in *La ida*)—and its voice; this representation would be incompatible with the establishment of the genre and would imply its end. Therefore he took the voice of the body par excellence from its user, that is, from the singer. And starting with that voice he mapped the other space of differences, circles, and turns, the space of the internal body of the texts of the genre.

> *New Patriotic Dialogue (1821)*
> Bartolomé Hidalgo
> Between Ramón Contreras, Gaucho of the Monte Guard,
> and Chano, Overseer of a Ranch in the Tordillo Islands
>
> CHANO
> What's up, friend Ramón,
> what are you doing in my district
> on that chestnut racehorse?
>
> CONTRERAS
> Friend, I'm getting him ready
> because I have to run
> against Hilario's sorrel.
>
> CHANO
> You don't say! If that's the way it is
> I'm going to put eight to four odds
> on this wild one.
> Look, friend, he's a horse
> that already at the starting line
> leans back the other way.
>
> CONTRERAS
> And how've you been since that day
> we were talking?
>
> CHANO
> Healthy but without yerba: [39]
> unsaddle your horse,

---

39. [*Yerba mate,* or just *mate,* is a South American tea; more than a drink, it is a social ritual. Mate is extremely high in caffeine, and contains an ingredient that allowed the gauchos, who drank it frequently, to subsist on a nearly all-meat diet. See the North American scientist Roger Payne's description of mate drinking and its paraphernalia and social

hang up your gear, and rest.
Take this rag, Mariano,
and walk with the yellow bay
and hook him up to the others.
That stretch between here and the Guard
is pretty hair-raising, huh?

CONTRERAS
And with so many downpours
the road is very rough,
and full of outlaws[40]
you're always bumping into;
the good thing is that I've sharpened
the poisoned knife to my taste.
With the tamers[41] I asked
the chestnut four questions,
and when he was eager
and raising hell,
I let the reins out full and I came away,
but always on the watch...
take the yerba, old friend
we'll keep on drinking bitter mate.

CHANO
And what about the motherland
that I'm so worried about?
Yesterday some officials
dropped by Pablo's
and while they were drinking mate

---

connotations. It is "usually drunk from a small gourd (*el mate*), . . . sipped through a sil-
ver-plated straw (*la bombilla*) whose tip is expanded out into a strainer so that the leaves
of the . . . yerba remain behind" (*Among Whales* [New York: Scribner's, 1996], 85). The
host pours boiling water onto the yerba in the gourd and passes it to a guest, who drinks
it and returns it to the host so that he may pour water for the next guest. *Trans.*]
40. [The Argentine term *malevo,* which I translate as "outlaw" or "outlaw gaucho," refers to vagrant or wandering gauchos who would attack or steal from ranches, other gauchos, or travelers. The word contains the word *mal,* "bad" or "evil." *Trans.*]
41. [That is, his spurs. *Trans.*]

they took a shot of cane liquor
and changed the mate water,
and read some notices
about King Fernando
anxiously requesting
through his deputies
that his sworn constitution
be recognized in these parts.

CONTRERAS
The rumor's been going around for days,
certainly they weren't deceiving you:
the deputies came,
and from the ship they sent
a whole heap of papers
in the name of King Fernando;
and the braggarts came...
the ba... those bad horsemen!
But friend, our Junta
gave a shout and pushed it out
and sent them a reply
much prettier than San Bernardo.
Ah, gauchos, scribers
on a cigarette paper!
When the others saw the gauchos weren't biting,
and that they'd been beat,
they raised anchor,
and, turning the ship around,
they left without saying goodbye...
May they go with two hundred devils.

CHANO
He's a clod,
our friend Don Fernando:
as I figure it,
he's so useless
he doesn't even know how to whistle,
sure as my name is Chano.

We dropped the price
of all his orders to nothing
and for our freedom
and its sacred rights
we left the countryside,
and came upon the enemy,
our ponchos ready for a fight
and jackknives in hand,
with our hearts in God
and the holy scapulary
of Our Lady of Carmen,
and crouching like a cat;
without heeding the bullets
or the strong cannon fire,
we struck each other in the mouth
and clashed together,
I like this one, I don't like that one,
and so we cornered them,
and at a shout: *Long live the motherland!*
we redoubled our courage,
and among shots and smoke and confusion,
among slaps and slashes
they began to slacken,
and so loose did they get,
that of all that great company
we left not even a memory.
For good measure, we threw in
some other battles
in which we also creamed them;
and if they don't believe it, they can ask
that liar Posadas
how he did down there in Las Piedras,
and there on the ships.[42]

42. [There were two battles of Las Piedras, and both are mentioned in the Argentine national hymn. In the first, of May 18, 1811, the Spanish captain Gervasio Antonio de Posadas lost to General José Gervasio Artigas; in the second, of September 3, 1812, Major

So Tristan would say... I don't want to
waste any more time shooting vultures,
because Tristan was much sadder
than that other poor loverboy.[43]
And Muesas at del Cerrito;
Marcó weak and bloodthirsty
at the battle of Chacabuco,
Osorio the strongman
there in the Cerros de Espejo
in the brawl at Maipú.
Speak up, Quimper and O'Relly,
and you others who are being so quiet now.[44]
Everything's free, Contreras,
if you know Fernando;
he keeps drawing
but only gets a lousy hand.
Isn't it ridiculous
him coming around now to threaten us?
He'd better not sleep too much,
friend, because his subjects
find the name of Liberty

General Díaz Vélez made a surprise attack on the royalist army, forcing it to flee with a
great loss of lives and equipment (see Hidalgo, *Cielitos y diá logos patrióticos,* ed. Horacio
Jorge Becco [Buenos Aires: Editores Huemul, 1963], 134). *Trans.*]

43. [The Spanish general Pío Tristan, who lost the battles of Tucumán (1812) and Salta
(1813) to General Manuel Belgrano. "Tristan" sounds like *triste* (sad), and, of course,
evokes Tristan of *Tristan and Isolde,* "that other poor loverboy." *Trans.*]

44. [This stanza evokes a number of the actions and figures of the wars of independence.
The Spanish brigadier Vicente María Muesas died in the battle of Cerrito (1812). In the
battle of Chacabuco (1817) on the Chilean coast of the same name, General San Martín
defeated the Spanish brigadier D. Francisco Marcó del Pont, governor of Chile. Marcó's
troops fled, and Marcó, left without food or means of escape, was taken prisoner and
later executed. In the battle of Maipú (1818), San Martín laid in wait on the plains of
Maipú, to the south of Santiago, Chile, while his enemy, General Mariano Osorio, expected him in the Cerros de Espejo. Colonel Manuel Quimper was defeated in Nazca,
Peru, by General Lavalle (1820), and the Spanish general Diego O'Reilly was defeated near
Pasco by Colonel Arenales (also 1820). *Trans.*]

to their liking,
and since he starts to get on his jammies
even while he's threatening us,
they've already taken him for everything
and cut him out of the game.

CONTRERAS
Oh, Chano, I'm afraid
that goes without saying.
What you've told me is the truth
and I can't deny it;
but *put yourself in this situation:*
that they're scheming
to see if we unyoke ourselves
from the rest, and then
they'll strip us of everything,
even our trousers.

CHANO
Friend, better not touch that subject
because the devils are in me!
Who could stand up to us
if we joined forces?
I'm not talking about that dolt of a king;
all the tyrants of the world together
with more soldiers than there are mares in our countryside
couldn't hurt us; but friend,
quarreling about how we get paid
has slowed us down some.
Ah, friend, how much precious blood
has been spilled! Contreras,
doesn't it hurt to see
how we Americans
live in perpetual war,
giving our enemy
such a good time
while our time is so bitter?
But I hope from this time forward

to greet the May Sun
in happier days,
united with my brothers.[45]
So there's no need to back down,
since brave San Martín is already
at the ports of Lima
with those tough boys,
soldiers in a bad mood,
and they tell me that in Lima
there are so many patriots
that Pezuela's out spying,[46]
and when he is defeated
our state will have to be changed,
because patriotism will be born again
in even the humblest hovel.

CONTRERAS
Yeah, you bet.
That's the moment we've been waiting for!
And as soon as it's over
right then we'll show up
with rifle and sabre
to beg a longshot
to stop throwing away what belongs to someone else
because it's a terrible sin
against the taste of the owner
to use what one hasn't been given;
and in good conscience (because
I'm a true Christian) I don't want
anyone to be damned
for such a reckless act.[47]

45. [The "May Sun" refers to the first national government, which the junta established May 25, 1810 and which replaced the Spanish viceroyalty system. *Trans.*]
46. [The Spanish brigadier Don Joaquín de la Pezuela, who defeated Belgrano at Vilcapugio and Ayohuma, later viceroy of Peru. *Trans.*]
47. [The "longshot" is General Carlos Federico Lecor, the leader of the Portuguese army, who dislodged Artigas's forces from Montevideo, January 20, 1817. *Trans.*]

CHANO

Right, Ramón Contreras!
Do you remember that holy mess
that we saw at Andújar
when General Belgrano
made the leg-guards break on the Spanish,
those bad horsemen?
The general sure screwed up
in that battle (without meaning to hurt us)
and we're still paying for it;
he wanted to be generous,
and he soon saw how he was tricked,
when the sworn Castro
took up arms against him,
and broke his vow,
staining his honor and his rank.[48]
Those generosities
have thrown us far off course,
because the tyrant assumes
that such strange behavior
is only a lack of justice;
but that's all past, friend,
and it won't be bad
if we finally learn our lesson.
For now, take out your knife,
let's polish off this barbecue
and then take a siesta,
so we can go to the Bald Indian's
to see if my piebald
has turned up in his herd;

48. [The colonel from Salta, Saturnino Castro, part of the royalist cavalry, swore before Belgrano after the battle of Salta that he would not take up arms against the patriots. This vow was broken by order of the Spanish general José Manuel de Goyeneche, and after the insurrection of Cuzco (1814), he wanted to support the American cause and incited his troops to revolt, but he was unsuccessful and was executed by his coreligionists. For this and other notes to the poem, see Becco's edition of *Cielitos y diálogos patrióticos. Trans.*]

several days ago that brute
slipped out of the pen.

They ate with great contentment,
and after their siesta
they saddled up loosely
and left at a gallop
for the hovel of Andrés Bordón,
alias the Bald Indian,
who served as a sad soldier
in the northern provinces,
and in the battle of Vilcapulgio
they shot off his leg.
They shouted at the fence where his property began,
the dogs raised hell;[49]
Bordón left his kitchen,
and helped them off their horses;
and what passed between them
we'll tell another time, more slowly;
for now the pen has grown tired.

The First System of Frames

In its emergence the genre reveals the operation that defines it: the connecting of two verbal zones, the "oral" and the written. In these zones enunciations, tones, names, and forces are distributed; functions and hierarchies are assigned. The first operation is to construct the word of the gaucho as "heard word": the verse register and the situation in which it is emitted fit inside oral culture. From outside of the text, *the written word* announces and defines the voices: "New Patriotic Dialogue. Between Ramón Contreras, gaucho of the Monte Guard, and Chano, overseer of a ranch in the Tordillo Islands." The title and subtitle above function as *the*

---

49. [When arriving at a ranch, the traditional greeting, "*Ave María purísima!*" (Hail Purest Mary!) was shouted from horseback, in expectation of the customary response, "Conceived without sin!" The presence of friends or strangers on the ranch was announced by the barking of the dogs, whom the owners hushed without leaving the house. (See ibid., 138 n.). *Trans.*]

first frame of the texts. *The second, internal, frame* is the textualization, at the beginning of the poems, of the oral context in which the song, or in this case the dialogue, takes place: the texts incorporate and represent the situation in which a cielito is sung or the occasion when the encounter and dialogue between friends occurs.[50] Thus there are two frontiers that establish the ring of the alliance between the oral and the written. One provides the title and the event, and the other deploys the oral scene of the body of the poem: the literary revolution, the incorporation into literature of a kind of interlocutory position that *had never before passed into the written* (the heard and never-written voice): the audience present in the song or ordinary dialogue in the moment of leisure, of visiting, the greetings, the offering of drinks. The passing into the written of the oral scene produces an effect of "reality." And moreover, these are the situations in which the continuum production-reception-reproduction characteristic of the traditional song or saying occurs. They constitute the space of oral art.

Outside, therefore, is a learned writer who writes and "reproduces" or "quotes" what the "oral authors" "sing" or "say." The exterior frame of the title, in the register of the written word, acts to introduce a formally direct

---

50. That is to say, the writer of the genre brings into the written text the unspoken context in which the song or popular saying takes place; this context is the most important thing from the point of view of the sociology of folklore: the size of the vocal group, the interrelation between the director and the chorus, the group's level of organization, et cetera. See Alan Lomax, "Folk Song Style," *American Anthropologist* 61 (1959): 927–954; also Dell Hymes, *Foundations in Sociolinguistics: An Ethnographic Approach* (Philadelphia: University of Pennsylvania Press, 1974), from page 128 on. It is recognized that popular culture is transmitted through meetings, conversations, celebrations, and ceremonies and that it is not considered "literature" in the context of traditional culture, which does not clearly separate aesthetic, practical, cognitive, and legislative functions. The gaucho genre imitates other features of traditional (oral) literature, forming an aesthetic of convention rather than one of originality; the authors appear as transcribers rather than as "inventors"; their frequently repeated pseudonyms are the masks they adopt in order to write these fictions of oral creativity. See Walter D. Mignolo, "Semantización de la ficción literaria," *Dispositio*, no. 15–16, 5-6 (Fall 1980–Winter 1981); reprinted in his *Teoría del texto e interpretación de textos* (Mexico City: Universidad Nacional Autónoma de Mexico, 1986). Mignolo uses gaucho literature as an example of the possibilities and difficulties that the semantization of the situational field presents: "In the orality of the enunciative situation a triple semantization is brought about: that of the situational field, that of the (oral) mode, and that of the social role" (161).

discourse. *The first rule of the genre is the fiction of the written reproduction of the Other's oral word as the Other's word* and not as the word of the one who writes. The difference is established at the outset and is the first thing that is written in order to construct the ring of the two voices: "New Patriotic Dialogue. Between Ramón Contreras, Gaucho of the Monte Guard, and Chano, Overseer of a Ranch in the Tordillo Islands." *The second rule of the genre is the construction of the oral space,* the frame of the "heard voice," in the interior space of the text. These two discourses or words, the learned writing and the "heard voice," are sharply differentiated. The learned frame of the title-subtitle, which may be extended and autonomized until it constitutes the "Letter to Don José Zoilo Miguens" or the "Four Words of Conversation with the Readers,"[51] postulates the "literality" or "originality" of the heard voice (or, in Hernández, the "copy" or "imitation"), in order clearly to differentiate itself from that voice. This learned frame is the writer's *own* word: in Hidalgo it is an impersonal and

51. Here are some other examples in Hidalgo:

Title: "Patriotic cielito. Composed by a gaucho to sing of the Battle of Maipú" (1818).

And the first stanza: "Little chords, don't deny me now, / grant me your favor, / and I will sing in this cielito / of the great battle of Maipú."

And another title: "A gaucho of the Monte Guard responds to the Manifesto of Fernando VII and salutes the Count of Casa-Flores with the following cielito in his language" (1820).

And the first stanza: "Now that I've put away the yoke / and closed the pen / I'm going to tune the guitar / to explain my desire."

Note the height of development that this system reaches in Ascasubi. In "Los payadores": "Seated in a circle around a campfire at the bottom of the trenches of Montevideo, singing the following verses, three Argentine youths and minstrels lamented, on the same day that they joined the ranks of the Defenders of the Plaza, abandoning the ranks of Rosas's besieging army under the command of General Oribe (alias Alderete)." And the oral scene: "A native of Entre Rios. Ay, in the name of God!... / a native of Entre Rios is going to sing, / tongue, don't be disturbed, / in such a splendid circumstance— / —in such a splendid circumstance; / I abandoned the tyrant, / now I'm with the Uruguayans, / and I'll be a free gaucho."

In Antonio Lussich's *Los tres gauchos orientales:* "Discussion among the peasants Julián Giménez, Mauricio Baliente, and José Centurión on the western Revolution in circumstances of disarmament and in the pay of the army, dedicated to Señor D. José Hernández." The letter to Hernández and his reply follow, dated respectively "Buenos Aires, June 14th 1872" and "Buenos Aires, Hotel Argentino, June 20th 1872."

informative written word that states the names of those who are speaking, what positions they occupy, and where they're from; Hidalgo wrote for the theater and was director of the Casa de Comedias in Montevideo. The written word "gives" the voice to the oral "locutor," who is constituted as a fold and interiority in relation to the written: as an effect of the subject. In this fictional relation the ring of the alliance between the written word and the heard voice that is the genre is traced. The two frames—the title that refers to the oral enunciation (*it is said twice* that a gaucho is singing or speaking: first the title defines the Other and then the Other defines himself) and the oral scene in which the dialogue between the gauchos takes place—contain the text itself, the enunciated, or written transcription of enunciation (of the) "gaucho": what the patriot "sings" or "says." And what he sings or says is the convergence or alliance between the two discourses: the report or celebration of political and military events, the telling of the revolutionary and military process, on the subject of some written news of the enemy, as in this New Dialogue. In the oral scene, rapidly transformed into convention (and therefore able to be parodied), the voice of the gaucho speaks of the Other, of the political, the official: it speaks of the public life of the motherland.[52]

Thus the intonation of the voice of the gaucho and the military and political enunciation are linked, and, moreover, this relation manages modern journalism's conjunction with the traditional context of oral diffusion. From the beginning, the genre appears as a form of popular journalism

52. The genre connects the public life of the rural masses, which is also their art (minstrel shows, games, songs, dialogues, refrains, proverbs), with the new public life of the revolution and the war. This last, constituted before the revolution, exists in newspapers, patriotic societies, theaters, et cetera, and responds more or less to J. Habermas's concept (*Historia y crítica de la opinión publica* [History and criticism of public opinion] [Barcelona: Gustavo Gili, 1981]). Like the public life of the proletariat as analyzed by Oskar Negt and Alexander Kluge in *Offenlichkeit und Erfarung: Zur Organisationsanalyse von burgerlicher und proletarischer Offentlichkeit* (Frankfurt: Surkamp, 1972), the public life of the gauchos is manifested *in historical moments of disruption:* crises, wars, revolutions, counterrevolutions, which imply social constellations of various forces. It is manifested in moments of rupture and violent contradictions. See also Rainer Nagele, "Freud, Habermas, and the Dialectic of Enlightenment: On Real and Ideal Discourses," *New German Critique* 22 (1981).

and in fact that is how it circulated, in pamphlets and leaflets. In its dialogues, it also circulated as a form of popular theater. Thus there are already two "genres" of the exterior space of the genre, one literary and the other nonliterary, and moreover, at the same time, there are already *the two subgenres into which the genre is divided from the beginning:* sung texts (cielitos) and spoken texts (dialogues). And one of the characteristics of this literature for the people, and for a new public, is that *it represents,* in its interior, *the forms of its circulation or reproduction:* a song, two peasants speaking, one of whom reads for the other, who cannot. What the writer says in the title, with his written word, is what those who "hear" the dialogue must do: quote, reproduce, place the written in dialogue with the voice. Orality constructed and written, presented as "transcription" or "copy," thus represents the desire for reproduction. The same thing happens with direct oral discourse: there is a fiction of direct discourse that inverts the field of "authors" and inclusions. The author is the one who constructs the oral as oral to include in its interior the written, political word—*his*—that appears quoted and reproduced by the voice of the gaucho. His word is thus translated into orality. Or rather, the "heard" is constructed in order to quote and reproduce the written inside itself. *This alliance* (and the set of the system of rings-alliances) *constitutes the logic of the genre.*

The alliance between the voice without writing and the learned word is constituted by the war: by the first appeal to the rural masses to give free rein to their antagonism against the common enemy, the foreign oppressor. In the moment of solidarity and of the foundation of the motherland, everyone's voice may appear. The logic of the genre, then, is a verbal conjunction that assumes a verbal division and confrontation. This is the genre: to share words, to divide words, to differentiate words, and to combat the words of the two cultures in the word / voice (of the) "gaucho." The gaucho gives his sung voice, the disciplined and public use of his voice as singer, and the writer gives his writing and his public—political and literary—word. In the texts of the war, the language-weapon unites in a ring with the written word, which is idea, project, and knowledge, giving the struggle meaning: liberty, unity, and equality in the eyes of the law. Hidalgo proclaims these principles and his patriotic word is founded with the voice and intonation of the patriotic gaucho. These are *the new protag-*

onists, the ideologue of the revolution and the soldier of the war, who unite their words in the emergence of the genre. The alliance between the two is the poetic and political conjunction between the new revolutionary culture and the traditional culture. The writing of this alliance postulated in reality and realized in literature constitutes the logic of the genre and the factor of its transformation in history: the distribution of the different parts of the verbal pact (which is political, military, juridical, and which may also be economic) modulates, according to the functions of written voices and the conjunctures of the war, until its end in *La vuelta de Martín Fierro.*

At the end of the dialogue there is a third, hybrid word: *a "gaucho" narrator* says that he is writing the dialogue that he "heard," and he says it at the end of the text and in the gaucho register: in the written-oral register of the word/voice (of the) "gaucho." This is a footnote, a distancing, of the final frame or last frontier, which will be developed in the genre in various intonations, sizes, and positions (for example, in del Campo and Hernández).

The system of frames (titles, subtitles, oral scene, final narrator) of the "oral" and "written" words turns around, following the circle characteristic of the uses (or of the twists and turns of the ruses): the voice of the writing says the opposite of what it does. It writes what it wants to have said and done. The formally direct discourse of the "heard word" is the genre's field of fiction, a specific type of fiction, in the form of a ring or circle, where the "authors" and the quotations or reproductions are precisely inverted and refer to each other, as if they were self-referential. Or specular. (Remember: this is also the fiction of the relation between, on the one hand, the word/voice [of the] "gaucho" of the genre, and, on the other hand, the other side of the logical exterior space of the genre, the space of the learned word.) And this is not simply a ring between the oral and the written but also between "saying" and "doing" with the voice. The writer appears as the first one to "reproduce" the oral in order to establish the chain of reproductions that must return the text to orality. This return not only stages once more the circular logic of the uses but also, in this dialogue, applies that logic to the relation between the written and the oral in order to constitute the fiction: the gaucho Contreras is the illiterate singer of cielitos, and Chano, the overseer, knows how to read and write.

The Second System of Frames

These are Chano the overseer's first words (and notice that he has a son or peon, Mariano, to whom he gives orders) after the sketching of the oral scene (through greetings, references to horses, *some lack, in this case of yerba mate,* and the description of the journey Contreras has made to visit him):

> And what about the motherland
> that I'm so worried about?
> Yesterday *some officials*
> dropped by Pablo's
> and while they were drinking mate
> they took a shot of cane liquor
> and changed the mate water,
> *and read some notices*
> about *King Fernando*
> anxiously requesting
> through his deputies
> that his sworn constitution
> be recognized in these parts.
>   (Ll. 37–48; emphasis mine)

These are the first words of the gaucho Contreras:

> But friend, *our Junta*
> gave a shout and pushed it out
> and sent them a reply
> much prettier than San Bernardo.
> Ah, *gauchos, scribers*
> *on a cigarette paper!*
> When the others saw the gauchos weren't biting,
> and that they'd been beat,
> they raised anchor,
> and, turning the ship around,
> they left without saying goodbye...
> May they go with two hundred devils.
>   (Ll. 61–68; emphasis mine)

In the words of the learned overseer Chano, the officials read King Fernando's notices as they drink mate (like the gauchos in the dialogue—Contreras brought the yerba that was lacking); in the words of the illiterate gaucho Contreras, the gauchos of the junta write their response on a cigarette paper (such as the cigarettes they themselves are surely smoking). Once again there's a ring between the oral scene, reading, and writing, and between the military and the political gauchos. The transparency of Hidalgo, the founder, allows the texture of leaps, frontiers, alliances, inclusions, exchanges, spaces, and orders to be read.

In the same dialogue there's another space, of those who have neither voice nor word. This is the world of silence, the final margin. It occurs in the oral scene, *before the first words of Chano the overseer* about the officials' reading *and after the last words of Contreras*—when the final narrator who says that he is writing and ending the dialogue takes over. Before Chano's first words, Contreras describes his journey to the ranch where Chano is overseer:

> And with so many downpours
> the road is very rough,
> and full of outlaws
> you're always bumping into;
> the good thing is that I've sharpened
> the poisoned knife to my taste.
> *With the tamers I asked*
> *the chestnut four questions,*
> and when he was eager
> *and raising hell,*
> I let the reins out full and I came away,
> but always *on the watch...*
> take the yerba, old friend
> we'll keep on drinking bitter mate. (Ll. 23–36; emphasis mine)

He not only gives Chano the yerba mate he wants but also speaks of evil.

And *after Chano's last words,* which refer to the barbecue they will eat and the siesta that will follow (a return to the oral scene and to the silence of dream), *the narrator,* who heard, who saw, and who writes, *takes over,* and *this is his text:*

They ate with great contentment,
and after their siesta
they saddled up loosely
and left at a gallop
for the hovel of Andrés Bordón,
alias the Bald Indian,
who served as a sad soldier
in the northern provinces,
and in the battle of Vilcapulgio
they shot off his leg.
They shouted at the fence where his property began,
the dogs raised hell;
Bordón left his kitchen,
and helped them off their horses;
and what passed between them
we'll tell another time, more slowly;
for now the pen has grown tired.

The text constitutes its interior space with *all its words* (the oral and the written voice): it divides reading and writing in the oral-written body of the poem *in order to unite them against the Spanish oppressor.* But there is more: literature begins when the music ends. *It is constituted*—and on this it constitutes its internal space—on two silences, or rather on only one silence at the initial frontier and *on all silences* at the final frontier. On the one hand there's Contreras's reference in the oral scene, after the greetings, to the outlaws; and on the other, the reference, written by the narrator who hears and sees, to the one who can no longer be a soldier. The separation between Contreras, the patriotic gaucho, and the outlaws, the illegal gauchos, constitutes *the first verbal confrontation* of the genre, that which gives birth to it. In order that the writing of the alliance, of the word/voice (of the) "gaucho," may exist, there must be a differentiation and a division in the field of the voice: an "evil" voice, which in Hidalgo's transparency is silence, no voice, or a voice unheard and never written, which is the "evil" meaning of the word "gaucho," the legal meaning of the illegal or deserting gaucho; and another "good" voice, that of the patriot. Contreras the patriotic gaucho has his Other. The first pact of the genre is with the voice of the one who fears the outlaws, who has separated himself from them in

order to speak and sing, and who, therefore, may be attacked by them because he is their enemy, their opposite (Contreras counters them): they
are the illegals' bodies without a use and moreover without a voice, *those
who carry evil in their name* [53] and cause suspicion. The two meanings of
"gaucho," the legal and the illegal, the useful and the useless, the patriotic
and the antipatriotic, *separate and articulate the set of the genre,* which is a
treatise not only on written words, heard voices, and their meanings but
also on the division of the voice of the Other and on good and evil—a
treatise on the motherland.

In Hidalgo the gaucho's voice must separate itself, like an enemy, from
the outlaw gauchos and illegals and connect itself, like a friend, with the
one who is no longer a soldier: this is the final frontier of the "New Patriotic Dialogue." There are also two times involved: one before the war and
the military alliance (the time of the "delinquent"), and one after them,
with the "sad soldier." Between the useless and the already used bodies,
between *enemies and friends* (another of the fundamental materials of the
genre), the alliance of the patriot's voice with the one who writes—or the
construction of the voice of the patriot gaucho by the one who writes—
takes place.

A synthesis of the cosmos of frames: on the one hand there are the two
central voices of the patriots: reading (which is oral, starting from the written) and writing (starting from the oral), which are the voices of Chano
and Contreras (and also the first ring between the title-subtitle and the
oral scene). And on the other hand, on each side—at the beginning, and
at the end—are the two nonvoices, or silences, of the outlaw gaucho (body
without use) and of the soldier without a leg (body already used). There
the silences are defined by the uses of bodies, as enemies (he who fright-
ens, who makes Contreras take out his knife), and as friends (he who is attacked by the violence of the war against the Spanish enemies).

The opposite extreme from the outlaws' position is occupied by the no-
voice of Andrés Bordón, alias the Bald Indian: notice the opposition between the nature of the outlaws and the name, surname and nickname, of
one of the friendly Indians in the interior. In Hidalgo the Indians are also
allied with the Spanish: "Cielito, heavens, yes / keep your chocolate / we're

53. [In Spanish, the word *malevo* contains the word *mal,* or evil; see above, n. 40. *Trans.*].

all pure Indians here / and we only drink mate," it says in "A Gaucho of the Monte Guard Responds to Fernando VII's Manifesto and Salutes the Count of Casa-Flores with the Following Cielito in His Language," 1820. This Bald Indian without a leg tires the pen of the narrator who writes. For the one who survived the fear and violence of the war (the end of language), the body that is not whole cannot emit a voice that can write itself: this is the furthest margin of the voice. *Each of the voices,* the one who sings and speaks (Contreras) and the one who writes (the narrator), *separates itself from another that can attack and silence it.* The place of violence against bodies exists on either side; the place of the silence of fear and of death, the final end of language. Two enemies touch at the margins of silence: the Other gauchos, the outlaws, and the foreigners of the war who amputated the leg of the Bald Indian with a bullet. The definition of the enemy, of the enemies of the patriotic gauchos, is located in silence, the text's initial and final frontier, the material on which it is written.

But the silence of the soldier without a leg, *which issues from the kitchen,* is also *a second silence:* that of loss and of the consciousness of loss. And *a third:* the final silence of the other oral scene, which begins outside the text but which is also written ("and that which happened between them"). Friendship, laughter, celebration: music between gaucho friends. The silence of pleasure. The silence of death, of the final end of language, and the silence of pleasure are filled, respectively, by the voices of the gauchos of *La ida* and *Fausto.*

(A final digression on silence: Contreras, in front of the outlaws, "with the tamers / [asks] the chestnut four questions." That is to say, *he speaks to his horse with his spurs,* until "[the horse] raises hell." The Bald Indian contains the scream of amputation inside himself, and this time it's the dogs who raise hell: "They shouted at the fence where his property began, / the dogs raised hell; / Bordón left his kitchen, / and helped them off their horses. . . ." This is not simply about the relationships of contiguity so fundamental in poetry or about relationships in general: there's an outcry of animals on both sides. It is also about coreferentiality, *which is only set in motion by silence:* Chano and Contreras's scream is the same as the scream of amputation.) [54]

54. "I see someone pointing a gun and say 'I expect a report.' The shot is fired. —What! was that what you expected, so did that report somehow already exist in your expecta-

Note on Names and the Final Silence

"New Patriotic Dialogue" is Hidalgo's second dialogue; the first is titled "Interesting Patriotic Dialogue" and is also from 1821. It is subtitled "Between Jacinto Chano, Overseer of a Ranch in the Tordillo Islands, and the Gaucho of the Monte Guard," and already in this very subtitle there's *a footnote from the author:* "The overseer Chano has recently arrived at the Monte Guard, and the dialogue takes place in the house of the peasant Ramón Contreras, the gaucho of the Guard." The author's footnote replaces the word "gaucho" with the word "peasant," and gives this person a name: Ramón Contreras. The subject of "Interesting Patriotic Dialogue" is the law and inequality before the law. In "New Patriotic Dialogue," exactly the opposite takes place: Chano lacks the "Jacinto" of the first dialogue, and Contreras visits *him.* At issue, as we have seen, are the oral and written word and their relations with each other and with silence. In this dialogue the "footnote" is a literal metaphor: it is the final part of the text, its foot, its lowest point, but written by the third voice, that of the "gaucho" narrator who saw and heard what the gauchos said and who states that he is the one writing the dialogue. While Chano and Contreras take a siesta, this final narrator gives the Bald Indian a name. He takes the silence in repose of those who speak and write, he has those who are having a dialogue go to sleep, in order to visit, in their company, the sad amputated soldier and give him the silence of the text, of the genre: the silence of the voice, of music, and of writing. There in the middle of the silence the narrator constructs a cosmos: he gives a name to the one without a voice and

---

tion? Or is it just that there is some other kind of agreement between your expectation and what occurred; that that noise was not contained in your expectation, and merely accidentally supervened when the expectation was being fulfilled? —But no, if the noise had not occurred, my expectation would not have been fulfilled; the noise fulfilled it; it was not an accompaniment of the fulfillment like a second guest accompanying the one I expected. —Was the thing about the event that was not in the expectation too an accident, an extra provided by fate? —But then what was *not* an extra? Did something of the shot already occur in my expectation? —Then what *was* extra? for wasn't I expecting the whole shot?

"'The report was not so loud as I had expected.' —'Then was there a louder bang in your expectation?'" (Ludwig Wittgenstein, *Philosophical Investigations.* G.E.M. Anscombe, trans. Oxford: Basil Blackwell, 1968, 442; emphasis in the original.)

tells his story. He calls him *Andrés*—a name that contains the root that means "man" (as in the word "androgynous")—and *Bordón* (which is not only "burden," or refrain, the "line repeated at the end of every stanza," but also the thickest string of the guitar, the bass string, the string of the lament). Because of this his pen has grown tired. He replaced the author: he gave the amputated soldier a name during the silence of those the author named.

The system of silences is a hierarchical system, of transferences of names, hell-raising, and periods of rest. First, in his own, learned word, in the prose of the title and subtitle, the author takes the name "Jacinto" away from Chano. This is the name of the learned gaucho, the overseer who knows how to read and write. The author transfers this (pen) name to the narrator who writes the heard voice of the gauchos. He transfers a silence to him, the first silence. The narrator, in turn, silences the dialogue between Chano and Contreras, the names and voices sung and written by the author: he sends them to take a siesta. And this silence of heard voices is given, in the form of a name, to the one who lacks something, to the amputee without a voice. The narrator gives the amputee the name of "man" (Andrés) and the name of "singer" or of music (Bordón), and he also gives him *an alias, an Other, his Other,* the silence of the Indian: the bald silence of the Indian, the final silence that contains all the others. He constructs the gaucho genre once more *from the other side of the circle,* at a lower edge: the amputated gaucho singer in league with the Indian. This ceremony of names is written in verse and in the word/voice (of the) "gaucho" that is the narrator. Again, this hierarchy communicates everything through silences and names. While the names of Chano and Contreras appear in the first frame, in the learned prose of the author, the final name of the sad soldier and the Other, the Indian, appears in the last frame, in the verse of the narrator who ends the text. And this narrator not only gives names to the one who lacks them but also tells his story, in silence. He tells of the scream of amputation, of the end of the word and the attack on the body: fear, evil, war, enemies, *in the hell-raising* (here of dogs) that Contreras has been carrying in silence ever since the beginning, when he ran into the *outlaws* (ll. 25–26). The narrator constructs a coreferentiality with Contreras: "and in the battle of Vilcapulgio / they shot off his leg. / They shouted at the fence where his property began, / the dogs raised hell" (ll. 233–236).

The Bald Indian is the lowest margin of Contreras (who is on the other side of the circle), and the final narrator is the lowest margin of the author (who is on the other side of the text). The gaucho genre has been reproduced, at a lower point and in silence.

Hidalgo not only distributed the voices but also included the (silent) voices of another possible genre of the future.

Hidalgo's spectrum of distribution of voices—the specter of Hidalgo distributing the voices—unfolds in the demarcations between the silences of the outlaws and the amputee (at opposite extremes); the two voices of Chano and Contreras (at the center of the dialogue); the learned word of the title-subtitle; and the written voice of the final narrator.

Between one text and another, in the difference between the learned word of the writer, the written voices, and the nonvoices (that may later be distorted voices of other languages or screams of animals), is the internal space of the genre, with its good and evil. The turns of the interior space of the genre (its historical dimension: the extent of the white and sky blue ribbon) are framed by the various extensions, variations, transformations, and perversions of Hidalgo's basic spectrum. They are framed in the differences between, on the one hand, the learned word of the title-subtitle and those who possess the differential voice of the gaucho, which is both "oral" and written, and, on the other hand, those who occupy the silences of Hidalgo's margins. *For example:* the "gaucho" nonvoices (and notice again the Bald Indian and think of the screams and impossible animal voices of the Indians in *La vuelta*) *make a revolution,* a turn, and reappear as *central voices* in other texts of the genre. The voice of the "outlaw gaucho" who attacks the "patriotic" gaucho Cielo, who reads and writes, in Ascasubi's "La refalosa" [The slippery one]; the voice of the soldier without a leg in the "Cielito of the Retired Blandengue" (anonymous); and the voices of Martín Fierro (singer, soldier, ex-soldier, and outlaw) and Cruz (metaphorically amputated by the army: the commander took his wife away from him) in *La ida, where they unite and form an alliance.* The figures of the margin of a text may fall in this way into the interior space of the genre, *which contains the texts and is at the same time the space between the texts, in their margins.*

Each demarcation of the system of frames may be unfolded and turned around. Hernández's *final narrator* ends Hidalgo's dialogues as the author of the footnote to the subtitle, but in Hernández he is expanded and placed in precise locations. He's the one who remains when Cruz and Fierro go into exile with the Indians, the one who says: "he's a cloth woven with strings of woe, / every gaucho you see" (ll. 2309–2310). Or he's the one who refers to his own writing and his own book at the end of *La vuelta,* as he discusses the civilizing project: "the gauchos ought to have houses / and a school and a church and their rights" (ll. 4827–4828). And *La vuelta,* which is the genre's maximum point of expansion, in order to construct a perfect sphere, extends the margins to such a degree that there, *in the actual interior of the text* (in its space, even if "only" in the frame of the door of the pulpería), *a learned locutor appears: the ox with the missing horn,* the maverick there's one of in every herd, "the professor," *the liberato.* The learned locutor's word erupts in the middle of the Second Son's song, to correct his voice and teach him the other register. This is the furthest, final margin of the genre: if this education is imposed, if there is no longer a differential voice of the gaucho, if the word of the state's linguistic unification silences the other word, the genre ceases to exist as such: as the space of the word/voice (of the) "gaucho." At this point, at this final margin, the furthest frontier of the interior space of the genre touches the texts of the genre, and thus it is now possible to move on to another genre, to theater, to the novel, or to the story.

Thus these voices—mute, distorted ("Other" voices), sung, spoken in dialogue, and written—not only frame the borders or margins of the voice in the texts but are also at the same time the borders of the word/voice (of the) "gaucho." These borders serve to define the word/voice as a written voice with meaning: the voice of the alliance that adds another word to the definition of the law, against the nonword/voice (of the) "gaucho." The voice of the alliance adds the name that is lacking—for example, that of Cruz in *La ida* or that of Picardía in *La vuelta.* The genre is the war of definitions of the word/voice "gaucho" (of the meaning of the word "gaucho"), according to the transparent system of distribution mapped out by the ingenious Hidalgo—as Amaro Villanueva calls him—or Hidalgo's genie.

The ring between the two spaces (the "written" space of the title and the "oral scene"), the two positions and enunciations and the mutual citations, generates a proliferating duplication, the signature of the genre. To write a register that is not the one of the one who writes is to split the enunciation, and to connect the situation of the locution with the political enunciated is to split it a second time. This duplication produces the conjunction of two (asynchronous) temporalities and two kinds of dialogue. Each time and each dialogue refers to a word and to its culture. *The two temporalities are:* the large, traditional time of the oral situation, composed of repetitions and rituals (uses, refrains, games; the recurrent, rhythmical time of the cielito), and the precise time of the political conjuncture and the event (and also the historical time of the process of the revolution and the war). The genre conjugates these times and the passage from one to the other: *it is a treatise on modernization.*

The two types of dialogue constitute the fundamental interlocution of the genre, even in the apparently monologic ("sung") texts. While dialogue appears as the "natural" and familiar word par excellence,[55] the genre exploits two of its possibilities, constituting them as the axes of the construction of the texts: dialogue as conversation between friends and allies, as information and persuasion (the didactic dialogue), and dialogue as dispute between enemies (dialogue as polemic and war). In this double use of dialogue the two cultures are once again joined in wedlock: the popular zone, that of the written voice of the gaucho, dramatizes the hostile dialogue with the enemy and comprises *the polemological register* of the genre in its "sung" area; this is the basic position of the cielitos and of "sung" texts in general: the language-weapon, *the Contreras position.* The area of the learned word (the written translated into orality) is *propagandistic and didactic,* directed at the gauchos insofar as they are allied; it constitutes the basic position of the dialogues: the language-law, *the Chano position.*

The result of these conjunctions (the communal local with the public, orality with the written, the two times, the two dialogues) *produces an event that is unique in our culture:* the popularization and "oralization" of the political (and of the written, "the literary") and the politicization, and

---

55. "The most notable characteristic of the folk song is its orientation toward dialogue," writes Jan Mukarovsky in "Detail as the Basic Semantic Unit in Folk Art" (1942), reprinted in his *The Word and Verbal Art* (New Haven: Yale University Press, 1977). On dialogue as the "natural" word par excellence, connected to the direct perception of the interlocutor, see Lev Jakubinski, "Sul discorso dialogico" (1923), in *Teoria della letteratura in Russia, 1900–1934,* ed. E. Ferrario (Rome: Editore Riuniti, 1977).

the writing, of the oral-popular. The gaucho genre implemented this conjunction: it constituted a literary political language, politicized popular culture, and left its founding mark on Argentine culture. And it also popularized and oralized and politicized and Argentinized the writings of European culture. There is no text of the genre that doesn't contain them: from Hidalgo's paraphrase of *The Social Contract* to the telling of the opera *Faust.* And European literature, the translated written word, may appear in the genre in the form of a literary tendency (above all in the writers of the genre who also wrote cultured poetry—Hidalgo's neoclassical poetry and del Campo's romantic poetry), or of a "civilizing" political program translated into gauchesque orality (such as the glosses of the *Comercio del Plata* in Ascasubi), or of a series of anti-European mottos, as in Luis Pérez. There is not a single text of the genre that does not include the European word and culture of which it writes. In a work that may appear alien to this word, such as *La ida,* it is possible to speculate that its publication *together with* "El camino transandino" ("Containing at the end an interesting memoir on the transandean route"), a proposal for modernization written in the learned word, served precisely to reestablish the constitutive duality of the genre in autonomous texts connected by contiguity. *La ida,* in order to be able to include *all Hidalgo's silences,* had to pass Chano *to the text on the side.*[56]

If one reads "El camino trasandino," one may encounter the particular

---

56. See Adolfo Prieto, "La culminación de la poesía gauchesca," in *Trayectoria de la poesía gauchesca,* ed. Horacio J. Becco et al. (Buenos Aires: Plus Ultra, 1977). Prieto discusses the genre's double intentions—artistic, political, social, and others, undeclared: "These intentions, inhibited or censored in a variety of ways, do not make their imprint in the surface of the text, but they may be discovered, without speculative excess, if other indicators are considered. It would seem strange, for example, if coincidence alone were responsible for the inclusion of the tract, *Memoria sobre el camino trasandino,* in the first edition of *El gaucho Martín Fierro.* The tract has no thematic relation with the poem and does not appear to serve any purpose apart from padding the volume or providing wider circulation for a journalistic article. Curiously, however, it happens that this article is a clear articulation of the philosophy of material progress as understood by the liberalism of the time and that the development of the postulates of material progress necessarily led, among other consequences, to the extinction of the gaucho" (101). ["El camino trasandino" only appeared with *La ida* in its first edition (1872); after the publication of *La vuelta* (1879), *La ida* and *La vuelta* were published together, and "El camino" was dropped out. *Trans.*]

hue of Hernández's liberalism, which may also be seen in "Four Words of Conversation with the Readers" in *La vuelta*. In this sense, there is no ideological change in Hernández between *La ida* and *La vuelta*. His liberalism has to do with the combining of "nature" (and this category may take on various different hues) and "reform" or progress. The article centers on the search for a natural passage across the Andes to Chile that would allow the construction of a railroad. Hernández provides a history of the explorations since 1605, dwelling especially on the expedition of the Chilean José Santiago de Cerro y Zamudio in 1803, followed by the expeditions of Esteban Hernández, the mathematician de Souillac, and Luis de la Cruz. According to Hernández, the Commission of Exploration's expedition, which provided the impetus for the article, follows an itinerary identical to that of earlier expeditions: "As we can see, this Zamudio, who discovered it, *was not looking for a new route* so that he could bombastically designate it as his own . . . but was rather proposing to *restore* the road that passed between Buenos Aires and the kingdom of Chile in ancient times." Zamudio's passage is a natural one, and Hernández adds: "In order to promote commerce, progress, and the unity of both countries, science and progress have only to use what nature has made." "Draw for the Republic the dividing line that nature has marked out, conquer the desert, allow it to overflow with the activity of industry, wealth, commerce, and civilization, and the great problem of the passage across the Andes is resolved by 1802" (from the version of Antonio Pagés Larraya, *Prosas de* Martín Fierro [Buenos Aires: Raigal, 1952], 224–225).

This particular liberalism, this alliance between what nature does (or the wisdom of the gauchos' heard voice, that is, their culture, which, in the nineteenth century, is like nature) and what progress does, is also the logic of the genre.

But there is something else in "El camino." Hernández discusses the depredations of Indians, who have almost completely depopulated San Luis and who bring "fire, desolation, and death to the inhabitants of the countryside. 12 or 15 leagues from Rosario there are deserted pampas, vast plains, where rural property is under constant threat of being carried off by savages" (220). Barbarousness, for Hernández, is Indians. There can be no doubt here: the learned author does not concur with Fierro and Cruz's final exile in Indian country (or with its strange utopia with idleness at its center, which Fierro enunciates before he leaves). Indians are barbarousness because they attack rural property and leave certain provinces depopulated. This is another place of barbarousness, the opposite of Sarmiento's and Hidalgo's.

This discussion of "El camino" again recalls *Facundo,* the historical guide of the genre. Like *Facundo,* "El camino" is a historical text, a political text of opposition (it is also a text of opposition to Sarmiento's government, to *Facundo*'s final project). The two texts use the same words: "barbarousness," "savages," "civilization," and "progress." And "El camino" is also a literary text, which appears beside the classic. Hernández says of the passage to Chile:

> But it was not constructed and what was desired couldn't be done. Since that time silence has stretched out for a hundred years in the deserts of Patagonia and in the Andean region. In 1872, as in 1600 and in 1700, expeditions continued with the same lack of topographical data, with the same difficulties, inconveniences, and dangers as in the time of earliest discovery.
>
> Perhaps some day our Nation will have governments that dedicate to this essential element of any progress, the treasures and lives that they now sterilely sacrifice to oppress the people!" (219)

He tells Sarmiento the same thing that Sarmiento himself said in *Facundo:* "Let us ask the people for just and progressive governments, and liberal Congresses, and the desert, which now surrounds us on all sides as an impenetrable barrier to civilization and commerce, will cease to choke us" (220). This is the moment in which Sarmiento, president of the Republic, has put a price on Hernández's head. The latter has gone with López Jordán into exile in Brazil and another language.

And after this, suddenly, Hernández writes a story; a piece of contemporary cinema and literature and also a part of *La vuelta.* This is a story of mystery and of names:

> We will conclude by mentioning a circumstance which perhaps will not fail to present something original and curious. In the itinerary that we have published, we came across a place designated by the significant name "Hanged Sailors." Is this name an invention of fancy?

What "Hanged Sailors" have there ever been in these remote regions, in the center of these masses of stone, perpetually covered with snow? May it be presumed that this name has been given with some *appropriateness*? Would it be possible to search for its *origin*? Is it perhaps *commemorating* one of those terrible tragedies for which the vast solitudes of America—its dark jungles, its immense deserts, its rivers, its mountains—have so often been the theater? It is not possible to rend *the mystery in which the secret hides,* but this reminds us of a curious antecedent.

Don Luis de la *Cruz,* in his 1806 voyage from Chile to Buenos Aires, passing through the same places that have recently been explored all over again, *reports the following story that an Indian told him:* "That an English ship was wrecked in the Boca de Linagbeubé, at a considerable distance from the sea, that the Indians did not see them come in, and that walking along the shores of a river, they found the English people by their footprints; these people were rather numerous, and had taken shelter in the river gorges. That they were carrying chickens, pigs, sheep, and other animals unknown to them. That the English remained there for some time, and when they least expected it, they disappeared."

In 1807 *the censor's commission,* named by the Consulate to make a judgment regarding this voyage, *mocked Cruz's declaration,* but in spite of this, perhaps it is not too venturesome to imagine that *an intimate relationship exists between the Indian's story and the name* of the place that has attracted our attention, a relationship that allows one to assume *the unfortunate end of the unhappy castaways,* lost in that endless solitude, surrounded on all sides by dangers, and victims in the end of the barbarousness of its inhabitants. (226–227, Emphasis mine)

First the names: among the chain of voyagers are Esteban *Hernández,* de Souillac the mathematician, and Luis de la *Cruz.* And an Indian told Cruz the story. This is the very Hernández who is with Cruz and the Indians; and already here is the end of Cruz and his relation with the garrulous Indian (he who speaks both languages), who wants to be a Christian, who saves Fierro and Cruz, and who falls victim to smallpox and infects Cruz (ll. 871–930). The unfortunate end of the unhappy castaways. That is to say: the text beside *La ida* contains *La vuelta*. And there is yet another relevant episode in *La vuelta*—it immediately precedes Cruz's infection and death and involves the little gringo captive with sky blue eyes: "There was a little gringo captive— / always talking about his ship— / and they drowned him in a pond / for being the cause of the plague… / His eyes were [sky blue] / like a wall-eyed foal" [translation adapted for clarity] (ll. 853–858). "Hanged Sailors": the name unleashed in Hernández—along with his own and Cruz's proper name—the future invention, *the definition of barbarousness in the future book.*

As we can see, in Hernandez's text there is a liberalism (an "association") that is different from Sarmiento's, and above all, there are other names, other futures, and another possible literature.

In "El camino" Hernández is inspired by the mystery of a name ("Hanged Sailors") and within this mystery he sketches the future book, the "barbarous" part of *La vuelta* that includes Fierro and Cruz's life with the Indians and the death of Cruz, who is infected by the bilingual Indian (he who speaks both languages and therefore both cultures or tones). For Hernández, the secret name "Hanged Sailors" contains three characters and three languages: the Indian who told Cruz the story, the person who wrote the name on the 1807 itinerary to Chile, and the gringos, the Englishmen from the ship. In *La vuelta* he kills them all: the Englishmen as represented by the little gringo captive who always spoke of the ship, the Indian, and Cruz, all victims of the same evil—the plague. The world of barbarousness is the world of horror and of the mystery of the name. Hernández has interrogated the mystery of barbarousness in order to write the barbarousness of the future book, which is also his own present of Indian thefts and depredations.

For Sarmiento, as for Hernández, barbarousness and mystery meet in the name; Sarmiento passionately interrogates the mystery, or the terrible shade, of the dead Facundo. Like Hernández, he interrogates the past in order to place the barbarousness of the present, or the barbarous part of his present book, within it: the horror of Quiroga and Rosas. And in the last chapter of *Facundo* he constructs the future (the future of an illusion, the illusion of a future) on *the symmetrical negation* of the present. We do not need to go to *Facundo* as a whole or to its final chapter; this activity of construction occurs in our anthological fragment, which offers an example of what is still taught as literature and contains the entire book within itself. In this fragment the present, *the verb in the present tense* that accompanied the name "Facundo," and that accompanied the first "afterward"—or rather, *the present that accompanied the future in the past* of 1810, with the small motherland and the sun—was symmetrically opposed to the last "afterward" of Quiroga and Rosas, the "afterward" of *the past perfect* of the death and the shade of the motherland. (The past perfect is the mode of finished past action, whose effects continue and extend into the present: a past-present "afterward.") And there was also Ocampo, "afterward president of Charcas," who commanded a regiment in the imperfect of the small motherland. At the time that he wrote *Facundo*, Sarmiento was excluded from the governments of both the small motherland and the large motherland. If this figure is inverted (blazons or their fields often appear backward) it contains the specific equation of Sarmiento's afterward or illusion. In relation to the present, the future is symmetrical, alternative, and polar. And the future also implies the inclusion of the present. From the government of the small motherland, with Ocampo, to the government of the large motherland, with Quiroga and Rosas (or from the afterward in the imperfect to the afterward in the perfect), *Sarmiento writes his own political future.* The governor of the province is above, and the president of the large motherland is on the shield. In *Facundo*, Sarmiento writes not only the project of the future country but also his own future, which is the present of Hernández's *La ida.*

Facundo is a symmetrical text of binary oppositions that names and defines itself. Binary oppositions, symmetries, blazons and their fields, and, moreover, an intermediate zone made of two. In the first place, a specific mix of opposing elements, and in the second place, a void: a desertion. This is how the fragment from our anthology—which is still taught as literature—is constructed.

And here the differences between our day and Sarmiento's text and between the latter and the genre may emerge, in the relation between the frontiers of the text and the place of the political. Sarmiento is writing before the definitive establishment of the state, during the war for definition, and his learned, written word *is* reality. His text, symmetrical and closed, doesn't close: it leaps the frontier again and suddenly acquires a dazzling, blinding reality. It transforms the two zones of exclusion of which it writes into reality and fills them with the future history of Sarmiento, governor and president, and his realized dream. Or, in other words, before 1880 the nongenre has the capacity to leap over the margins of texts and make a turn in order to appear as political reality, because it is written in the same language with which what is thought or constructed as "political and historical reality" is written. The learned word is reality and thus it may realize the dream.

By contrast, the genre has another kind of relation to frontiers and margins, and thus the place of the future is different there. Texts do not pass from the written voice of the Other, which is their subject, into historical reality, because only the learned word, which is reality and future, may accomplish that leap over borders. Thus, in their very interior, these texts descend and leap over the opposite frontier, constituting the future text of the genre in the form of barbarousness, often without realizing it. The genre is all illusion, desire, and future, because it is an eagerness for alliance with the voice of the Other, but its writers were not the ones who made that alliance a reality. They didn't hold the chance of fulfilling the dream in their hands, in their biographies: none of them would become a father of the motherland. Thus rather than leaping from the written into political and historical reality they leapt over the margin in the written's interior and descended: *they wrote the literature of the future* (Macedonio's future book). They put illusion in the present book and, often without realizing it, they also put barbarousness in the book that was to come. The difference between the genre and other literature is defined by the place of the political and of the political future in the margins of both words. The nongenre is future reality; the genre, the literature of the future.

Hidalgo had already written the future genre in the character of the sad amputated soldier, in whom the man-singer or man-musician is in alliance with the bald silence of the Indian. Silence was given voice on the other side of the circle and in the future text of the genre. Hidalgo's final text, of the names for the silence of those without voice, is filled by the future of *La ida*, in which Cruz, metaphorically amputated by the army (the commander took his wife and, with her, all women), forms an alliance with the Indian who speaks both languages. The lowest border of the genre is the other side of Hidalgo's circle, full of voices, and the other side of *La ida*. Thus, with *La ida* and "El camino transandino," Hernández writes *La ida*'s future book, Hidalgo's future book, *Facundo*'s future book, as well as the critique of *Facundo*'s future book, which is Sarmiento's fulfilled dream. And in his present moment Hernández says the same thing Sarmiento says to Rosas in *Facundo*'s present, but this time with the names of Sarmiento's ministers, secretaries, the names of the *subordinates* that are exactly the place of the writers of the genre. Sarmiento's minister of war appears in *La ida,* and in "El camino" de Angelis appears: Rosas's Other, *his learned alias,* he who writes for a European audience and is European and does the work of a historian and archivist. He is Rosas's European or Rosas's Sarmiento or Rosas's Chano. On the subject of José Santiago de Cerro y Zamudio's voyage to Chile in 1803, Hernández writes in "El camino": "We still have a manuscript of his voyage, and the official memo in which he reports to Virrey on the success of his exploration: a document which to our knowledge has never been published, since Angelis doesn't even have an itinerary of Zamudio's voyage in his collection, and such an itinerary, of course, would hardly meet the conditions of clarity and exact description that we should expect" (218). Pedro de Angelis, who persecuted and silenced Luis Pérez, the author of the *Biografía de Rosas* in the word/voice (of the) "gaucho," was the author of the *learned biography* of Rosas (as Sarmiento was the author of the learned biography of Facundo): *Ensayo histórico sobre Rosas,* 1830.

In Hernández, as in Sarmiento, the writing provides a title, naming and defining the very book that is being read. And Hernández and Sarmiento share the same void, that of the name of San Martín (he who definitively founded the motherland and who was exiled in another language, on the other side of the ocean), who was dead by 1872. San Martín crossed the Andes to Chile using a natural passage. "El camino transandino" gives *El gaucho Martín Fierro a learned title,* and does it *in the future,* with the vocabulary of progress and civilization and *with a translation from the French "chemin de fer."* Beginning with the void of the name of San Martín and the future of the passage or of the future railroad of the natural passage: (San) Martín *and* (The transandean passage) *of* Fierro.[57] This is the learned name of the genre and of *La ida,* the name of progress built on the

---

57. [A pun on the French *chemin de fer,* railroad, or literally, path (*camino*) of iron, and the name *Fierro,* iron in Spanish. *Trans.*]

absence of the patriot's name and of the gaucho's voice, and on the future of the transandean *chemin de fer*. The natural passage of the liberator is united with the railroad of progress. The title names a future book that defines the present book. And in the mystery and secrecy of the name "Hanged Sailors" Hernández inserts the future book, *La vuelta*, in its place of barbarousness. Thus he has simultaneously constructed in the future and in the past the double face of the genre and the alliance that defines it. (Like San Martín, Hernández was named José, and he was born in 1834 during Rosas's regime, on the Perdriel ranch in the district of General San Martín, belonging to the Pueyrredóns, the anti-Rosist part of his family.)

Each text and each moment of the genre may be read from and with another that allows it to be read and at the same time is read by it.

II. On the Side of the Master, on the Side of the Gift[58]

"A Small Preliminary Cruise toward a Reconnaissance of the Joyce Archipelago" On the Island: A Study on Montage

> In the Orient, as in all parts of the world, newspapers were preceded by illustrated leaflets, which usually narrated, in ballad form, some extraordinary event (earthquake, crime, the assassination of a bandit). These leaflets almost always had pictures.
>
> This type of leaflet is still in circulation in parts of Mexico (especially in those areas where newspapers are lacking). The vendor himself sings the ballads as he sells the leaflets which describe, in heart-rending terms, a criminal's repentance before his execution, or the death, on such and such a date, of a popular general. At times these are called *lamentos*. (Sergei M. Eisenstein, "Nature Is Not Indifferent," in S. M. Eisenstein, Noam Chomsky, and others, *Le montage*, ed. Change 1 [Paris: Seuil, 1968], 35)

---

58. [There are two meanings of the Spanish *don* in this heading: first, a respectful title for a man; second, a gift; there is a play between acknowledging "the important man" and giving the gaucho a voice. Together, the two ideas suggest paternalism: the important man, to whom respect is due, is the one who gives, who grants favors. *Trans.*]

The Anarchist's Universal Grammar

MITSOU RONAT: Your linguistic discoveries have led you to take positions in philosophy of language and in what is called "philosophy of knowledge." In particular, in your last book (*Reflections on Language*), you were induced to determine the limits of what is *knowable in thought;* as a result, the reflections on language became transformed virtually into a philosophy of science. . . .

NOAM CHOMSKY: Of course, it is not the study of language that determines what is to count as a scientific approach; but in fact this study provides a useful model to which one can refer in the investigation of human knowledge.

In the case of language, one must explain how an individual, presented with quite limited data, develops an extremely rich system of knowledge. The child, placed in a linguistic community, is presented with a set of sentences that is limited and often imperfect, fragmented, and so on. In spite of this, in a very short time he succeeds in "constructing," in internalizing the grammar of his language, developing knowledge that is very complex, that cannot be derived by induction or abstraction from what is given in experience. We conclude that the internalized knowledge must be limited very narrowly by some biological property. Whenever we encounter a similar situation, where knowledge is constructed from limited and imperfect data in a manner that is uniform and homogeneous among all individuals, we can conclude that a set of initial constraints plays a significant role in determining the cognitive system which is constructed by the mind.

We find ourselves faced with what may seem a paradox, though it is in fact not a paradox at all: where rich and complex knowledge can be constructed in a uniform way, as in the case of knowledge of language, there must exist constraints, limitations imposed by biological endowment on the cognitive systems that can be developed by the mind. The scope of attainable knowledge is linked in a fundamental way with its limits. (Noam Chomsky, *Language and Responsibility, Based on Conversations with Mitsou Ronat* [New York: Pantheon, 1979], 63–64)

Hidalgo's Transparent Life

The Stain of Paternal Difference, the Stain of the Motherland

He was born in Montevideo in 1788, son of Juan José Hidalgo and Catalina Ximénez, both natives of Buenos Aires and of very modest origins. . . . In 1817, Joaquín de la Sagra y Pérez called him "little mulatto." In a way, this assertion coincides with Father Castañeda's; in 1821, the latter called him "dark Montevidean" in the pages of the "Matron Commentator," adding "that he aspires to what they call equality, to which there are certain physical impediments." Hidalgo then published a pamphlet, *The author of the dialogue between Jacinto Chano and Ramón Contreras answers the charges put to him in* The Commentator, the only piece in his life that he published with his initials, "B.H."

Did any African blood flow in his veins, or were "little mulatto" and "dark" simply unworthy epithets of contempt? What were his "physical impediments"? (Lauro Ayestarán, "La primitiva poesía gauchesca [1812–1838]," in Bartolomé Hidalgo, *Cielitos y diálogos patrióticos: Documentos literarios* [Montevideo: Arca, 1977], 90–92)

The Subordinate in the House of the Founding Father

In 1803, Hidalgo began work as a subordinate in the business of Martín José Artigas, the father of the commander. . . . (92)

Between Weapons and Letters

. . . and in 1806 we find him employed as an intern in the Ministry of Real Hacienda. During the English invasions, he fought in the battle of the Cardal . . . when the English were chased out, Hidalgo returned to his post in the ministry. . . . In 1811 he accompanied Artigas's troops to Paysandú and Salto. . . . In the month following Alvear's entry into Montevideo . . . he was named postmaster. When the Argentine forces withdrew in 1815, the new national government of Otorgués named Hidalgo Acting Minister of Hacienda, a post that he shortly left to fill the position of chief clerk in the same ministry. (92–93)

Aesthetics

At this time, Hidalgo was already in contact with the muses—rhetorical, high-flown, patriotic muses. . . . In the pages of the periodical *Gazeta de Montevideo,* which supported hispanic domination, he was branded as "an uppitytalker". . . . His *Marcha Nacional Oriental,* the first of his works that survives, was written two months later.

On January 30th, 1816, his one-man piece *Sentimientos de un Patriota* was performed in the Casa de Comedias, and almost immediately he was named director of the same theater. (93)

Theme of the Traitor and Hero?[59]

On January 27th, 1817, Lecor entered Montevideo with Portuguese troops, and Hidalgo became the censor for the Casa de Comedias. . . . With exquisite cruelty, or perhaps with the writer's complicity, the baron de la Laguna put Hidalgo, whose verses against the Portuguese still resounded in patriots' ears, to the task of correcting the literary texts to be performed at the Casa de Comedias. . . . In March 1818, he immigrated to Buenos Aires. (96)

Exile and Genre: The Border Space

Hidalgo's most transcendent period of creation encompassed the last three years of his life. In 1820 he wrote his last cielitos, which were sold in the streets as leaflets, and, the following year, his three patriotic dialogues. (97)

---

59. [This heading is a reference to the story "Theme of the Traitor and Hero," from Borges's collection *Ficciones.* This brief story involves patterns of events that seem to repeat themselves mysteriously in widely divergent times and regions; the blurring of the line between history and fiction; and the censorship, cover-ups, and betrayals of "truth" that occur in both history and fiction. Like Hidalgo, Borges himself endured a kind of censorship or political betrayal when, during the Perón dictatorship, he was demoted from director of libraries to poultry inspector. *Trans.*]

The china[60]

He married Juana Cortina of Buenos Aires, May 20th, 1820. (Ibid.)

The Final Resting Place: Light, More Light

Suffering from pulmonary tuberculosis, he died in the outskirts of Buenos Aires, in the small village of Morón, November 28th, 1822. "His end," writes Falcao Espalter (*El poeta uruguayo Bartolomé Hidalgo: Su vida y sus obras* [Madrid, 1929], 63), "was so obscure that on his death his corpse became the material of legend, since no one knows where his sad bones came to rest. It may be that poverty, which, like a friar of the order of Saint Francis, accompanied him from the cradle to the grave, mixed Hidalgo's still-warm ashes in the common grave. But this same oblivion, this supreme misfortune, is the garment of immortality in the eyes of the Spirit: among the piled-up dead, his bones will give out light." (Ibid.)

The Anarchist's Universal Grammar

MITSOU RONAT: But that is not the same definition of human nature, it is no longer a matter of defining a psychology of individual character.

NOAM CHOMSKY: Certainly, we can distinguish between theories that assign a determinate social status to particular individuals or groups by virtue of their alleged intrinsic nature (e.g., some are born to be slaves), and theories that hold that there are certain biological constants characteristic of the species, which may, of course, assume very different forms as the social and material environment varies. There is much to be said about all of these matters. It seems to me that one might suggest, in a very speculative manner, that such factors as the ones I have mentioned entered into the success of empiricism among the intelligentsia. I have discussed this question a bit in *Reflections on Language,* stressing the crucial and sometimes

---

60. [The woman of the gaucho. *Trans.*]

overlooked point that speculation about these matters of ideology is quite independent of the validity of the specific doctrines in question; it is when doctrines of little merit gain wide and unquestioned credence that such speculations as these become particularly appropriate.

In *Reflections*, I also mentioned that even at the earliest stages it is not so obvious that empiricism was simply a "progressive" doctrine in terms of its social impact, as is very widely assumed. There has been some interesting work in the past few years, for example, on the philosophical origins of racism, particularly by Harry Bracken, which suggests a much more complex history. It seems that racist doctrine developed in part as a concomitant of the colonial system, for fairly obvious reasons. And it is a fact that some leading empiricist philosophers (Locke, for example) were connected to the colonial system in their professional lives. . . .

Bracken has suggested, plausibly it seems to me, that racist doctrine raises conceptual difficulties within the framework of dualist beliefs, that is, if they are taken seriously. Cartesian dualism raises what he has called "a modest conceptual barrier to racist doctrine." The reason for that is simple. Cartesian doctrine characterizes humans as thinking beings: they are metaphysically distinct from non-humans, possessing a thinking substance (*res cogitans*) which is unitary and invariant—it does not have color, for example. There are no "black minds" or "white minds." You're either a machine, or else you're a human being, just like any other human being in essential constitution. The differences are superficial, insignificant: they have no effect on the invariant *human essence.*

I think it is not an exaggeration to see in Cartesian doctrine a conceptual barrier—a modest one, as Bracken carefully explains— against racism. On the other hand, the empiricist framework does not offer an analogous characterization of the human essence. A person is a collection of accidental properties, and color is one of them. It is thus somewhat easier to formulate racist beliefs in this framework, although it is not inevitable.

I don't want to exaggerate the importance of these speculations. But it is worth investigating the question whether colonial ideology did in fact exploit the possibilities made available by empiricist doctrine to formulate more easily the kind of racist beliefs that were employed to justify conquest and oppression. (Chomsky, *Language and Responsibility*, 91–93)

Voiceover

The conceptual apparatus of the genre necessitates the reiteration of a difference, toward a lower point.

The written lives of the writers of the genre have gone through Hidalgo's transparent sequence: sons of a difference, because of which they have been accused; dependents in the house of a master or founding father; exiled from the motherland.

The difference that condemns one to condemnation for being different, the stain in the paternal house (Castañeda, son of a Spanish merchant, accuses Hidalgo, a mulatto, or the Spanish judge accuses Luis Pérez), constitutes a synthetic set of differences that may be identified with the division of the motherland in each moment. This is the alterity of the motherland as an irreducible difference: that which incites it to war. Whites and mulattos, Spaniards and inhabitants of Buenos Aires or the provinces, unitarists and federalists, exiles and those who remained: these words and phrases cannot be united. Writers carry these differences inscribed within themselves, and these differences are not only based on those of the motherland but also constitute the axis of the genre in its previous stage. The war between unitarists and federalists, which is Hernández's stain (he had a federalist father, a unitarist mother), is dramatized in the genre by Pérez and Ascasubi, among others. And Ascasubi's own war—Spanish father, provincial mother—is spoken in Hidalgo's texts. In their own lines, these texts themselves simultaneously speak the previous genre and the future difference.

The universe of differences is also the universe of paradoxes, juxtapositions, and montages. That which in the previous genre is war, or the impossibility of unity, becomes, in the lives of the writers and in their families, the alliance itself. These writers are sons of a rent in the fabric and of the uniting of words in war (scandals of the language); the genre's drama is their own. Differences, alterities, condemnations, alliances of differences, and wars because of differences are simultaneously founded and pulled apart. In this movement they encounter the writing of the genre in the voice of the Other as a war and an alliance of the impossible.

The writers of the genre have been subordinates, or scribes in the master's house—masters, men of good name, or founding fathers (and del Campo and Hernández were subordinates in the houses of the motherland—Masonic or legislative). The history of this dependence and the hierarchies it assumes is the history of the genre and also of the founding fathers, from Artigas (as told by Hidalgo) to Alberdi (as told by Hernández). The writers of the genre are secondary or minor; they have no titles and they place their writing (or their "heads," as Hernández writes to López Jordán) at the master's service. The name of the founding father and the alliance between the writers' writing and this name constitute them and constitute the genre. This alliance also places Shakespeare's dramas about founding fathers inside the genre: assassinations, treasons, exiles, representations, reproductions, prefigurations.

The writers of the genre wrote during the passage through the loss of the motherland. Their exile carried them to the other motherlands of the genre, to Uruguay or to Brazil's gaucho south. And when they were not exiled, as in the case of Pérez, they were excluded from the house of the founding father (and condemned to prison and silence), or, as in del Campo's case, his own father was exiled.

The conceptual apparatus of the genre necessitates the reiteration of a difference, toward a lower point.

The writers' lives are reproduced downward and in more than one direction: they not only follow Hidalgo's transparent sequence but also return to write in the differential voice of the gaucho. In the world of war and alliance, this voice speaks its own stain, its dependence on a master and loss of a space. But this voice is itself different, dependent and excluded in relation to the written word. Therefore, within the genre, the writers are master.

The reiteration of difference toward a lower point constitutes the genre's scandal of logic. Dependence on the master (he who has what the Other doesn't have: name, titles, or, in the genre, written word) follows a hierarchical and antagonistic relation that is, at the same time, horizontal and equal in the ring of the alliance. The pyramid of masters and the horizontal equation of masters coexist: scandals of the language and of geometry.

The Anarchist's Universal Grammar

MITSOU RONAT: But you met Michel Foucault, I believe, during a television broadcast in Amsterdam?

NOAM CHOMSKY: Yes, and we had some very good discussions before and during the broadcast. On Dutch television, we spoke for several hours, he in French and I in English; I don't know what the Dutch television viewers made of all that. We found ourselves in at least partial agreement, it seemed to me, on the question of "human nature," and perhaps not as much on politics (the two basic points about which Fons Elders interviewed us).

As far as the concept of human nature and its relation to scientific progress was concerned, it seemed that we were "climbing the same mountain, starting from opposite directions," to repeat a simile which Elders suggested. In my view, scientific creativity depends on two facts: on the one hand, on an intrinsic property of mind, and on the other, on a combination of social and intellectual conditions. There is no question of choosing between these. In order to understand a scientific discovery, it is necessary to understand the interaction between these factors. But personally I am more interested in the first, while Foucault stresses the second.

Foucault considers the scientific knowledge of a given epoch to be like a *grid* of social and intellectual conditions, like a system the rules of which permit the creation of new knowledge. In his view, if I understand him correctly, human knowledge is transformed due to social conditions and social struggles, with one grid replacing the other, thus bringing new possibilities to science. . . .

His position also involves a different usage of the term *creativity*. When I speak of creativity in this context, I am not making a value judgment: creativity is an aspect of the ordinary and daily use of language and of human action in general. However, when Foucault speaks of creativity he is thinking more of the achievements of a Newton, for example—although he stresses the common social and intellectual base for the creations of scientific imagination, rather than the achievements of an individual genius—that is to say, he is thinking of the conditions for radical innovation. . . . In the historical perspective of Foucault, one no longer seeks to identify the innovators and their specific achievement or the obstacles which stand in the way of the emergence of truth, but to determine how knowledge, as a system independent of individuals, modifies its own rules of formulation.

MITSOU RONAT: In defining the knowledge of an epoch as a grid or system, doesn't Foucault draw near to structuralist thought, which also conceives of language as a system?

N.C.: To reply properly it would be necessary to study this matter in depth. In any case, while I have been speaking of the limitations imposed on a class of accessible theories—linked to the limitations of the human mind that permit the construction of rich theories in the first place—he is more interested in the proliferation of theoretical possibilities resulting from the divergence. . . .

M.R.: What were the political disagreements between you and Foucault?

N.C.: For my part, I would distinguish two intellectual tasks. One is to imagine a future society that conforms to the exigencies of human nature, as best we understand them; the other, to analyze the nature of power and oppression in our present societies. For him, if I understand him rightly, what we can imagine now is nothing but a product of the bourgeois society of the modern period: the notions of justice or of "realization of the human essence" are only the inventions of our civilization and result from our class system. The concept of justice is thus reduced to a pretext advanced by a class that has or wants to have access to power. . . . In this respect I have a very different opinion. A social struggle, in my view, can only be justified if it is supported by an argument—even if it is an indirect argument based on questions of fact and value that are not well understood—which purports to show that the consequences of this struggle will be beneficial for human beings and will bring about a more decent society. Let us take the case of violence. I am not a committed pacifist, and thus do not say that it is wrong to use violence in all circumstances, say in self-defense. But any recourse to violence must be justified, perhaps by an argument that it is necessary to remedy injustice. . . . We were in apparent disagreement, because where I was speaking of justice, he was speaking of power. At least, that is how the difference between our points of view appeared to me. (Chomsky, *Language and Responsibility*, 74–80)

Two Biographies of Writers of Gaucho Biographies

Luis Pérez

Accused on the Basis of Origin
The War against the Other Dependent of the Founding Father
Theme of the Traitor and Hero

We have no information about the date of his birth, and only know that he "saw the light of day" in Tucumán, as he expresses it in an article that he published in *El clasificador* or *El Nuevo Tribuno* of January 10, 1831, to respond to accusations that he was a native of Spain. . . .

Luis Pérez becomes a serious enemy of Pedro de Angelis at the beginning of 1834. . . . He has just published a virulent leaflet in which he charges against de Angelis with the fury of a bull:

"Next Sunday a new issue (of *El Gaucho Restaurador*) will appear. Its publisher has been treacherously slandered and insulted by the *gringo,* the *wop,* the traitor *Pedro de Angelis,* by this vile man who was *unitarist* in Rivadavia's time, *an insurgent* with Lavalle, neutral with Señor *Viamont,* a Restorer with Don Juan M. de Rosas, and always a traitor, always treacherous; by this *evil man* who justified the barbarous assassination of the valiant Maza of Buenos Aires; by this man who came loaded with sheets of music to our beaches and who now believes himself authorized to insult all the sons of this land, the true Americans, the inhabitants of Buenos Aires."[61]

. . . In the Nation's General Archives we have found a document that confirms that the chief of police received an official notice on April 21, 1834, ordering the detention of the publisher of *El Gaucho Restaurador.* . . . Later his name is lost in anonymity. (Ricardo Ro-

---

61. [De Angelis was a music teacher when he first came to Argentina from Italy. *Trans.*]

dríguez Molas, *Luis Pérez y la* Biografía de Rosas *escrita en verso en 1830* [Buenos Aires: Clío, 1957], 3, 12, 14; emphasis in original)

José Hernández

Vive the Paternal Difference, of the Motherland
The Dependent in the House of the Founding Fathers
and in the Houses of the Motherland
Theme of the Traitor and Hero
Exile and Genre: The Border Space

November 10, 1834. José Rafael Hernández y Pueyrredón is born on the Perdriel ranch (district of General San Martín). The house belongs to Victoria Pueyrredón Camaño, elder sister of the poet's mother. . . . The poet is the son of Rafael Hernández de los Santos and Isabel Pueyrredón Camaño, both of Buenos Aires. . . . The maternal family is of definite unitarist affiliation; the paternal, of active federalist militancy. (Aurelia C. Garat and Ana María Lorenzo, "Biochronology of José Hernández," in *José Hernández* [Essays collected in honor of the centenary of *El gaucho Martín Fierro,* 1872–1972. La Plata: National University of La Plata, School of Arts and Sciences, 1973], 9)

Isabel is the oldest sister of Brigadier Juan Martín de Pueyrredón, an already mythical figure for the young nation: he fought against the English at Perdriel itself, then against the Spanish. Later he was the supreme director of the United Provinces and thus belonged to the party first called directorial and then unitarist; it is probable that his entire family shared his ideas, except perhaps for young Isabel, who decided to marry a member of a federalist family who was certainly a federalist himself. . . . (Noé Jitrik, *José Hernández,* La historia popular 23 [Buenos Aires: CEAL, 1971], 10–11).

March 1858, Paraná. Hernández is a bookkeeper in the business of Ramón Puig (father-in-law of Ricardo López Jordán).

May 1859, Paraná. Hernández wins the competition to occupy the post of stenographer in the Senate of the Confederation. "To my stenographer's pencil, I used to say, I owe my constitutional studies" (Rafael Hernández, *Pehuajó,* . . . , p. 82).

1860. Secretary to Juan Esteban Pedernera, the vice president of the Confederation (there are letters from Pedernera to Urquiza in Hernández's own hand).

1861. He joins Masonic Lodge Littoral Sanctuary No. 18 and in 1862 is elected secretary.

February 16, 1868, Corrientes. Letter from Hernández to Urquiza: "The Hernandez family have never been traitors. In recent years when there have been no accolades for us, I could have sought refuge in the opposing ranks, but no one has ever seen me vacillate in my political faith, desert my companions, lose heart in the struggle, or surrender even a greeting to the enemy. . . ."

August 20, 1868, La Paz. Letter from Hernández to Urquiza: ". . . given the gravity of the situation . . . I think it's come to accepting the benevolent offers of Your Excellency, entreating him to carry his good faith so far as to impart to me all those ideas that in his seasoned judgment may lead us to the laudable objective we propose. . . ."

October 7, 1870. Holograph card from Hernández to López Jordán, signed "Your friend": ". . . Urquiza was the Tyrant-Governor of Entre Ríos, but more than anything, he was the Traitor-Chief of the Great Federalist Party, and his death, deserved a thousand times over, is a tremendous, exemplary justice for the party that he sold and sacrificed so many times. . . . For the last ten years you have been the peoples' hope. . . . Count on me, I am entirely at your disposal and at a word from you I will be at your side. . . ."

March 10, 1871. López Jordán and Hernández cross the Uruguay River into exile. They settle in Santa Ana do Livramento, a Brazilian town on the Eastern frontier.[62]

In their peaceful immigrant life, Hernández improvises verses, plays the guitar, and displays his creole skill in singing duels with Juan Pirán. . . .[63]

62. [See note 6 above for a summary of the historical context referred to here. *Trans.*]
63. [A minstrel form, derived from the medieval *tenson,* in which one singer asks a question and another answers until one of the singers silences the other and wins. *Trans.*]

> End of February 1872. Hernández arrives in the city of Buenos
> Aires from Montevideo. He stays in the Hotel Argentino. . . . He re-
> ceives assiduous visits from José Zoilo Miguens. Antonio D. Lussich
> interviews him. His family continues to reside at the ancestral ranch
> where he was born. (Garat and Lorenzo, "Biochronology")

Voiceover

Relations between Literature and Reality:
Two Oral Autobiographies

If the motherland is almost coterminous with the genre during Rosas's regime, then a Rosist gauchesque seems redundant. Only when it becomes
necessary to mobilize the rural masses, around 1830, do Pérez's dailies cir-
culate freely. At this time, European culture, the opposite of the gauchesque, is also needed as a dependent in the master's house. Pérez and de
Angelis each wrote a biography of Rosas, one from the space of the heard
voice and the other from the exterior space of the genre, that of the written word. Pérez's biography is in verse and narrated by a gaucho in whose
name the names of Hidalgo, Chano, and Contreras are inscribed. This
gaucho biographer first tells his own life story, and this is the first time in
the genre that the popular plot of the oral autobiography appears: the gaucho's encounter with the party, followed by his detention and conscription, mistreatment in the army, and desertion. This story leads directly to
La ida, the other oral autobiography. From a linguistic point of view, Pérez
is the least gauchesque of the gauchesques, because his literary language
has few gaucho inflections; it is rather a popular, almost urban, language.
Is this language of the gauchos then "more real"? Is language the only
thing that connects literature and reality? Pérez is also the only writer in
the genre who constitutes a new alliance, between the gauchos and the inhabitants of the slums on the outskirts of the city (or between the country
and the city, from the bottom up):

> My object is to entertain
> the youths of the slums on the outskirts of town:
> I don't care if I am criticized
> by the scholars and city slickers.

Pérez also gave blacks a voice.

The Rosist writer of the genre was annihilated by de Angelis, the European scribe in the house of the founding father.

Introduction to the Stories of National Liberation
Theme of the Traitor and Hero: Joyce in Borges

In the theater of an oppressed and tenacious country, the hero signs his own death warrant; the traitor's execution is the instrument of the motherland's emancipation. The story copies and parodies history, history plagiarizes literature.

The plot of Borges's story "Theme of the Traitor and Hero" (set in Ireland, with allusions to Parnell, to Yeats's *Fergus*—*quoted* by Joyce in the first chapter of *Ulysses*—to the druids and their doctrine of metempsychosis, to Vico's cycles) resembles the "real," historical assassination of the traitor-hero of the emancipation; it *reproduces* the "literary" assassination of Shakespeare's *Julius Caesar* according to a *translation* from Gaelic; parts of *Macbeth* have also been *copied* into it. This assassination, in which the people participated in a *reproduction* of the Swiss Festpieles, itself *prefigured* Lincoln's assassination. The investigator who discovers the historical truth enters the fabric of written history: he hushes up the truth and dedicates a book to the glory of the hero (and his writing had also prefigured this book).

The Anarchist's Universal Grammar

> MITSOU RONAT: To which philosophy do you feel closest?
> NOAM CHOMSKY: In relation to the questions we have just been discussing, the philosopher to whom I feel closest and whom I'm almost paraphrasing is Charles Sanders Peirce. He proposed an interesting outline, very far from complete, of what he called "abduction" . . .
> M.R.: Abduction is, I believe, a form of inference which does not depend solely on a priori principles (like deduction), nor solely on experimental observation (like induction) . . .
> N.C.: Peirce's ideas on abduction were rather vague, and his suggestion that biologically given structure plays a basic role in the selection of scientific hypotheses seems to have had very little influence.

To my knowledge, almost no one has tried to develop these ideas further, although similar notions have been developed independently on various occasions. Peirce has had an enormous influence, but not for this particular reason.

M.R.: More in semiology . . .

N.C.: Yes, in that general area. His ideas on abduction developed Kantian ideas to which recent Anglo-American philosophy has not been very receptive. As far as I know, his approach in epistemology has never been followed up." (Chomsky, *Language and Responsibility*, 113)

The Sign of Three

The concepts of Firstness, Secondness, and Thirdness are rather simple. Giving being the widest possible meaning, with the end of including ideas as well as things, and the ideas that we may imagine having, as well as those that we really have, I would define Firstness, Secondness, and Thirdness in the following way:

Firstness is the mode of being of that which is what it is, definitely and without reference to any other thing.

Secondness is the mode of being of that which is what it is with respect to a second thing, but to the exclusion of any third thing.

Thirdness is the mode of being of that which is what it is, by relating a second thing and a third thing to each other.

. . . The idea of a present moment, whether it exists or not, conceived of naturally as a moment of time in which no thought may be produced, from which no detail may be separated, is an idea of Firstness.

. . . In general terms, genuine Secondness consists of a thing acting on another thing: of brute action. I say "brute" because if the idea of any *law* or *reason* appears to any degree, Thirdness is present.

. . . If you consider any ordinary triadic relationship, you will always encounter a *mental* element. Brute action is Secondness, and any mental aspect implies Thirdness. For example, analyze the relationship contained within "A gives B to C." What is giving? It does not consist of A's placing B at a distance from himself and C's then collecting B. No material transfer need occur. It consists of A converting C into the possessor, in accordance with the *Law.* There must be some kind of law before there can be any kind of gift or giving, such as the law of the strongest. But let us now suppose that the gift consists merely in that A puts B down and C later picks it up. This would be a degenerate form of Thirdness, in which Thirdness is added from the outside. When A abandons B, there is no Thirdness. Nor is there when C picks up B. But if you say that these two acts constitute a unique operation, by virtue of B's identity, mere brute fact is transcended and a mental element is introduced. . . . In its genuine form, Thirdness is the triadic relation that exists between a sign, its object and the interpreting thought, which is in itself a sign, if this said triadic relationship is considered as a sign's mode of being. An *interpretant* sign mediates between the sign and its object. . . . (Charles Sanders Peirce, Letter to Lady Welby, October 12, 1904. Translation from *Obra lógico-semiótica* [Madrid: Taurus, 1987], 109–120; emphasis in original)

A Genealogy of the Genre: Places and Names

Father Castañeda's Other Gender/Genre

Castañeda's first journalistic incursion as editor and director of a magazine occurred on an uncertain date near the beginning of 1820 during the anarchy resulting from the collapse of the directorate. It was a forthright and virulently antifederalist periodical, essentially in opposition to Artigas: "The Gauchipolitical, Federiguerilla, Chacauco-Uruguayan Disillusioner, Goat-Protector, and Slut-Republicanizer of all good men who live and die uncared for in the nineteenth century of our Christian era". . . . Almost simultaneously with the preceding, Castañeda brought out another magazine, with an equally mumbo-jumbo title: *The Theophilanthropical Mysticopolitical Awakener,* "dedicated to Argentine matrons and through them to all the persons of their sex who people the face of the earth today and will people it in the centuries to come": it appeared on April 1, 1820, and was composed in epistolary form. Castañeda pretended to receive letters from matrons, which he answered and commented on in a strong antifederalist and antiuni-

tarist tone. . . . To critique federalism he devised a constituent as-
sembly made up exclusively of women, one per province, as well as
a female Charrúa Indian to serve as secretary.

In the following year, 1821, with *The Disillusioner, The Awakener,
The Supplement to the Awakener,* and *The Holy Chronicler* simultaneously underway, Castañeda felt himself with a surplus of forces
and brought out another magazine, which had the strange name
The Matron Commentator of the Four Journalists. Since it carries no
date, Zinny assumes that it is from the beginning of that year. The
prospectus that announced its appearance presented it as a magazine with a direct, colloquial style, and declared that it did not accept male correspondents, since it was not disposed to enter into
a polemic with the "learned." (Miguel Angel Scenna, "Un fraile de
combate: Castañeda," *Todo es historia,* no. 121 [June 1977]: 17–18)

Hidalgo's Names: Jacinto Chano and Ramón Contreras

In Luis Pérez

> In the name of God
> and of the Virgin of Rosario
> I begin to tell my story
> as a gaucho of Salado.
> I was born of *Juana Contreras,*
> wife of *Pedro Lugares;*
> in the bush I learned to read
> as my parents ordered.
> And I knew how to read and write
> when I reached the age of twelve.
> I learned how to break a horse
> so I could make a living.
> And on my fifteenth birthday
> I enlisted as a soldier
> in none other than the Company
> of Captain *D. Juan Chano.*

(A poetic biography of Rosas entitled "El Gaucho," published in
1830 by Luis Pérez; reprinted in Molas, *Luis Pérez,* 17; emphasis in
original.)

If Father Castañeda was capable of creating innumerable figures to speak for him, Luis Pérez, and later Ascasubi, were no laggards in this regard either. Pancho Lugares Contreras (sometimes called simply Contreras); Juana Contreras, Pedro Lugares, Chano, Panta the Minkraiser, Chanonga, Mr. Grimace Maker, Antuco Gramajo, Ticucha, Don Cunino, Don Alifonso, Jacinto Lugares, Chingolo, Juancho Barriales, and Lucho Olivares among the whites; Catalina, Uncle Juan, Franchico, Juana and Pedro José, and Juana Peña among the blacks—these are some of the masks Pérez used in his journalistic theater. (Olga Fernández Latour de Botas, "Estudio preliminar," in *El Torito de los muchachos—1830* [Buenos Aires: Antonio Zinny Bibliographic Institute, 1978], xix)

In Hilario Ascasubi . . .

"Dialogue between Jacinto Amores and Simón Peñalva, describing the first of the civic celebrations in Montevideo for the swearing in of the Constitution in 1833."

"1843. Magazine: *El gaucho Jacinto Cielo.* Fourteen issues. Charity printing."

"May 25, 1844. Memories of the glories of the motherland as told by the Argentine gauchos Chano and Contreras in the trenches of Montevideo, May 25, 1810."

"Dialogue between two soldiers from Buenos Aires, Ramón Contreras and Salvador Antero, in General D. Manuel Oribe's encampment, eight months after laying siege to Montevideo. Montevideo, 1849."

. . . with the Other Aesthetic and Its Places

In 1855, a new project—audacious, revolutionary for its time, possesses Hilario Ascasubi's imagination. In the Hueco de las Animas, according to an obscure tradition, the colonial church organization had designated a site for the construction of a grand theater or coliseum. . . . This was a costly and hazardous enterprise, which Hilario Ascasubi entered into with enthusiasm. . . . According to an accounting statement, in that year and part of the next, Ascasubi paid the company 185,000 pesos in installments, and owed another

18,833. All of it was devoured by those eighty box seats, that special women's section, that paradise, that *ceiling* of dancing nymphs surrounded by caryatids, that central chandelier with four hundred lights, and the water tanks, and the gas installation with its inflated bills. . . . Finally, on April 25, 1857, the Colón Theater was inaugurated. . . . Ascasubi was ruined, but this was his day of triumph. A contemporary journalist, referring to the architectural crowning of the coliseum, said that it deserved to be called "*Aniceto the Rooster's crest.*" (Manuel Mujica Lainez, *Vida de Aniceto el Gallo (Hilario Ascasubi)* [Buenos Aires: Emecé, 1943], 120–124)

In 1862, during General Mitre's presidency, Colonel Ascasubi was sent on commission to Europe. His mission was to recruit men by contract and send them to Buenos Aires to defend the frontiers against Indian invasion. . . . He settled in Paris. For more than ten years he lived in the French capital and successfully discharged his duty. . . . In March 1864, he came back to Buenos Aires . . . and arranged with President Mitre and General Gelly, the minister of war, to return to Europe. On this occasion he was able to make a dear wish come true, one that stirred his poet's fancy. In November of the previous year, he had visited, for the first time, Alfred de Musset's mausoleum in the cemetery of Père Lachaise and had read there the verse in which the French poet expresses his sole wish, after death, for the tutelary shade of a willow over his grave. En route again to Paris, Ascasubi carried with him a weeping willow. On July 4, 1864, he wrote to Paul de Musset, the poet's brother, telling him of the fact, and on the 15th of that month, in a very simple act, he left the Argentine tree in front of the illustrious sepulchre with this message:

An American poet brings you
this willow, whose pleasant shade
falls on the slab of your tomb,
like a kiss that the River Plata sends the Seine.

(Eleuterio Tiscornia, "Ascasubi," *Poetas gauchescos* [Buenos Aires: Losada, 1940], 17–18)

Ascasubi's Name and Place in del Campo

> At the hour of vespers,
> for four or five nights now,
> I've seen a line of carriages
> in front of the Colón The-a-ter. (Ll. 201–204)
>
> (*Fausto: Impresiones del gaucho Anastasio el Pollo en la representación
> de esta ópera,* 1866 [Buenos Aires: Colihue, 1981])

> When the fine horse whinnied
> Laguna turned around
> and cried out: —Good God!
> Isn't that El Pollo [the Chicken]?
> —The Chicken, no; that time is over,
> (answered the other peasant),
> now I'm an old cock, brother,
> with teeth like a fish-hook,
> the soil itself is denied me,
> to the very last grain. (Ibid., ll. 51–60)

> Jaca: an old rooster, *F.* 57. Ascasubi had used the same term
> in *A Gallo,* pp. 67, 115, and in *Paulino Lucero,* p. 137. (Tiscornia, "Vo-
> cabulary," in *Poetas Gauchescos,* 288)

Del Campo in Hernández: Two Places

The Letter-Prologue . . .

> As for the rest, my friend, I hope that you will judge it with benev-
> olence, even if only because Martín Fierro doesn't go to the city to
> tell his companions what he has seen and admired on May 25th or
> a similar occasion; although some references to such things, as in
> *Fausto* and various other works, are certainly of great merit, but
> these also relate the works, disgraces, and misfortunes of their lives
> as gauchos, and you are not unfamiliar with the fact that this matter
> is more difficult than many imagine. ("Letter to Don José Zoilo
> Miguens," prologue of *La ida,* December 1872)

... and the final resting place

> November 7, 1880, Buenos Aires. Cemetery of the North. Burial
> of the remains of Estanislao del Campo: "It is worth noting that this
> was the only time that Hernández spoke over a grave ... this excep-
> tion with del Campo proves the strength of the love and esteem in
> which they held each other." (Rafael Hernández, *Pehuajó*, ... , p. 78)
> (Garat and Lorenzo, "Biochronology," 41)

> Thursday, October 21, 1886. Hernández dies in his country house
> in Belgrano, twenty days short of his fifty-second birthday. ...
> October 22, Buenos Aires. Burial at the cemetery of La Recoleta,
> at 4 PM. Luis V. Varela and Lucio V. Mansilla speak, among others:
> " ... I assert that when the fame of many of our great men of the mo-
> ment has been buried in the dust, the name of Martín Fierro will en-
> dure in the memory of the people, and that José Hernández will not
> have died, even if his remains have vanished." (Ibid., 48 – 49)

Voiceover

Two Extreme Aesthetics against the Fathers of the Genre
Castañeda and Joyce

Father Castañeda, the fascist who accused Hidalgo of being a mulatto and
made fun of Artigas's titles ("Chacauco-Uruguayan Disillusioner, Goat-
Protector, Slut-Republicanizer") and of the lives of Lavalle and Hidalgo
("Biography of the Ingenious Hidalgo, Juan Lavalle and other matters for
those who like reading about horrors"), is not a strictly gauchesque poet.
He belongs and does not belong to the genre—like Joyce's novels, genres
that aren't genres. Rather than naming the gauchos, Castañeda named
himself (pseudonyms: Brother Cipriano, Bartolo the Stupid, Brother Rab-
bit, Confucius, and various others). Rather than entering the house of any
founding father as a subordinate, he entered the house of the Father of all
motherlands, in order to add the title of father to his name and to use it to
attack all the founding fathers of all motherlands. Instead of oscillating between weapons and letters, he was a "friar of combat": he condensed the
two alternatives into one. As Hidalgo was distributing the voices to found
the genre, Castañeda confronted this genre with the Other gender/genre;

he opposed the voice of the gaucho with the voice of the matrons. He put the master in the service of the ladies: he chose the other possibility of the female Other and he had no successors. He wrote during the period of anarchy and his succession of fidelities, infidelities, and betrayals is such that which political sector he really belonged to is unknown. General Lucio Mansilla Sr. spoke over his grave.

Castañeda is the Argentine Joyce of titles, the Joyce of the title of Michel Butor from the first volume of *Repertoires* ("Small preliminary cruise toward a reconnaissance of the Joyce archipelago"): he became Joyce through his titles. Only there could he confront the scandal of Hidalgo's language with the scandal of his own; only in titles did his languages go crazy, producing mixtures, contaminations, and diatribes. And titles are where he embraced all of space-time. Like Pérez, he was prohibited from publishing his lampoons and it was recommended that he be imprisoned.

Four scenes

1. He was the son of Don Ventura Castañeda, a Spanish businessman settled in Buenos Aires, and of Andrea Romero Pineda, a lady of old Buenos Aires stock and profound religious devotion. He saw the light of this world in 1776 and his first years passed under the indubitable influence of his mother, who transmitted her robust faith to him and wished to see him enter the priesthood. This influence carried such weight with him that, at age eleven, he entered the Franciscan monastery, intent on devoting his life to God. The separation from his nuclear family was neither easy nor pleasant. For the boy and his mother, it necessitated a real tearing away, especially for the former. . . . (Scenna, "Un fraile," 8)

2. He had extremely novel ideas about the position of women in society. In a time when the female sector of humanity occupied a secondary, subaltern place, Castañeda affirmed that the presence of women was not only fundamental but also indispensable in any social and political action, and he would address himself to women in his sermons, exhorting them to fill the position that belonged to them. (Ibid., 10)

3. A birth, as in Joyce's *Ulysses*

One day Don Francisco Xavier de Riglos arrived for a visit at the Monastery of Saint Francis, accompanied by a daughter in the advanced stages of pregnancy—so advanced, that in the middle of the civilities she began her labor. It was necessary to proceed with all speed in that holy place. Brother Francisco gave up his cell so that the lady could be attended to, and there she gave birth. Meanwhile, Castañeda went to sleep at his mother's house. The next day *La gaceta* announced in a scandalized tone that the friar had spent the night outside the monastery. Immediately the accused took up his pen and replied: "Know that the daughter of the magistrate was giving birth and that it was not right that I witness it, since I don't want to be witness to women's labor but rather to men's, so that I may tell the public when the Antichrist is born, who must be the son of guerrillas like you." (Ibid., 19)

4. The joyces' madness?
   A theory of fascism?
   A biography of Sade?

This poor lunatic, whose insane literature was admired by Restoration sympathizers, was the unwitting instrument of the apostolic party.

For reasons of elemental decency, the governor prohibited him from publishing lampoons and asked the provincial head of the Franciscans to keep him locked up in his monastery; confusing an evil passion with what was already incurable mental illness, he believed that the unfortunate man would repent. (José Ingenieros, *La evolución de las ideas argentinas* [Buenos Aires: Editorial Futuro, 1961], 1:245)

The Relationship between Life and Literature in the Genre:
The Problem of Parody

Estanislao del Campo occupies the other extreme. He's the one who turns the genre around for the first time, who parodies it, and thus he marks the first point, or hole, in which the exterior space and the interior of the genre are the same. This is the first turn of the white and sky blue ribbon. And this catastrophe also changed the relation between writers and genre, between life and literature: the writers' biographies, their written lives, came to form a part of the genre.

Del Campo is the first to read the genre as "literature," and therefore the first to take its writers as writers. Here are two of his gestures:

(a) *He turned around what he took from his father in the genre.* From Ascasubi, from Aniceto the Rooster, Ascasubi's name in the genre, he made Anastasio the Chicken. Strangely, he also changed his father's space in the genre. His setting is not the country, the usual place of the genre, but rather the city's theater, the Colón, where Ascasubi's aesthetic and life, which were in opposition to the genre, were located. And he divided the names' position between the title, subtitle, and body of the text in such a way that the last turned the first two around. Rather than making the name of the gaucho the title, as Ascasubi did, del Campo gave his title the name of the opera—or of Doctor Faust. And he also divided the gaucho of the subtitle into "being" and "calling himself." ("The gaucho Anastasio the Chicken's impressions of the performance of this opera"): when he presents and identifies himself in the gauchesque verses, the teller of the opera is no longer a chicken but rather "an old rooster." Or perhaps he's his own father. Parody is the son's aesthetic.

(b) *He also turned around what he took from his own father in real life.* Del Campo didn't go into exile—his father did, following Lavalle and his remnant, while del Campo himself was educated, during Rosas, in the *Federal Academy of Buenos Aires:*

> 1834. Romualdo Gregorio Estanislao was born in Buenos Aires on February 7, the son of Colonel Juan Estanislao and Gregoria Luna.
> 1840. Colonel del Campo accompanies Lavalle's remnant to Potosí, later going on to Chile.
> 1849. He completes his studies in the Federal Academy of Buenos Aires. His father returns from Chile after nine years of exile. (Noemí Susana García and Jorge Panesi, "Chronology," *Introduction to Fausto* [Buenos Aires: Ediciones Colihue, 1981], 9–10)

And not only did he enter the house of some founding father of the motherland as a subordinate, but his woman was the niece of the same General Lavalle whom his father followed into exile, into the loss of the motherland. In other words, he placed himself in his own house—in marrying the Lavalle woman, he married the lateral daughter of his own father's founding father.

> 1850. He begins work as a subordinate in Manuel Albornoz's store. Later he will work in Mariano Brantes's store and after that in Balcarce's warehouse. Here he has the opportunity to deal with men from the countryside: imitating their style of expression, he writes his first poems. His favorite poet: Hilario Ascasubi.
>
> 1858. He is named private secretary to Governor Valentín Alsina.
>
> 1863. He is designated secretary of the Chamber of Deputies of the province of Buenos Aires.
>
> 1864. He marries General Lavalle's niece, Carolina Micaela Lavalle. (García and Panesi, "Chronology," 11–14)

Parody's fundamental activity is the rupture or widening of frames and borders. Del Campo widened the borders of the genre to such a point that with his work the biographies of the writers of the genre came to form a part of the geneology of the genre itself. Del Campo's parody and aesthetic of festival and laughter (a *hilarious* aesthetic), turn around again in *La ida*: Hernández couldn't write without *Fausto* and named del Campo's title in the letter-prologue, that extension of the subtitle, to situate himself at the other pole, in the place of loss and tears.

And Martín Fierro, with the name the genre gave him, spoke over del Campo's grave, the place of silence and tears, to return his laughter to him, turned around. And also to give his name, the name of Martín Fierro, to his rooster's tomb.

Essai sur le Don (1923)

> In the systems of the past we do not find simple exchange of goods, wealth and produce through markets established among individuals. For it is groups, and not individuals, which carry on exchange, make contracts, and are bound by obligations; the persons represented in the contracts are moral persons—clans, tribes, and families; the groups, or the chiefs as intermediaries for the groups, confront and oppose each other. . . . We propose to call this

the system of *total prestations.* Such institutions seem to us to be best represented in the alliance of pairs of phratries in Australian and North American tribes, where ritual, marriages, succession to wealth, community of right and interest, military and religious rank and even games all form part of one system and presuppose the collaboration of the two moieties of the tribe. The Tlingit and Haida of North-West America give a good expression of the nature of these practices when they say that they "show respect to each other." . . . We are here confronted with total prestation in the sense that the whole clan, through the intermediacy of its chiefs, makes contracts involving all its members and everything it possesses. But the agonistic character of the prestation is pronounced. Essentially usurious and extravagant, it is above all a struggle among nobles to determine their position in the hierarchy to the ultimate benefit, if they are successful, of their own clans. This agonistic type of total prestation we propose to call the "potlatch." (3–5)

    . . . Holmes makes the acute observation that the Toaripi and Namau languages, the one Papuan and the other Melanesian . . . have "only a single word to cover buy and sell, borrow and lend." Antithetical operations are expressed by the same word. [It is not that the operations are antithetical, but rather that they are two forms of the same reality.] (30–31) [64]

    . . . "[The obligation to give] is the essence of the potlatch. A chief must give a potlatch for himself, his son, his son-in-law or daughter and for the dead. He can keep his authority in his tribe, village and family, and maintain his position with the chiefs inside and outside his nation, only if he can prove that he is favourably regarded by the spirits, that he possesses fortune and that he is possessed by it. The only way to demonstrate his fortune is by expending it to the humiliation of others, by putting them "in the shadow of his name." (Marcel Mauss, *The Gift: Forms and Functions of Exchange in Archaic Societies,* trans. Ian Cunnison [New York: Norton, 1967], 37–38)

---

64. [This last sentence, which I have translated, appears in the Spanish version of Mauss's essay but not in the English version. *Trans.*]

The Anarchist's Universal Grammar

> MITSOU RONAT: I remember reading [Kenneth Hale's] study of a game of antonyms, where each speaker must replace words by their opposites, according to certain rules . . .
>
> NOAM CHOMSKY: Yes, that is one example. What emerges from his work is very interesting, undoubtedly. These games could not have been invented simply to pass the time: they respond to fundamental intellectual needs. It has also been suggested that the proliferation of the extraordinarily complex and intricate systems of kinship may have no explanation in terms of social function . . .
>
> M.R.: Thus he is opposed to the functionalism of Lévi-Strauss, which links the kinship system to exchange . . .
>
> N.C.: Perhaps these kinship systems satisfy an intellectual need. They may be the kind of mathematics you can create if you don't have formal mathematics. The Greeks made up number theory, others make up kinship systems. Hale and others report informants who are exceptionally gifted in kinship systems, just as mathematicians can be gifted. These discoveries belong to anthropology, but naturally to psychology as well. They show how human beings create cultural richness under conditions of material privation. As far as these language games are concerned, children are said to have no difficulty at all in learning them. They seem to be linked to rites of puberty. All very strange and fascinating. (Chomsky, *Language and Responsibility*, 60)

Voiceover

In the universe of the gift, the genre is a system of total prestation: of economic, juridical, political, and literary alliances, inextricably intertwined. It is the alliance of "two motherlands" or of two parts of the motherland, in a pact to make war on the enemies of the motherland. A system of alliances between juxtapositions and montages, and a system of exchanges in which the one who writes places within the voice of the singer (the one without land or name) what he doesn't have, the written word. The one who writes gives the singer writing, and with it a name, a title other than "vagrant" or "outlaw." And with this title, he gives the singer the name by which he defines himself: patriot, in Hidalgo's case. The writer writes this voice in order to ask it for what he himself lacks: justice and equality, against the motherland's stain of difference. The heard voice of the Other is also the writer's voice and his word; in the juxtapositions and montages of the game of the alliance, the singer and the writer are and are not the same.

The writers' written lives constitute a language whose meaning depends on the figure of the gift, with its two faces. "Gift" designates operations that only seem antithetical: they are nonhierarchical hierarchies, the abolition of hierarchies or inversion of hierarchies. To give writing and receive the voice are two sides of the same coin, like the same meaning in two different languages. And the moment of the biographies is exactly the point at which the gift may be returned. The writers' lives are read and defined from the position of the writer who succeeds them and from the position of the gaucho biographies that they themselves wrote.

The history of the genre is the movement of devolution from the heard voice to the writers that gave it writing. This is the movement of its history because time and future are necessary so that the sequence or ring of the gift may close, and the gauchos, from inside the genre, may restore their voice to those who wrote it. The category of the future, along with the categories of the gift and the alliance, designate a logical movement of potential unification by juxtaposition and montage. These are the constitutive categories of the genre. The cycle of reciprocity opened by Hidalgo is closed with Hernández, where the name of the gaucho names the one who named him: "Yesterday Senator Martín Fierro passed away," a journalist wrote when Hernández died (Horacio Zorraquín Becú, *Tiempo y vida de José Hernández, 1834–1886* [Buenos Aires: Emecé, 1972], 323). The folkloricization of *Martín Fierro,* its passage from reading into the voice, into song, and into collective memory, closes the sequence of the gift opened with Hidalgo's voices and silences. Martín Fierro's life story is identified with Hernández's. Thus the oral biography of the gaucho determines the montage and is at the same time the shared biography of the writers of the genre. And this voice not only came to return a name and a life story, but in itself it also conveyed the name Hidalgo gave it: patriot. Beginning with *Martín Fierro,* and retroactively, the voice and name of the gaucho were transformed into signs of the motherland.

Thus the written oral biography of the gaucho and the written life of the writer of the genre can be the same: two collective graphies that carry the stain of the motherland's difference.

The Anarchist's Universal Grammar

MITSOU RONAT: Can one consider as "external" the questions posed by sociolinguistics?

NOAM CHOMSKY: It is conceivable. I'm not sure what these questions are. One can imagine that the definition of a language or a dialect could be one such question. It seems doubtful that these are really linguistic notions.

What is the "Chinese language"? Why is "Chinese" called a language and the Romance languages, different languages? The reasons are political, not linguistic. On purely linguistic grounds, there would be no reason to say that Cantonese and Mandarin are dialects of one language while Italian and French are different languages. . . . So what is a language? There is a standard joke that a language is a dialect with an army and a navy." (Chomsky, *Language and Responsibility*, 190)

In some way it must be imagined that, in speaking of "Chinese thought," we meant to refer to the structure of thought determined by national or racial traits. In reality, we simply wish to signal the set of representations and the system of thinking that the Chinese use, above all, in the humanistic and superstructural realms. The particularity of this system of thought is profoundly rooted in the history of the future of social formations through which present China formed itself. It is also rooted in the particular social phenomenon according to which the forms of reflection related to the most ancient stages of social development are not displaced by other more modern forms (even as they are "canonized" by tradition), but rather are enriched by the experience of succeeding stages, and are not surpassed, owing to the respect and esteem accorded to the perfection that is reached in them." (Sergei M. Eisenstein, "El mago del jardín de los perales," in his *Cinematismo*, ed. Domingo Cortizo [n.p., n.d.], 237)

Chapter Two

Challenge and Lament, the Intonations of the Motherland

Inside the Internal Space of the Genre

Four Definitions of the Genre and Its Internal Space

First. The genre is the alliance between a heard voice and a written word. Its enunciations are not sentences or propositions but rather the relation between intonations and meanings.[1] The alliance is a relationship of poetic and political forces among voices and meanings produced by the genre's enunciations; it does not exist prior to or outside them. The logic of the alliance, then, assumes a fictional modality: it is desired and postulated, an ought-to-be written as an is. Each time the enunciations of the genre construct a specific kind of alliance, it's because there is no exact correspondent in reality. Postulation, which identifies an ought-to-be with saying and being, makes the alliance real within the genre. This is the modality of the contract, the pact, and the legal cross-examination—it is also the modality of the genre's internal space: there is no before or outside as such, and its postulation is its production.

Second. What makes the genre possible, between independence and the definitive establishment of the state in 1880, is the existence of at least two sectors competing for hegemony; each one calls on the gaucho as an ally against the other. In other words, there must be a war of definitions; in the genre the war is for the definition of the word/voice "gaucho." The internal space of the genre is therefore a polemical space, governed by the logic of debate: the alliances' poeticopolitical constructions are repeatedly re-

---

1. [The Spanish word *tono,* which assumes a special significance in this chapter, has a wider range of meanings than its most obvious English counterparts, *intonation* and *tone.* Tono may refer to spoken inflection, the stylistic tone of a written text, or a particular mode of expression. Ludmer's use of the word encompasses all of these meanings. At times one meaning is more dominant; at others, all meanings are in play. While none of these three English words—intonation, tone, or mode—is fully adequate, I have chosen intonation because Ludmer's use of the term originates from, and remains rooted in, the heard voice, with its particular inflections, unreproducible in "translation" to the written word. *Trans.*]

futed and undone. The use of the word/voice (of the) "gaucho" and the enunciation and debate of the alliance are two aspects of the same reality. And the debate of the alliance is the debate over what place the gaucho should occupy, how to use his body, what laws should govern him, to whom he should subordinate himself, and who should educate him. To put it another way, the discussion of the gaucho's place and function in society and of the type of relationships that may be established between him and the other, political and learned, sectors takes place within the genre. But this discussion is not parliamentary, journalistic, or merely political: it is argued in the word/voice (of the) "gaucho," in the space of its emission, its directions and meanings. Or it is argued in the construction of the voice and its intonations in determined discursive situations, with a particular treatment of certain significant matters such as the subject, the modalities of identification of the event, and its position in space-time. This debate occurs each time the voice of the gaucho "speaks" or "sings" in the texts and each time it occupies its assigned place in the alliance. The debate's terms and its utopian resolution are one and the same, to the degree that the ought-to-be is the is in the conjunctions, linkages, distances, and cultural and verbal exclusions. The war of definitions links the texts together and sketches a diagram that represents the internal space of the genre, where the texts debate not only with their contemporaries but also with their predecessors and with the descendants who rewrite them. This effect of a generalized, massive polemic constitutes the internal space of the genre and gives it a particular form: that of one of the parliaments before the establishment of the state.

Third. Alliance is a complex category, which in the internal space of the genre designates an apparatus for the distribution of the positions of heard voices, and of their intonations, which is governed by an apparatus for the distribution of written meanings (a rationale or a system of interests) in relation to the uses of words and bodies. The set of relationships between the intonations and the meanings not only constitutes the genre's enunciated, that of the alliance, and its internal space, but also functions as an apparatus of unification, of inclusion and exclusion: as an apparatus of the state. Between independence and the state, the genre does not cease to represent the state.

Fourth. Alliance is not only enunciation, word/voice (of the) "gaucho," postulation, pact, war of definitions, parliament, and apparatus of the state but also something more. Beginning with the heard voice of the gaucho, the alliance articulates the internal space of the world of subjects using the motherland: the intonations of the gaucho's heard voice are the voices of the genre's subjects and also the intonations of the motherland. These intonations, the material of the internal, voiced space of the genre, are the very intonations that the minstrels' heard voice gave the genre: the challenge and the lament. And they are the positions with which the alliance was constructed: the categories that articulate the public and political spaces of the motherland—those that the genre in its emergence introduces, with Hidalgo's work—with an intimate space in which subjects are heard. (This is precisely the difference between gauchesque texts and the heroic odes of the abstract men of the motherland, such as the national hymn.) The motherland makes itself intimate with the intonations and positions of the voice in the challenge and lament; they link effects of universality with effects of inclusion, of interiority. In them the outside is doubled in an inside that is coextensive with it. This is the form of the internal space of the genre, curved and in a perpetual diagonal.

And Four Formulas for the Intonations

First. The category of the intonation (the challenge and the lament) is not limited in this treatise to the words that the gauchos address to their rivals or enemies or to the subject's position in symbolic degradations and exaltations. Within the intonations, a world order (with its justice and its values) is postulated. The challenge and lament are articulated with this order that imparts meaning, as if the words that the Others—the gauchos—hurl at their enemies or address to their allies need a code to be deciphered. The alliance's enunciated is constituted between the heard intonations of the challenge and lament and their orders (rationales, hierarchies, and justice).

Second. The genre debates the direction not only of the intonations (that is, to whom challenges and laments should be addressed) but also of the uses of bodies and of the meanings of certain words (these are debated anew each time they appear). And this debate is sustained by a universal reason located in a specific space that is both logical and real. Each time a text of the genre allows a challenge to be read, it establishes a position of the body of the voice, of the body that sings or speaks (the positions of the patriotic singer, the learned gaucho, the ex-soldier, the soldier, the outlaw, the amputee) in an area or space, and it gives meaning to the very words that it emits: in Hidalgo, these are liberty, equality, courage, gaucho, and motherland. The words are the same and the opposite in *La ida*—in the other universal order which it sustains.

Third. The intonations hold a central place in the genre. They both sustain and decipher an ambiguity that the language of the challenge and lament itself produces and in which it inserts itself. In the challenge or the lament the gaucho throws a double meaning at the Other or a meaning that has several different translations, which may be deciphered with different codes or reasons. And this ambiguity, which is often read in the verbal play at all possible levels of the language, remains there, floating. The ambiguity of the challenge and lament, its verbal work, the possibility of changing direction, of turning around, is installed in the very center of the word "gaucho" and its two meanings or directions, which is one of the axes of the genre. In both the challenge and the lament, there is something like a battle for a logic of identity or being, which may be read in the prelude to *La ida.*

Fourth. In the genre, the challenge and lament (two intonations of the heard voice and two positions facing power and the law), militarized, politicized, and each linked to a universal reason or a system of interests, are always directed against the enemy of the one who writes. The challenge is the military and political language-weapon; the lament introduces the language-law. Modulated, quoted from one text to another, their location changed, the two intonations represent the universe of the heard voice in the genre. Furthermore, when they again assume the disguise they wore in their oral source, the intonations open two traditions of our culture: those that gave form to the milonga and the tango.

The Preludes or the Code of the Intonations

It is in the preludes that hearing begins. Now the voice becomes clearer and the substance of its sound may be perceived: intonations, heights, intensities, types of attack, and tempos. In this experiment with codes, "prelude" designates Hidalgo's founding texts (the first cielito in which a gaucho sings and the first dialogue in which two gauchos converse) and also the prelude of *La ida*. The relationships between the heard intonations and their meanings or codes may be read in the preludes because they are the internal border of the genre's and the texts' internal space.

The genre's two preludes, in Hidalgo and in *La ida,* are each other's opposite; their codes or logics are located at opposite extremes. *La ida* is the only text that gave voice to Hidalgo's silences and voices simultaneously. The text is performed by all the possible positions of the challenge and lament, and not only those of Chano and Contreras, because it occupies the complete spectrum of Hidalgo's voices and nonvoices; the learned Chano is installed in the text on the side, "El camino trasandino." *La ida* is the exact reverse of the emergence of the genre and the last text before the constitution of the state; the reverse of *La ida, La vuelta,* is the state within the genre, and it directly represents the state's constitution. *La ida,* then, speaks the voices and codes that the state needed to silence in order to constitute itself, which are inverse to the voices and reasons of those of the birth of the motherland. Moreover it is the text without which there is no genre because it closed the ring of the gift: it allowed the written to be folk-loricized (it was sung in pulperías) and allowed the heard voice and its intonations to be returned to the writing from which they came, from the voice of the minstrels. In the preludes, the use is the gift.

(This essay on heard voices and their codes in the internal space is a first fold toward *La ida*. Its form is a diagonal grid; a work with fractions and the figure of the diagonal that Cantor drew between 0 and 1 in order to demonstrate that the set of real numbers is infinite and not quantifiable. The space between 0 and 1 is precisely the internal space of the genre, the space between the birth of the motherland and the state, and also the space of *La ida* which contains all of it.)

The Patriotic Singer's Challenge

In the interior of the voices' system of distribution, a system of distribution of the voices' intonations and positions is now revealed. There are at least three intonations in Hidalgo's first cielito where it is said that a gaucho sings ("Cielito Composed by a Gaucho to Sing of the Battle of Maipú," 1818):

> *The first intonation:*
> Cielito, heavens, yes,
> the toad said to the frog,
> sing as you please tonight;
> and we'll see each other tomorrow.
>
> Cielito, I say no,
> friend Fernando, don't kid us;
> if the motherland must be free,
> then why are you going backward?

> *The second intonation:*
> Long live our freedom,
> and General San Martín,
> publish his renown
> with your bugle ringing.
> Cielito, heavens, yes,
> our noble independence
> was fought and won
> at the battle of Maipú.

> *The third intonation,* in the same cielito:
> As the fifth of April ended,
> the two armies met
> fighting in the Maipú River,
> which became like a fraction.

> *The initial quatrain and the final chorus, respectively:*
> Little chords, don't deny me now,
> grant me your favor,
> and I will sing in this cielito
> of the great battle of Maipú.

Cielito, heavens, yes,
long live the authorities
and also long live me,
so I may sing the noble truth.

There are three positions framed by the true story of the singer,[2] who possesses the only "I" of the text and ends it in alliance with the authorities. This singer has not participated in the battle.

In Hidalgo, the system of distribution of intonations and codes is clear: there is a popular, "oral" voice, which is addressed directly to the enemy, challenging him; a "high," solemn, written voice, which gives meaning and direction to the oral intonation, guiding it; and a narrative, chronicler's voice. This is a *fiesta*, a celebration of victory.

Popular oral culture is inherently rebellious; it constantly demonstrates a situation of domination and subjection, although in an indirect way and with a disguise different from that of the ambiguity of the Other culture. From the beginning, the genre exhibits the rebellion and protest contained in two intonations or positions of the traditional gaucho culture, the challenge and lament. And it disposes of any ambiguity or disguise by directing that rebellion against the enemy. These two intonations are linked, in turn, with the historical conjunctures in which Hidalgo's first gauchesque cielito and his first dialogue appear.

The challenge forms part of the ritual of the minstrel song and is addressed to the other singer, demanding a competition to determine who is better. It is a struggle for titles: the very definition of symbolic war. This challenge may also be read in the prelude to *La ida;* in the minstrel song of *La vuelta,* the black's challenge is suppressed and told by the narrator: "It was a clear challenge." The challenge carries the duel, which for Clause-

2. In oral cultures, one of the signs of truth is created by giving the texts another organization that is superimposed on the linguistic organization: *verse* may indicate that what is being said is not only the content of the communication but also something more, with the denotation of practical truth (fables and myths appear in prose for the most part). This phenomenon may be seen in proverbs and more generally in the system of customary laws. On this point, see Yuri M. Lotman and A. M. Piatigorsky, "Text and Function," *New Literary History* 9, no. 2 (1978): 233. Also see Louis Chevalier, *Classes laborieuses et classes dangereuses à Paris pendant la première moitié du XIXème siècle* (Paris: Plon, 1958), chap. 3: "L'opinión populaire."

witz is the essence of war,[3] into the realm of the performative; the singer addresses his agonistic enunciation to the Other, and this aggression serves to identify the rival, the enemy. With the challenge we enter the polemological space of oral culture, the space of the word-action, and the interior of the voiced space of the genre.[4]

The challenge is a movement of exaltation and degradation of language that transfers hierarchical differentials to universes outside of meaning: animals and body parts. It unfolds a series of divisions and equalities that the genre integrates as forces and power relations. The challenge is the place of linguistic deviation, of ambiguity, and at the same time the place of relationships of force. These are relationships not of mere violence but of that which precedes and represents it: a verbal action about or against verbal or future actions. The challenge is also the exhibition of one's own courage and the mocking of symbols of power; within it, everything can turn itself around. The challenge thus forms a part of what has variously been called satire, counter-theater (E. P. Thompson), carnivalesque (M. Bakhtin), or elements of antagonism and resistance in popular cul-

---

3. "War is no more than a duel on a grander scale" (*On War*, bk. 1, chap. 1); in the birth of the genre, war appears as the original form (the very structure of communication), and the dialogue of weapons is the dialogue par excellence. In the challenge, moreover, the ally-enemy distinction appears as a strategic category; see André Gluksmann, *El discurso de la guerra* (Barcelona: Anagrama, 1969).

The challenge is one of the rituals of the minstrel song; it is also found in Rio Grande do Sul, and more generally in Brazilian penny books. See Paul Zumthor, *Introduction à la poésie orale* (Paris: Seuil, 1983), 221; N. Anido, "*Pajadas* et *desafíos* dans le Rio Grande do Sul," *Cahiers de littérature orale* 5 (1980): 42–170; Bianca Maria Gnerre, "Dal contrasto medievale al 'desafio' de 'cantadores' nella letteratura popolare brasiliana," in *Letteratura popolare brasiliana e tradizione europea,* ed. Luciana Stegagno Picchio (Rome: Bulzoni, 1978).

On the recurring images of the challenge and the exchange of boasts that often ends in a fight, see Eneida Sansone de Martínez, *La imagen en la poesía gauchesca* (Montevideo: Universidad de la República, 1962), 293 on.

4. On the polemological space of oral culture, see Zumthor, *Introduction,* and especially Walter Ong, *Orality and Literacy: The Technologizing of the Word* (New York: Methuen, 1982). The agonistic dynamic of the processes of thought and expression in oral culture has been fundamental in the development of Western culture, where it was institutionalized by the art of rhetoric and by Socratic dialogue.

ture (B. Canal Feijóo, L. M. Lombardi Satriani, A. M. Cirese, S. Hall, R. Darnton, P. Burke and others).[5]

In Hidalgo's text the one who sings strips the king of his title and horizontalizes relationships, which is the condition of confrontations in traditional culture; the singer calls his enemy "my friend the king" and thereby establishes equality. In the challenge a world order or a change of world orders is announced. The animals of fables—a different genre—maintain the informal address, the song, and the future threat. The symbolic war is sung by the patriotic gaucho who will later be called Contreras.

The genre constructed the enunciation of the war, the language-weapon, with this verbal duel that maintains antagonism: it gave direction, objectives, and space to the words of the popular rebellion, placing them each time in a scene and *linking them with a universal code. This is the second intonation* in Hidalgo's text: the written voice of the motherland, renown, freedom, independence, and the hero San Martín. This is the heroic moment in which reason and literature speak of what they write for everyone, gauchos and learned people alike; the universal rights of man and of the citizen speak, placed in the entire space of the motherland. The solemn code gives a point, in the double meaning of signification and direction, to the oral intonation. *In the first place* the code gives a precise meaning to the word "freedom" by transferring it to the motherland. In the voice of the gaucho, this word could have another meaning, namely this: *to be free was to not serve.* This is the meaning of freedom in the prelude to *La ida,* in the anonymous "Cielito of the Retired Blandengue," and in Lussich's *Los tres gauchos orientales:*

5. See E. P. Thompson, "La sociedad inglesa del siglo XVIII: ¿Lucha de clases sin clases?" in *Tradición, revuelta y conciencia de clase* (Barcelona: Editorial Crítica, 1979); M. Bakhtin, *Rabelais and His World* (Bloomington: Indiana University Press, 1984); L. M. Lombardi Satriani, "Dinamica culturale e stratificazione sociale," in *Sociologia della letteratura,* ed. F. Ferrara et al. Atti del primo convegno nazionale (Rome: Bulzoni, 1978), and also by Lombardi Satriani, *Reggio Calabria: Rivolta e strumentalizzazione* (Vibo Valentia: Qualecultura, 1971); A. M. Cirese, *Cultura egemonica;* S. Hall, "Notes on Deconstructing 'The Popular,'" in *People's History and Socialist Theory,* ed. R. Samuel, History Workshop Series (London: Routledge and Kegan Paul, 1981); R. Darnton, *The Great Cat Massacre and Other Episodes in French Cultural History* (New York: Random House, 1985); P. Burke, *Popular Culture in Early Modern Europe* (London: Temple Smith, 1978).

> But they call me a bandit
> because I don't want to serve,
> I could never suffer
> having the harness put on me;
> I'm free like the cold pampas wind,
> and I've always lived free,
> I was free when I left
> the house of my father;
> with no other dog barking at me
> than my own destiny. (Ll. 2238–2247)[6]

Hidalgo's gaucho's word, his challenge, says "If the motherland must be free," that is, *he conjugates the verb* for the motherland, while the word of reason's code, that of the second intonation, says "our freedom": it uses the abstract universal. *In the second place,* the written word in a solemn intonation names the war hero who directs the popular rebellion against the enemy: this is the figure of the officer who commands in the genre. Between the oral intonation and the written system two values play: the courageousness of the gaucho, who directs his voice to the enemy, and the written courage, which this courageousness directs and is directed by.

In Hidalgo the maximum separation is produced between the oral intonation and the written code that gives it a point; each one is a literature and a language, or two incommensurate levels of the same language.

The oral intonation and its meanings converge at Maipú, the event and the battlefield. *The third voice,* which is the voice of the titles and subtitles, *informs the audience.* It is almost impersonal, enunciated by a popular chronicler who narrates the battle. Hidalgo worked directly with the written word, with San Martín's *Parte de batalla,* published in *La Gaceta* on April 22, 1818 (*El Censor* published it on April 25). He omitted San Martín's lengthy enumeration of the difficulty in gaining positions and also of the patriot losses (San Martín: "I calculate our loss at a thousand men"). The

---

6. This quotation is from the first edition of *Los tres gauchos orientales* (Buenos Aires: "La Tribuna" Press, 1872). In the 1877 version there are variants: "But they call me bandit / Because I play with the Indian cutlass, / Because this ringing of Diana / Sounds fierce in my ear, / I'm free like the cold wind of the pampas, / And I've always lived free, / I was free when I left / the belly of my mother / with no other dog barking at me / than my own destiny . . ." (Montevideo: Marcha, 1972).

challenges and the oral intonation fill the void of the *Parte*'s technical details and losses.[7] The narrative voice links the intonation of the challenge with the solemn intonation in a specific space of convergence: that of the punctual, conjunctural event (a battle, a patriotic or enemy announcement, a celebration) and its telling. The type of construction and representation of the situation constitutes another fundamental material of the genre and is one of the axes of its historical change.

The political, poetic, military, and patriotic alliance is thus constituted; the first gauchesque verses are organized as mosaics, cubist texts, or Riemann's spaces, with leaps in the semantic structure characteristic of folklore. In Hidalgo, these leaps are the result of the *relationships of contiguity* of the two cultures' signs in the field of their convergence.[8] This is also the style in which the prelude to *La ida* is written. These signs are differential and hierarchical: the challenge against the Spanish oppressor in the oral intonation, the telling of the real event in the intonation of the oral chron-

7. See Ana María Amar Sánchez, "Las versiones de la historia en la gauchesca," *Filología* 22, no. 1 (1987). Comparing Hidalgo's cielito with San Martín's *Parte,* she shows the constitutive relationship of the genre with historical facts drawn from journalism. Hidalgo returns to rework this relationship in "Relación de las fiestas mayas," 1822. Sanchez also analyzes the relationship between Luis Pérez's *Biografía de Rosas* and de Angelis's biography of the same title.

This relationship is constant; journalism forms one of the materials of the genre, as basic source of information but also as learned discourse. Ascasubi worked with facts from the *Comercio del Plata;* del Campo took the script of the opera *Fausto* from the *Correo del Domingo* and from *La Tribuna;* Hernández worked with his own articles and Alvaro Barros's articles from *El Río de la Plata.*

8. Since the genesis of the folkloric work begins with an accumulation of traditional motifs and formulas, a process of change through the recombination, addition, and loss of details is produced; units are linked to form a whole in the manner of a mosaic. This construction also explains the brusque transitions of intonations (from praising to insulting, for example) produced by the addition of a mere stanza. The result is a property typical of oral literature: the constant oscillation of the semantic contexture. Contradictions, incongruities, and discontinuities are not mistakes but rather the result of the juxtaposition of motifs: the folkloric work combines signs and does not reproduce the "real" relationships between things. See J. Mukarovsky, "Detail as the Basic Semantic Unit in Folk Art," 205. In the letter-prologue to *La ida,* Hernández says that the gaucho expresses himself without logical connectives: he identified the gaucho "mentality" with this trait of folk literature and thus demonstrated that the genre works with the texts of oral culture when it is often believed to be working with the "real gaucho."

icler, and the meaning, the universal meanings and values or instances of cohesion, in the solemn, written intonation—the universal rights of man are a literature unto themselves. The public, like the texts, may divide it- self: each sector would recognize itself in the intonation of what it says to the other (the gauchos to the enemy, the universal values and the story to the gauchos), and, at the same time, each intonation would represent this voice's posture, direction, and place in the alliance.

To put it another way, the intonations of the voices are simultaneously verbal actions, positions, and functions in the alliance. The violence of the popular voice is disciplined and civilized—directed at the common en- emy, militarized, given a commander, and associated with the written principle that gives it meaning. It becomes licit, permitted passion, the use of legitimate violence. This is where the use of the gaucho's voice and the use of his body read each other inextricably.

In the preludes of Hidalgo and of *La ida,* which provide the codes to the intonations of the genre, *the use is the gift.* With the challenge to the en- emy, Hidalgo writes the illuminist utopia of human equality and freedom for the gauchos: he gives them "reason." For example, his singer invokes his "little strings," not God, in order to sing. God has died, and freedom, equality, and independence constitute the new universe of the mother- land. The code that the mulatto Hidalgo gave to the gauchos' voice to found the genre gives meaning to these words and conjugates them with the motherland as the subject. This utopia of the man of reason is incar- nated in Chano, the learned gaucho who appears in Hidalgo's first dia- logue using the intonation of the lament.

Here an undecidable variable is introduced into the treatise. Hidalgo would have taken the intonation of the lament from the minstrels but not the intonation of the challenge, which he would instead have taken from one of the two categories of learned literature of his epoch, that of satires and rondelets, and would have combined that category with the other cat- egory of solemn odes: *satire and the utopian impulse mutually implicate each other.*[9] Hidalgo's text would not be the genre itself but rather a pre-

9. Hidalgo, like Castañeda, would have mixed the "high" and "popular" levels of the learned literature of his epoch, as they appear in *Lira Argentina* or in *Telégrafo Mercantil.* On one hand would be the neoclassical hymns, odes, and sonnets, including Hidalgo's

lude to the genre. Without viceroyal and illuminist literature—or, rather, without the contamination in the voice of the Other between the two separated categories of this literature—there would be no genre.

Lament of the Learned Patriot

This treatise would like above all to be an anthology on or of the motherland. Or a reading primer. I propose the following text as the first chapter of the first-grade reading primer:

> So with this understood
> lend me your attention
> and I'll tell you how
> this poor heart feels;
> like a turtle-dove
> that's lost his mate
> and goes from branch to branch
> proclaiming his grief,
> so am I, going from ranch to ranch
> and from deserted village to shack,
> sad, with no rest,
> singing, with a hoarse voice,
> of the work of my motherland,
> of the rigor of my fate.

---

own "Unipersonal," which appeared in *Lira,* and on the other hand the world of satire, with the refrains, rondelets, invectives, and romances that the periodicals of the epoch exchanged from 1820 on. In its emergence, the genre would be a combination of the two eighteenth-century traditions that were present in that moment; the innovation would be the combination. The genre would then be a place where levels mixed and barriers were transgressed.

   With respect to the debate on whether satirical texts are "literary" in character (for Juan Cruz Varela they are not literature and in 1827 he eliminates them from *Lira*) and on the place of the oral popular in cielitos (e.g., R. Rojas, in *Historia de la literatura argentina* [Buenos Aires: Kraft, 1960], chap. 9, p. 410, shows the popular character of Riverola's romances as antecedents of the cielitos, and Juan María Gutiérrez, in *Los poetas de la revolution* [Buenos Aires: Academia Argentina de Letras, 1941], unties the cielito from the popular line of the Spanish romance), see Silvia Delfino, "La razón contra la pasión ¿un fracaso de los ideales?" *Teoría y crítica* 3 (April 1988).

> In the ten years so far
> of our revolution
> to cast off the chains
> of Fernando, the braggart,
> what advantage have we won?
> I'll tell you, with your permission:
> stealing from each other,
> increasing the discord between us,
> everyone wanting to govern,
> and, from faction to faction,
> wandering without knowing that we wander;
> with the result, in conclusion,
> that even the name of peasant
> seems to have a bad taste.
> And, in its place, I see only
> eternal rancor
> and a gang of poor people
> who, put in a corner,
> sing to the sound of their misery...
> Misery is not a bad sound!
> ("Interesting Patriotic Dialogue," ll. 69–102)

This is from Hidalgo's first dialogue of 1821, and the lament, the divided motherland, misery, theft, the name of the peasant (or the gaucho: they're synonymous in the text), and the social difference before the law that follows them enter the genre with such violence that it appears that the genre begins here, that this is its real explosion into being, and that here the gaucho master and the motherland cry together for the first time. And, moreover, it appears that for the first time the writer of the genre represents himself in a text, in the figure of the one who knows because he has the written word. And that this representation introduces at the outset the problem of the relation between literature and the people. The dialogue is constructed according to a specific order: it is the didactic sequence of the genre.

Jacinto Chano simultaneously inaugurates the tone of the lament and the figure of the one who knows in the genre. He is a *singer* (like Contreras, he possesses the oral code and its tones); he is an *old man* (he has what for the gauchos was the very essence of knowledge: experience); he is an *over-seer* (Hidalgo tells us this in the written word of the subtitle and in the footnote); and he is "*book-larned.*" Chano is the equal and two times the superior of Contreras (by virtue of being an old man and an overseer), and moreover he possesses the written code, which transforms the illiterate gaucho into the Other. Contreras recognizes Chano's wisdom and superiority, and recognizes it, as well, as just.[10]

This is the first step in Hidalgo's transparent, didactic, illuminist sequence: the legitimizing of the knowledge of the one who knows by the one to whom the lesson is directed. And, between the two, there is a code of difference.

The dialogue coincides with the division of the motherland, the struggle for power, theft, the difference before the law and the difference within the very name of "peasant" or "gaucho." The tone that Hidalgo now takes from oral culture is the lament: the bird or the dove of the romances and the minstrels who also sing of their affliction in the first sextina of *La ida.* The lament in the genre is the tone of loss, division, the breaking of a pact, difference before the law and the differential law. It is uttered between equals, and it is connected with the folk theme of happy days gone by, with fatalism, and with the cruelty of fate, all of which are at the core of *La ida.* This is the prepolitical complaint of the subalterns, of their defeat and impotence: *the dominated position of the dominated,* and it is found throughout almost all the oral tradition.[11] And the code that in Hidalgo gives meaning to the tone of the lament and that together with it

10. "Everyone knows / that Chano, the old singer, / is a man of reason / wherever he goes, / and that a sentence of his / is like one from Solomon" (ll. 63–68). And, "You, a man with book-larning, / thanks to your mother, I say to you; / that although I compose cielos / and am half-minstrel, / I give you my weapons / because you know more than I do" (ll. 107–112). "Interesting Patriotic Dialogue" (1821), in *Poetas gauchescos,* ed. E. Tiscornia (Buenos Aires: Losada, 1974), 47–48.

11. See P. Burke, *Popular Culture,* for the relationship between the *lamento,* the French *complainte,* and the German *Klagen,* which express the sorrow of the lover and the widow, the repentance of the criminal, or the cruel destiny of the sailor. Moreover, the lament over the difference in justice accorded to rich and poor appears, among other places, in southern Italian folklore: "Cuddinari ed amicizzia—Si teni 'nculu 'a giustizia"; see L. M. Lombardi Satriani and M. Meligrana, *Diritto egemone e diritto popolare: La Calabria neglo studi di demologia giuridica* (Vibo Valentia: Edizioni Qualecultura, 1975).

constitutes the enunciation of the alliance is the egalitarian, written law of the rights of man. Chano laments because the law is not carried out; he is the overseer of the egalitarian law of equality prior to the law, before all liberty: "and, as long as I don't see / that the crime is punished / without regard for rank, / I say we'll be free / when my old nag talks" (ll. 176–180), that is, when a genre acquires that which defines the Other.

In sum, in Hidalgo the lament, the heard tone, unites with the code that gives it meaning, which is the written law of equality before the law, in the voice of Chano, the one who knows. In order to be able to inaugurate the lament he introduced the learned gaucho (or the learned gaucho introduced himself) in the texts, and thus he established *a new alliance* in addition to the political, *the didactic alliance.* This alliance covers the abyss between the oral tone of the illiterate minstrels and the written code of the rights of man, and it exists through this distance. The difference in codes (or the definition of the other as the one who lacks something that the one who defines him and who writes has) can only lead to didactic literature.

The one who knows how to write in alliance with the lament, then, enunciates, for the one who has only heard it spoken,[12] the law of equality before the law. He has a teaching methodology: he moves between the abstract thought of the universals of man and the concrete example of differences before the law, which has as its setting the space of the gaucho's work. Example and narration are conflated in the literature for the people. *And in this space of the gaucho, in the very moment in which the one who knows how to write gives the other the law, he defines the crime:* "a gaucho steals some spurs, / or spirits away some old nag, / or lightens the load / of some peasant a little: / they arrest him, they treat him . . . / and like a bandit and a bad guy / and send him with some trouble to a prison. / The law is carried out, / and that makes me happy / . . . So now let's turn to some fat cat: / . . . What does he declare? / —That it's a lie, / that he is a man of honor. / And the dough? / —Who knows, the state lost it. / The prisoner goes out to the street / and the trial is over. / And you call that equality? / Son of a bitch! . . ." (ll. 319–347).

12. Contreras says: "Well, I've always heard it said / that, before the law, / I'm equal to all men," and Chano: "Essentially that's how it went, / and in printed papers / it was published everywhere. / But it has its difficulties / with respect to execution" (ll. 311–318).

The double meaning that is always in play in the challenge and the lament is now that of the crime, theft. And it is the crime that establishes the division, always in play in the lament, between the legal and illegal gaucho. The double meaning of the lament is also that of the crime, which must be punished, as the gauchos must also be inculcated in the world of work. Paradoxically in the dialogue, Chano's function as overseer refers to a conjuncture of peace: the war is over and now the gaucho is required to fulfill other obligations. Subordination to a military superior is replaced by subordination to the overseer and to the law: the use of the body for work in the country and the definition of the crime of theft in the very space in which the body is used. Or the convergence of the heard tones and their codes in the space of the use of bodies (and Chano is the one who visits Contreras): the challenge on the battlefield, the lament in the work field.

Hidalgo's transparent didactic sequence has been completely fulfilled in the alliance of the lament with the law of equality: the legitimizing of the world of the one who knows how to write on the part of the other; the lament for the difference before the written law (oral tone); the enunciation of the written law of equality before the law; the definition of theft and its punishment, and the division of gauchos into legal and illegal. If there is a didactic alliance, if there is an alliance, it is because there is no exact correspondence to reality. To inculcate in the gauchos the category of their crime is one of the meanings of the lesson, with lament, in a conjuncture of peace.[13]

13. The total time of the genre, the time of the process of political and juridical unification, becomes minuscule and textual in political conjunctures, as the sectors fighting for hegemony before 1880 go through moments of crisis, of radicalization of conflict, of war, of conciliation and pacification. Political conjunctures form part of the genre because the genre itself defines itself as political and of the political moment. The texts before *Fausto* are accurate and journalistic: they record battles, celebrations, peace treaties, and the appearance of decrees, and they function as chronicles. This specificity of the political moment that the genre manifests is shared, with variations, by all Argentine literature prior to 1880. The difference is in the action of the conjuncture on one hand and in its textual representation on the other. The latter is what is transformed throughout the history of the genre and it is what leads to the first mutation: with *Fausto*, dates are left behind and the genre appears as "literature."

The political conjuncture, which allows the polemical system of the genre to be typified, could be another theoretical fiction. It is a means of connecting the war of

Hidalgo's dialogue is hierarchical, and not only with the typical didactic-illuminist hierarchy of written knowledge. The texts that put the lament and also the language-law in the voice of the gaucho work specifically with hierarchical divisions and differentials. Chano speaks from above and below, each time with a specific posture: *he orders* the horse

---

definitions taking place in the gaucho's voice and its space with the war of definitions taking place between independence and 1880. It is also a means of postulating a category external to the genre that is transformed, by means of its logic, into something close to the genre. In political conjunctures, the genre seems to give form to the historical field. Political conjunctures decide the terms of the debate over the uses of the bodies of gauchos and over their integration into civilization, and they define the ever-shifting place of the writer. Only the differences of the political moment can notice the differences between *La ida* and *La vuelta,* between the two versions of Lussich's *Los tres gauchos orientales,* between Ascasubi's *Paulino Lucero* and *Santos Vega,* up through the definitive silence of Luis Pérez. And, in the first place, only these differences can notice the differences between the founding texts: Hidalgo's first cielito (1818, the war against Spain) and his first dialogue (1821, end of the war and the beginning of internal divisions). And the differences between challenge and lament.

In other words, what may seem an ideological or political change in a writer is due, from the point of view of the genre, to a change in political conjuncture: each time, various things are spoken of in different moments and positions, and therefore each time, the combination of voices and words in alliance varies. The theoretical fiction of political conjuncture as an external-internal element (the genre is a set riddled with holes) therefore represents the variable in the positions of locution and action, and their relations, in the texts. Political conjunctures influence situations, interlocutory circuits, hierarchies, degrees of antagonism, types of story, and characters: they integrate a multiplicity of data in the complex system of the genre.

The play of political conjunctures may be schematized as the sectors vying for power go through moments of war or peace, and as the sector to which the writer lends his voice finds itself in power or in opposition. In each of these moments there are two possible positions.

In the *conjuncture of war* the writer's voice gives meaning and direction to the violence. The texts are weapons (the classic example is Ascasubi's *Paulino Lucero*); they send a signal to the enemy and exalt the gauchos' leaders. This is about creating political and military unification against the enemy using the voice-body of the gaucho. In the *conjuncture of peace* the voice of work and of law, of the lesson and of political critique, emerges: this is about creating a juridical unification against the delinquent, the "bad gaucho."

The genre's own debate is thus located inside each conjuncture. In the conjuncture of war, crisis, and mobilization, the use of the gaucho's body and space is disputed: should

from Salvador, son or peon, with the use of the appropriate linguistic difference, the informal you ("come on, bring me the gray horse, / tighten my cinch" [ll. 13–14]); *he informs and instructs* the gaucho, who questions him and surrenders Contreras's arms to him, and *he also "humbly" asks* the authorities for reform and action: for justice, reason, and union. *And only then,* when he directs his request to the authorities, *does he call himself gau-*

---

he be a soldier or a worker? This debate is another debate at the same time: who commands and directs the gauchos? The agrarian sector, damaged by indiscriminate levies, reacts against the exclusive use of the gaucho as soldier: the voice is raised against the military power and the texts acquire the minstrel-like form of a life history and are tinged with anarchy, especially when the discourse is enunciated from the opposing camp. The gauchos seem to "sing" and "speak" for the whole of rural Argentina: the paradigmatic texts are "Cielito of the Retired Blandengue," Luis Pérez's *Biografía de Rosas,* and *La ida.* On the other side of the debate, from the sectors that postulate a politicomilitary or exclusively military alliance, as in Ascasubi, the gaucho festivalizes the war and exalts its heroes and leaders (and it is the gaucho of the opposing army who laments and suffers oppression and coercion).

    Anarchism or militarism: the difference can be read in the relations between locution and action. In the first case the voice that sings has participated in battles and in the life of the army and tells of horror and losses; in the second case the voice narrates battles and victories with journalistic distance and exalts the military leaders. The construction of alliances and the system of tones differ radically in each case.

    In the conjunctures of pacification or of accord between sectors, writers take on a fundamental function. The debate revolves around the education and civilization of the gauchos and the separation of legals and illegals. The writers don't lend their voices directly to any political sector but rather seem to speak for themselves (as the gauchos seem to speak for themselves against the army in conjunctures of war), filling specific functions: law, education, language, poetry. They debate who knows or who educates and the legitimacy of their knowledge. The texts of conjunctures of peace distance themselves from the events of the moment and connect themselves to the learned literature of the period (theater in the case of Hidalgo, who inaugurates the dialogues; romantic melodrama in *Santos Vega;* picaresque novel in *La vuelta*). The discourses confronting each other are *Christian moralism,* which clearly divides the gauchos into good and evil by nature, and *reformism,* which records the gaucho's protest of injustice in the application of the law and proposes institutional reform. This is about inculcating in the gauchos the law of civilization and the state. *Santos Vega* (like the texts of Castañeda) reproduces or quotes the voice of an absent priest who sends his Christian message to the gauchos, while in Hidalgo's first dialogue and in *La vuelta* the one who knows is present in the text, reciting the law and enunciating his reformist program. In both cases the gauchos must abandon their oral code or law of custom and therefore change the category of their crime.

cho and say that he is not asking anything for himself *and constitute himself as the representative of the motherland from below.*[14] In other words, in the presence of those from above he puts himself below and is a gaucho, and in the presence of those from below he puts himself above and is a learned person. Hierarchies, divisions, translations, masters, examples, and the representation of the motherland in the relations between literature and the people.

The hierarchical system of the dialogue, the alliance of the lament with the code of written law that gives it meaning, and the didactic alliance that translates this law into the oral code, *connect a "lawless" orality (without land or writing) with the word of the one who knows and who represents it.* And they contain one of the foundational nuclei of the genre as literature for the people: that which translates the egalitarian law into the verbal register, with the intonation of the voice of those in whom it must be inculcated. *Or into the voice of those to whom the egalitarian law is given:* the use is the gift in the codes of the preludes.

From this point forward, the genre will be the scene of a real war, which is still going on: who educates, and with what law and crime. Only *La vuelta* repeats Hidalgo's sequence in its totality and varies it to infinity, with a Chano without writing; that is to say, without the difference of the code, but with three sons and a black man, the Other, as listeners. Hidalgo's first dialogue contains not only *La vuelta* but also *La ida*, with the

---

14. "Peasants of all kinds, / pardon my story; / it's the child of a pure / wish and a good intention. / Valorous generals / of our revolution, / government to which I give / all my veneration: / may God give you his grace / in all your actions / so that you may correct the plan / that for so many years was wrong; / so that justice and reason / shine from all our decrees; / so that he who works may be paid, / he who deserves it may be rewarded, / in an eternal war on discord, / and therefore I think, yes, / we will be free men / and enjoy the most precious / gift of the earth. / Americans: union. / I ask you humbly, Lord, / a gaucho with a rough voice, / who hopes for nothing from the Motherland, / no prize nor recompense, / who cares nothing for riches / because he has no ambition" (ll. 353–380).

The gauchesque dialogue will appear henceforth as the engine that communicates between and connects the various social sectors with the inclusion of at least three discursive directions articulated by "the one who knows" (the most characteristic example is Antonio Lussich's *Los tres gauchos orientales*). The fact that Pérez and Hernández, the writers most linked to popular material, do not write dialogues, might be explained by the centrist or mediating quality of the dialogue structure as Hidalgo creates it.

same relation among the tone of the lament and the law, the name "gaucho," and the category of crime. But there the written law is the differential law, that of military service, of vagabonds and levies. The relation between the lament and the place of knowledge in Chano's very voice is thus radically opposed to the other motherland between two reasons or codes, the code of the voice that sings and laments and the written code.

The Logic of the Singer

In the prelude to *La ida,* the voice of the singer (or its tones), the word of the singer (or its code of meanings), and the voice (of the) "gaucho" are established as identical. The presentation of the singer, the first step in the ritual of the minstrel contest, unfolds this identity; the singer is the singer of the code of oral culture, and at the same time, indissociably, a singer who presents himself as illiterate, brave, a gaucho, and a persecuted gaucho. The parallel between the sequence of identities, or chain of reasonings of identity on the one hand, and the code of oral culture on the other, concludes with the mutual implication of the tones, challenges, and laments. To sing and to define oneself as the one who sings, to narrate the code, and to demonstrate that the tones derive from each other—these constitute the same movement.

Everything is in the song, says the singer at the beginning, and this should be taken literally; this is the foundation of the prelude and of *La ida.* The song, public voice of oral culture, articulates that culture in its self-referential immanence. Everything is in the song *and the song is everything.* To sing the song is, like living life or telling a tale, a self-engendering and self-sufficient etymological figure that seems to leave no remains, and because of that it can be the representation of totality in language: the doing (singing) coincides completely with what it does (song) and who it is (singer).[15] In the song is the whole life of the one who sings, from birth

15. See Noé Jitrik, "The Song in José Hernández's *Martin Fierro*" (in *El Fuego de la especie. Ensayos sobre seis escritores argentinos.* Buenos Aires: Siglo XXI, 1971). Jitrik maintains that the aesthetic gesture consists precisely in *bringing everything to the song:* "The recitative is, in short, the figure of the poem's unity, the summary of all the planes that come together to give it a form that allows the maximum operativity of the set" (14). He refers to the intonation, linking it to the tradition of the genre: "the presence of this subject in

to death, and the song itself is the telling of this life, because life and song are the same. In the song are the allies, those who help with the song (God and the saints, the allies of religious beliefs), and the rivals who are the other singers. The game, the economy of the roundup, and the use of bodies are there. In "to sing" and "singing," moreover, there is poetic variation. And the identification between the history of the subject who sings his being, and the code, which is the complete institution of the all-one culture of the oral space. *The song is the oral code;* the expression and at the same time the cultural cohesion of the community of gauchos, their public word: it contains their literature, their religious, social, juridical, economic, and sexual systems. In the song of the prelude, Hernández constructed the fiction of an all-one culture or a culture of identity: full, indivisible, without a state. And simultaneously he constructed its fracture and its division.

The all-one culture of the song is the rationale of the noncitizens, those excluded from the illuminist dream of liberty, equality, and fraternity. For the first time in the genre, a voice emerges that seems not to enter into alliance with learned culture, and it is a voice that founds itself with a rationale and a law that are in radical opposition to Hidalgo's human universals.

The challenge to the other singers is installed in the interior of the "all-one song." As in Hidalgo, it is a challenge between equals and for titles, for who is worth more. And who is worth more in the song is the same as who is more a man or who is more courageous: it is manhood that is always in play in the challenge. The singer defines himself now as courageous, according to the oral code of the song itself.

The challenge is always a position of the body of the voice in a determined space, and it gives meaning to the words that it hurls forth. In this

---

the poem appears perfectly natural given that gaucho literature emanates from the minstrel show, which went out singing; by speaking of song, the poet does nothing more than to take the origin of the genre upon himself, converting it into an essential invocation, much as occurs, perhaps, in poems that take poetry as a subject" (18). Jitrik analyzes all the elements of the preludes: pronouns, possessives, the natural character of song, universality, the complicity of the singer and the song, the risk that its elevation implies, the homologation of the song with life itself, and the fusion of the song and the culture. Clearly, we are only following his analysis.

challenge and in the meaning of "courageous" a kind of economy and a social and religious system may also be read:

> I'm a bull in my corral
> and a bigger one in someone else's;
> I always thought I was pretty good,
> and if others want to try me
> let 'em come out and sing
> and we'll see who's second best.
>
> I don't step to one side
> even if they come slashin' at my throat;
> I'm soft with the soft
> and tough with the tough,
> and in a tight spot no one
> ever seen me flinch. (Ll. 61–72)

Like that of Hidalgo, *La ida*'s demilitarized challenge draws support from the animal world, but here the animals are not the frogs and toads of fables. The use of courage as a weapon against rivals is also a weapon against animals. It manifests the schema of a fight between male rivals (bulls). That is, this is also a sexual rivalry in a specific space and specific type of property (the roundup) and with an economy of cutting the animals' throats. One's own and others' space is not land but the roundup. This is a poor pastoral economy, in which man defines himself against and in relation to animals,[16] and in which there are tough ones and soft ones.

---

16. The history of the challenge in the genre, and its relation to animals, constitutes another of the genre's histories. Around 1830, with Luis Pérez, with Rosas, the bull enters the texts: the titles of its periodicals state it directly: *El Toro del Once* (1830, 17 issues), and *El Torito de los Muchachos* (1830, 20 issues). In the latter, No. 17, October 14, it says: "There goes Cielito and Cielo too / Cielito of la Ensenada / He goes there with no motto / Let's give him a little butt." The use of the challenge and the representation of violence do not differ between federals and unitarists; the war of 1830 is also a war of challenges between enemy periodicals. Juan Gualberto Godoy replies to Pérez's *Toro* in his periodical *El Corazero*: "They say that this bull is very brave; / But what do I care, / Since even if he is, / I'll have to lasso him." And: "Toro's coming back to Camarones / He's wounded his ribs / From thousands of banderillas / They stuck into him" ("Al Toro," *El Corazero*, no. 2, Mendoza, October 23, 1830; reprinted in Félix Weinberg, *Juan Gualberto Godoy:*

The challenge for courage, for the appellation "courageous," is the challenge for a gift (for the use of a gift) from the father of the universe, precisely in order to defend oneself from animals; *it is at one and the same time the law of courage and the law of defense.*[17] In the poem of gifts of canto XIII (which closes the mark of the canto opened by the prelude, because it is what precedes the smashing of the guitar), the oral religious

---

Literatura y política. Poesía popular y poesía gauchesca [Buenos Aires, Solar/Hachette, 1970], 191).

Echeverría's *El matadero* also centers on the bull, or on one decision about the bull that metaphorizes another decision; the text can only polemicize about Lent and meat with the literate federalists, the priests, from the point of view of the literate layperson.

17. In a world in which everything is expressed in terms of force, the gaucho can conceive of no other form of resistance: his force is his virtue. He must be courageous to exist and to resist an always adverse fate. The concept of courage derives from necessity, as does that of banditry: it's a curse and a destiny, not a vocation. The customary code of courage is a structural phenomenon of pastoral society. See Eric J. Hobsbawm, *Bandits* (New York: Delacorte Press, 1969). Banditry, as a form of rebellion within peasant societies, seems to appear in moments of transition and modernization: it's free, unmarried men who don't own land who refuse to submit and see themselves as forced to stay outside the law. Banditry and millenarianism, the most primitive forms of revolution and reform, go together, according to Hobsbawm, and they emerge as figures of protest against the forces that destroy the traditional order. The coincidence of dates between *La ida* and *Solané* (a play by Francisco Fernández, based on the Tandil assassinations: see Hugo Nario, *Tata Dios: El Mesías de la última montonera* [Buenos Aires: Plus Ultra, 1976]) seems to demonstrate Hobsbawm's hypothesis. In *Rebeldes primitivos* (Barcelona: Ariel, 1968), Hobsbawm states that the bandit is protected by local opinion, being a state criminal for some abduction of a woman, an "honorable" homicide, or the revenge killing of a policeman. He is honored by his peers because he defends his law and his justice. Ernest Mandel (*Delightful Murder: A Social History of the Crime Story* [London: Pluto Press, 1984]) discusses parts of this thesis of Hobsbawm's, especially the fact that the bandits were "illegals" who respected the moral and juridical order of the peasant community. Mandel asserts that there were smugglers or traders who sometimes exploited the peasants, allying themselves with the local landowners against the centralized power; it was easier for a peasant to trade with this class of bandits than with nobles and merchants, and therefore the bandits were not denounced. There were also impoverished preproletarians, vagabonds, who embodied a populist rebellion as much against feudalism as against a nascent capitalism. This is why the tradition of stories about rebels and dramas about bandits is so widespread in world literature: in China it is found in the epic of the twelfth century, *On the Shore of the River.*

system of differential hierarchies may be read, as well as the definition of "man," by his difference from the animal world. In this poem man defines himself as different from and superior to all living things and to animals not only by virtue of language and understanding ("but He gave more to the Christian / when He gave him understanding" [ll. 2165–2166]) but also, above all, by virtue of his courage. This has to do with defining the macho man: "And since He gave the wild beasts / such great fury / that there's no power that can win over 'em, / or nothing that can scare 'em, / the least He could give man / is the courage to defend himself" (ll. 2173–2178). This is the gift of the father of creation that is also fought over in the canto, because the gift of courage is the gift of justice, as it is in Hidalgo. The equivalence of the challenge to the rivals in the canto and to the animal and human rivals, in the space of the property of the roundup and in the track left by the throat-cutting, again reveals an all-one culture, with a single schema of rival or potential enemy. In *La ida* Fierro's challenges and crimes, as well as those of Cruz, follow this schema.

In the prelude's chain of definitions and tones (singer, courageous), the definition of the "gaucho" comes next, *and this definition derives from differential language:* "I'm a gaucho, so you'll know / this is straight talk: / for me the earth is small / and I wouldn't mind it bigger; / no snake bites me / and the sun doesn't blister my brow" (ll. 79–84). The meaning of "gaucho" according to his language is free and without properties *in the entire space:* I am not a servant, I will not be used. And that is how the tone of the story's lament is installed, through the difference in the meanings of the word "gaucho" according to the gaucho's language and rationale, and according to the differential written law or rationale. The lament does not exist without difference before the law or differential law.

The prelude's chain of logic, as it appears in the succession of identities and their tones, is as follows: in a pastoral economy, those whose only property is work with animals and an oral code whose axes are "courage" and "liberty" are necessarily illegal according to the other code. There is a necessary structural connection between the economic structure of the pastoral society and its oral code: if the man is not courageous he does not belong to the community, and he must also be courageous in defense of his personal liberty, the other value of his language. And this connection necessarily generates a contradiction with *the law (or the necessity) of use,*

the law of vagabonds and levies. Law is necessity, and there are two contradictory necessities: on one hand the necessity or law of no-use, and on
the other hand the necessity or law of use or service. Between the differential value of the language and its code and the differential code of
vagabonds, a difference in the translation of "gaucho" is thus established:
"Now listen to a story / told by a gaucho on the run, / who as father and
husband has been / hard-working and willing, / and still the people / take
him for an outlaw" (ll. 109–114).[18]

Gauchos are free, courageous, landless men who must be respected.
They refuse to submit, to serve, defending this liberty with the law of courage (the "rebel soul" of Sarmiento's Facundo), and thus they appear
forced to remain outside the law. It is their very code, that is, their language and the tone of their challenge, that puts them outside the law and
gives rise to the lament. The two tones are thus two sides of the same phenomenon, which the other writers of the genre will separate. The sequence
of definitions is that of the tones and their syntax, and this sequence is also
that which the text follows in its narration. The oral code contains everything. The joyful affirmation of courage and total freedom as definitions
of "gaucho" is followed by the lament over this same definition viewed
from the law of service or use: delinquent. The gauchos are divided between two translations and two betrayals: to their own language-law or to
the other law, the law of the other language. Martín Fierro is a divided or
two-sided character. The lament for the division of the subject is also the
lament for the division of oral culture, between two codes. In La ida the
gaucho seems to speak alone, by himself, for the first time in the genre,
and his voice seems to be reproduced in shorthand by the stenographer
Hernández.

The entire genre may be read within La ida. Its emergence and its close
are there, because there its logic unfolds, a logic that is simultaneously that

18. The law of vagrants already figured in the laws of the Indies, and these laws allude to
unmarried men as possible candidates for vagrancy. The second law, title IV, book VII of
the Recopilación states, "The unmarried, vagabond Spaniards, mestizos, mulattos, and
black Indians who live among the Indians, having been ejected from the towns, and
guarding the laws and justice they punish excessively, with rigor, without exception,
obliging those who were officials to perform their offices . . ." (Gori, Vagos y malentretenidos, p. 10).

of the singer and that of the uses of the other's voice. The text of the prelude says that the use of the voice, the use of the body, and the use of meaning are coterminous. And it says this in one of the exemplary texts about double meaning, double use, and double interpretation. The voices of Martín Fierro and Cruz show that words mean different things according to the codes of the voices, according to who or which rationale uses them, and that the "gaucho" voice is defined in opposite ways by the language and the code that defines it. Thus, in the voice of the singer, the text puts face to face two juridical orders, two readings of each enunciation, and two meanings of each action.

Texts about double meaning, double translation, and the clashing of two codes are also texts about metamorphosis and silence. In *La ida* the tones of the challenge and lament touch their border and follow to the point of no-voice. The mute crime, the border of the challenge, marks the passage to the lament that follows it; tears, the border of the lament, mark the passage to the challenge or to the silence of exile. Hernández took the heard tone of the lament through the difference between the two codes or juridical orders to the extreme of the no-voice,[19] which is where Hidalgo placed the no-alliance. There the other genre opens, the Other. The logic of the persecuted singer concludes with the smashing of the guitar, silence, and exile to another language and another rationale, another genre: that of "the infidels." It is the loss of the motherland and the gaucho's passage to his other, who has another code, and who is also the enemy of his enemy.

In *La ida* there appears to be a political alliance without the alliance between the heard voice and the written word: this is the other extreme of Hidalgo. And in the prelude of *La ida* the singer and the bandit, or the per-

---

19. These are the two moments of total loss in *La ida*: "Nothin' was left of my place: / only the ruins were there! / Christ Almighty! It was enough / to break your heart! / And so I swore from then on / I'd be as mean as they come. // Who wouldn't feel the same / after sufferin' so much? / I don't mind saying I cried / my heart out like a[n abandoned] woman. / My God in heaven, if I wasn't left / sadder than Holy Thursday!" (ll. 1009–1020). The narrator who closes the text describes Fierro and Cruz's passage from the frontier into exile: "After they crossed it, / one clear morning, / Cruz told him to look back / at the last settlement; / and two big tears / rolled down Fierro's face" (ll. 2293–2298). [Bracketed material represents my adaptations and additions. *Trans.*]

secuted gaucho, appear to coincide.[20] Their tones are those of Hidalgo's no-voice; the challenge is directed not at the political enemy but at the rival, and the lament for the difference in translation of "gaucho" is enunciated from within the oral code and not the written law. The apparent no-

---

20. **Sarmiento and the Exterior Space**

"The singer incorporates the telling of his own exploits into his heroic songs. Unfortunately, the *singer,* although he is the Argentine bard, is not free to do them justice. He must also tell of the tracks of wounds he has meted out, one or two *misfortunes* (deaths!) that he had and some horse or girl that he stole. In 1840, among a group of gauchos on the shores of the majestic Paraná, a singer was seated cross-legged on the ground who held his audience moved and entertained by the long and animated story of his travails and adventures. He had already told the kidnapping of his sweetheart, with the travails he suffered; the *misfortune* and the dispute that motivated it; he was relating his encounter with the military squad and the wounds that he inflicted in his defense, when the rush and shouts of soldiers advised him that this time he was surrounded. The military squad, in effect, had closed in the form of a horseshoe; . . . the *singer* heard the shout without distress; he flung himself suddenly onto his horse, and throwing a searching glance around the circle of soldiers with their carbines at the ready, he turned the horse toward the ravine, covered the horse's eyes with his poncho, and drove in his spurs. A few moments later, the horse could be seen emerging from the depths of the Paraná, without a bridle, so that it could swim more freely, and the singer holding him by the tail, turning his face peacefully, as if he were in a boat with eight oars, toward the scene that he had left in the ravine. A few shots from the soldiers did not prevent him from landing safe and sound on the first island that his eyes discerned" (*Facundo,* chap. 2, "Originality and Argentine Characters").

Facundo marks the external border of the genre, with the entrance of its words into its heart. And it is a text about the frontier and about borders: the Paraná and its crossing represent them. Borders between lands, between oral and written codes, between the one who sings and what he sings, between the song and reality, and also frontiers between the world of the law and the world of the crime.

Sarmiento works on three levels: what he himself says about the singer as a delinquent gaucho, in which law and justice speak; what he says happened, in which reality speaks; and what he says the singer, who has no voice, says, in which indirect discourse speaks. Thus the relation between the codes that the tones of the voices of *La ida* have may be clearly read. As in *La ida,* the singer is a persecuted gaucho who recites the oral code.

The first to cross a frontier is the same singer who mixes his own exploits into his songs; he himself is a hero and his life and that of the Other belong to the same universe and thus may be mixed. He will also be the last to cross the other frontier.

The second to cross a frontier is Sarmiento. He says that his singer is an illegal and *he translates* a word from the oral register: "*misfortunes* (deaths!)." The translation empha-

alliance of codes in *La ida,* according to the fictional logic of the genre, would signal a real alliance. There is a problem with reality in *La ida.*

Between the polar opposites of Hidalgo's prelude and the prelude of *La ida,* which delimit the internal space of the genre, the divided motherland's war of challenges and laments may be found.

---

sizes the difference between the codes, because the word for "crime" is said in different tones and with different words (Sarmiento's admiration for the misfortune of the other!) on each side. There is a frontier between the two that only the translation may cross.

Next he crosses the frontier that brings him to the story and gives a date and a place to what he tells, which gives him an absolute statute of reality. On the shores of the Paraná, in 1840, he describes the singer facing his audience and says what he is singing about: Sarmiento's "stealing" of the girl is in the singer the kidnapping of his sweetheart and the singer tells it by saying *he worked and he suffered,* that is, with the tone of necessity or the law, and perhaps with the lament. And the misfortune is *a true misfortune,* a necessity of justice motivated by a dispute, as also happens in *La ida.* And the encounter with the army uses the law of the defense of one's courage and of the challenge with knives. The frontier between the song and its code on the one side and the outside of the other code on the other, is absolute: that which is a crime on one side is explained as duty and necessity, the law of its code, on the other side. This is the border that may only be crossed by translation, by different translations.

And at this very moment, when the two codes—the code of the armed law and the code of the singer—coincide and collide, there is another border or frontier between what the singer sings and what occurs in reality. The army arrives at the exact moment in which they arrive in the song itself, and with this the reality of armed law and justice erupts, *the sole rationale and real necessity.* This border may not be crossed; thus, the singer crosses the river to the other shore, to the island, in order to continue reciting the oral code.

The encounter with the army and the law told by Sarmiento (and by Hernández in the crucial moment of *La ida*) marks the crossing of another frontier. *It is the moment in which the singer emerges from the void of oral space* (emerges from having his words written in indirect discourse) and enters the reality of the written (in the no-voice of action). Only the collision with the law makes it possible to write the songs of the singer. Thus it may be seen here, as in *La ida,* that the singer of the code, or the persecuted gaucho (for they are the same), tells "the lives of infamous men that are only known through the archives of the police and of psychiatric hospitals."

Sarmiento confirms, in 1840, through this strange temporal relation that he has with the genre, what Hernández confirms in 1872: that the singer, who is the one who recites the oral code, is both persecuted and a bandit. In *La ida,* for the only time in the genre, this is the voice that sings.

The Challenges (on the Side of Use)

The First Fiesta of the Monster

The Slippery One
Hilario Ascasubi

Taunt of a *mazorquero* and throat-cutter,[21] one of the number besieging the plaza of Montevideo, to the gaucho Jacinto Cielo, gazetteer and soldier of the Argentine Legion, defender of that plaza

Hey, gaucho savage!
I don't lose hope,
and it's no joke,
of getting you to try
ting-a-ling and the slippery one.
I'll tell you how it goes:
listen up and don't be a scaredy—
for you, this little song
is sadder than Good Friday.

Any unitarist we catch,
we lash him down;
or else just leave him standing
while our comrades string him up
from behind
—mazorqueros, of course.
They bind
him with a double tether
so he's elbow to elbow
showing the world his birthday suit.
Savage!
Here's where your ordeal starts.

21. [A *mazorquero* is a member of the *mazorca*, Rosas's ruthless vigilante police force.
The mazorca enforced obedience to Rosas's federalist agenda through terror and assassination by throat-cutting (see Rock, *Argentina*, 106). See note 26, this chapter, for more
about the impact of throat-cutting on Argentine culture during the period of unitarist-
federalist struggle. *Trans.*]

Later after that, a three-ply leather thong
will hug his feets, like a horse
fastened up to a stake so neat,
and while he's standing there
we have him begging loud;
half-teasing, we let him have
a little jab,
and when he screams, we sing
the slippery one, and ting-a-ling
without a violin.

But we follow the sound
in the brass sheath
when we whet
the knife, and test
the point
on the nape of his neck.
That chicken savage jumps,
which makes us laugh,
and when some start to tear their shirts
and cry,
that's the best of all;
we feel as lucky
as our dear President.
And the cackle of joy
spreads far and wide
when we hear the pretty musicking
and the fun we're giving
to the savage we've got tied.

At last,
when we think the time is ripe
and we've had our fill
of fun, we decide
to stop his breathing;
and to do it right,
one grabs a lock of hair
while another

ties him by the hooves
like a young horse,
so if he moves
it's on all fours.

Meanwhile,
he's begging us in the name of whatever saint
might be up there in the sky;
and to comfort him and ease his fear
we cut across the veins
of his throat,
just a little below the ear,
with a well-sharpened blade
in what's called the mercy stroke.
And how does he say thank you?
—He starts to bleed,
a real treat,
and his eyes roll up in his head
from shock.

Ah, sissies!
We've seen a few
who bite themselves,
make gestures and faces
that'd make the savages scalp themselves,
then stick out their great big tongues—
among ourselves it's no disgrace
to kiss 'em
and make 'em half-satisfied.

What a high old time!
We laugh so much
we split our sides
to see how it even makes him shiver;
so we untie him
and loosen him up,
then pull him up short
to watch him do the slippery one.

He'll dance in blood
till he has a cramp
and falls down kicking
and shaking all over
—very proud—
till he's stretched out tight.
Inspired by this, we cut off a strip
of his skin that we know how to use
to make a razor strop.

Now we cut his ears,
his beard, sideburns, eyebrows, hair,
and scalped,
we leave him in a heap
to fatten up some hog
or vulture.
. . . .
So, my Savage,
now you see—
a mere nothing has to happen to you
to make you scream,
"Long Live the Federation!"
(*Paulino Lucero* [Buenos Aires: Estrada, 1945])

Hilario Ascasubi's "La refalosa" is a text well known to Argentines. Not only does it tell about the first fiesta of the monster but it also allows the reading of the construction of a murderous and brutal language, the representation of evil in language. It is worth looking at how this challenge works so that it may be taught in school. The voice of Hidalgo's outlaw gaucho (the one who drew his knife on Contreras) emerges from silence, *occupies the entire space of the motherland,* and for the first time the horror and the verbal scandal of the genre unite. This is the "motherland or death" universe, where bodies are amputated and killed. The text is written from exile.

In Ascasubi, in *Paulino Lucero* (which reunites in Paris all the periodicals and leaflets written during the war and the siege of Montevideo, from 1839 to 1851), the verbal violence of the challenge is extreme because the voice of the bad gaucho coincides with that of the political and military enemy: the two enemy voices converge against those that the genres have constituted. Ascasubi's paradoxical gauchesque (the scandal of the genre: that its enemy is gaucho) divides the voices of gauchos into a low, savage, or barbarous one, and a high, civilized one. It introduces a hierarchical difference into the language of the challenge, which lowers a margin and passes directly from the animal to the enemy's body. Which is the same one that he "transcribes." In Ascasubi's texts the enemies "speak" and "write" (as Luis Pérez had already done in 1830 in the "Testamento de Rivadavia"). The low language of the bad gaucho, as it is constructed by Ascasubi, is the other word of the Other, without name or supplement or alliance with literate culture: a murderous and brutal language. The division of the gauchos' register is political, poetic, and military. What is being contested is who commands them, who directs the meaning and use of their bodies. The federalists are outlaws directed by the outlaw gaucho Rosas, and in the epithets and insults that Ascasubi directs at him the precise meaning of "gaucho" *according to the law* may be read: delinquent. Rosas is that "outlaw, tenacious killer, coward and base / scoundrel"; a "bad gaucho," a "lying gaucho," [22] that is, a mazorquero, a "crazy person, thief, / soulless assassin." The unitarists, by contrast, *are led by the military, not by gauchos:* "And long live General Paz! / the one-handed man / who must bring the Gaucho Restorer [Rosas] / to the ground!" [23] *The army is on only one side.* Ascasubi's formula is: extreme militarization (the leader is always military), extreme moralization (the one who knows and can educate is the priest, and the last names of the gauchos are always Cielo [heaven], Lucero [bright star], Santos [saints]), and the extreme depoliticization of the voice (of the) "gaucho." In *Paulino Lucero* the political is militarized (the gaucho is used exclusively as a soldier and the political end coincides with the objective of the war),[24] and in *Santos Vega* the depoliticized voice

---

22. In "Retruco a Rosas," *Paulino Lucero,* 103, and in "Diálogo entre Paulino Lucero y Martín Sayago," ibid., 242.

23. In "Dialogue between two soldiers from Buenos Aires, Ramón Contreras and Salvador Antero, in General D. Manuel Oribe's encampment, eight months after laying seige to Montevideo. Montevideo, 1849," 327.

24. In Paz's *Memorias (póstumas),* chap. 36, 2:257, Paz refers to those who wanted Rosas's demise:

> In order to achieve it, they promoted resistance to the Argentine dictator with all their strength, and they busied themselves in finding him enemies, not only in the exterior,

is moralized; the center of the story is the division of twin brothers (a "natural," unmodifiable division) into a good, decent Christian one and a bad one, a thief and a criminal.

This challenge is the genre's lowest prior to *El fiord,* and it shows its border in the direct menace to the Other's body. There are no singers: this is a written challenge. And it takes place not between equals, as in Hidalgo or the prelude to *La ida,* but rather from below to above; it is written from heaven, and with a decisive hierarchical difference, that of the written code in the title. *"The Slippery One. Taunt of a mazorquero and throat-cutter, one of the number besieging the plaza of Montevideo, to the gaucho Jacinto Cielo, gazetteer and soldier of the Argentine Legion, defender of that plaza."* The one who threatens has no name or title, and the other has the name of Hidalgo's literate gaucho, Jacinto, plus Cielo (and the name of the Argentine Legion), the high space of the celestial and transparent cielitos of the motherland. Hidalgo's alliance has divided in such a way that the voice of the outlaw gaucho is directed solely and directly against the one who writes, the "gazetteer" (or against Chano, and not against Contreras, as in Hidalgo). This is also what happens, without a voice, in Borges's "Poema conjetural" or in his "El sur," and with a voice, in Borges and Bioy Casares's "The Fiesta of the Monster." The challenge of the monster is always directed at the body of the man of letters and heavens.

---

but also in all corners of the Republic. But in order to hide their activities, which I will not call antipatriotic, they surrounded themselves with the most impenetrable mystery respecting their course and their future plans, and they wished to rigorously *personalize the war,* without offering for the people's consumption more than generalities and words which, because they have been abused, are nearly meaningless.

As if Rosas had been eternal; as if after him no more tyrants could come; as if tyranny and freedom were two entities humanly organized and personified in Rosas and in them, respectively (note that these men called themselves *men of things* par excellence and not *of people,* as if things *were nothing,* and people *everything*), they wanted to persuade us that, with the dictator destroyed and them in power, everything would be accomplished, and that, therefore, there's nothing left to do but grab the spade and march forward with eyes closed, without asking even, *"What will we do once the blow is given?"* . . . To us the military officials, who will spill the blood of our compatriots . . . they only gave a glimmer of hope that our work had a more permanent goal, such as, let's say, the Constitution of the Republic. Isn't it admirable, I will say a thousand times, that with respect to these kinds of reticence, Rosas and his fiercest enemies are in perfect agreement? (Emphases in original)

The text is a challenge for the title "savage," or it is a contest for who is more "savage" (it is a counterchallenge for anticourage), and it may be said that it is constructed on the subtitles and emblems that accompany Rosist writing ("Long live the Holy Federation—Die, Unitarist savages!"), in order to turn them around. It must remake the inverse path of meaning and in order to do this it must pass the words through two writings; the threat is written and the gaucho Cielo must return "savage" to its first unnamed writer. The challenge, the meaning, is a two-way street. And the text directs each one of its written words against its own writers: live-die, holy-savage, unitarist-federalist.

War exists when enemies hurl at each other the same value with two different meanings. The center of the challenge in "La refalosa" is the debate over the double meaning or the double use of "savage" in relation to the use of bodies. This resembles the double use of the gaucho: soldier and gazetteer, mazorquero and throat-cutter. Besides the political alliance, the only thing that matters in "mazorquero and throat-cutter" is *the double use,* both economic and policing, of the body of the gauchos. It is an economic and criminal alliance. In Jacinto Cielo, by contrast, there is a single use of the body of the gaucho, as a soldier, because "gazetteer" is writing and ideas: *it is a military and ideological alliance.* The federalists are savages or barbarians who cut the throats of animals, and also animals and delinquents who cut the throats of men and sacrifice them as if they were animals, as also occurs in *El matadero.* The challenge and the animal world are mutually implicated in the genre. When Fierro, in the army, fails to receive his pay when everyone has already been called, he says, "To spill my guts / I saw the Major and went over to talk. / I edged up to him / and still actin' casual, / I said: 'Maybe tomorrow / they'll finish payin'.' // 'Whaddya mean t'morrow, or any other day,' / he snapped back at me. / 'The paying's already over with; / you animals'l never learn.' / I laughed and said: 'Me . . . I / ain't even got so much as a penny yet'" (ll. 739–750). But in "La refalosa," written from the major's point of view, it's the throat-cutting of animals that is in play, as in *El matadero.* The monster's challenge animalizes the Other, puts the animal into its language or body, and plays with a leap of the genre.

When words touch bodies it's off with their heads. The word of the outlaw in power is the one that "touches" or plays the instrument: ting-a-ling without a violin. It puts the language in the body and the body in the language, and its only goal or end is to silence. In "Isidora, federala y mazorquera," Ascasubi tells how the insane Rosas has Manuelita's friend killed by having her silenced, so that she will not tell what she has seen: "Kill the big sheep! / because if not, she'll leave and tell the world / that I'm already having convulsions." The story of "La refalosa" is that of the criminal traversing of a double body, half human and half animal. The words touch the parts of the body featured in the song twice. "Feets" and "hooves," "*cogote*" ["nape of the neck"] and "*pescuezo*" ["neck"]: the terms for human and animal kind alternate.[25] What is monstrous is the displacement of the killing of animals onto the human. The savage is the throat-cutting gaucho, barbarous, removed from his "natural" function, his economic and productive use, and carried to the political and policing use in order to kill men with civilized ideas. As a force of production, the body acquires relations of power; this power may be applied to a policing use, and the double use of the body, which is a double or triple alliance, constitutes the horror and the sinister inversion that found barbarism. The double use of the body or the double alliance without alliance with the written code of the rationale. This is the representation of the enemy, of the monster, in Ascasubi. It is the passage from the economic to the political alliance, *with the same function: to kill.* The horror of the transfer of the carnage of power over the bodies of animals onto the political and onto power over human bodies. When the savage gaucho occupies the entire space of the motherland he impedes access to the word through a mutilation that reproduces the supplication of Christ (the other meaning of Cielo, reinforced by "sadder than Good Friday" and "begging us in the name of whatever saint"). Illuminism has separated the two universes, that of ideas and that of bodies; the barbarian or savage affirms his identity; he focuses on the enemy's ideas, but in the enemy's body: he touches it and cuts it to pieces in order to kill the words of the law. Constructed from the point of view of the victim, from the point of view of terror, of the martyr's passion (or from the martyr's action, which is his passion without words), the monster's voice says the opposite of what Sarmiento wrote, quoting in French when he crossed the frontier of the motherland into exile: barbarians, ideas

25. [*Pescuezo* is a word for neck often applied to animals. *Trans.*]

can't have their throats cut. It rather says: I, the savage, cut the throat of ideas, which are heard words, voices in bodies. And it also says that the one who says that ideas can't have their throats cut is the one who exiles himself, removing his body. He takes it, along with his ideas and words, somewhere else.

"La refalosa" arrives at the border of the voice. In order to silence his victim, the monster founds his own language with the victim's body and reduces it to infantilism ("scaredy," "in his birthday suit") and to animalism, as he cuts the zone of the voice. Nomination and destruction of meaning, transparency of meaning, chorus of inframeaning: laughs, revelry, songs, "the pretty musicking," the presignifying fiesta of the monster. The federalist savages are having a fiesta, says Ascasubi, which is reminiscent of Hernández's *Vida del Chacho* (1863): "The unitarist savages are having a fiesta. At this very moment they're celebrating the death of one of the most prestigious, generous, and courageous commanders that the Argentine Republic has had. The Federalist party has a new martyr. The Unitarist party has one more crime to write in the pages of its horrendous crimes. General Peñaloza has had his throat cut . . . , and his head has been conveyed as a proof of the good performance of his assassin, the barbarian Sarmiento."

"La refalosa" is the first fiesta of the monster. The category of the fiesta is one of the axes of the genre and it signifies the ideal space of the use of bodies, the paradise of the uses of bodies. There is the fiesta of Borges-Bioy's monster, the orgiastic fiesta of *El fiord*, and also the "show" of the work on horseback on the estancia in *La ida*: "Why, that warn't work, / it was more like [a show], / and after a good throw, / after you'd showed your stuff, / you'd get a swig of likker / when the boss called you over" (ll. 223–228) [translation in brackets mine—*trans.*]. The fiesta is not only the ideal space of the use of bodies but also the very space of the alliance, or indeed the alliance itself: military, economic, political, policing, sexual. In the fiesta the one who commands is present, the chief: Rosas is there, in "La refalosa," as Perón is there in *El fiord*. Hidalgo's first patriotic cielito is also a fiesta, a celebration of military victory with San Martín. *The fiesta is the very center of the challenge,* and it may even be said that what is being disputed is in reality the word "fiesta" and its meaning.

In the war for the meaning of "savage" and "fiesta," words with two meanings like the bodies of the federalist gauchos, the text is constituted.[26] The word scans it and returns it to its source: federalists are savages, lawless barbarians who sacrifice Christians and heavens. In "unitarist savages" and in "holy federation" resides the political and ideological alliance of Rosas with the gauchos. For them, the "savages" were the Indians, non-Christians, without a code, who had to have their throats cut, and this was a holy work: the war of the oral community as a holy war. Next we will see the scene of the Indian's throat-cutting and his challenge in *La ida*. Rosas changes the meaning or the direction of the word "savage" and directs it at his political enemies: they are the atheist or infidel unitarists, like the Indians. This double use of the word ("savage") that designates the gauchos' enemy, applied to the political enemy, shows to what point Rosas is the genre in reality and how he uses its procedures.[27]

26. See Hayden White, "The Forms of Wildness: Archaeology of an Idea," in *Tropics of Discourse: Essays in Cultural Criticism* (Baltimore: The Johns Hopkins University Press, 1985). White reconstructs the geneology of the myth of the savage, which in the eighteenth century was "the noble savage." This notion includes the ideas of *madness* and *heresy*, the opposites of civilization and health. Civilization and humanity against savagery and animality. The savage is always the other, and supports complexes of changing symbols, which can have a religious, political, or economic content according to the epoch. White lays out the history of the concept beginning with the ancient Hebrews: since that time the notion of the savage has been associated with the desert, the jungle, and generally the uncivilized parts of the world. As these areas were conquered the notion became despatialized and underwent a process of psychic interiorization: the savage is thus the repressed, a projection of desires and anxieties, in the civilized man as in the primitive one. According to the different theories of the psyche, the idea of the savage delineates passages from myth to fiction and back to myth. The "savage" always appears as a threat to the "normal" man.

With respect to throat-cutting: it was a technique that both unitarists and federalists made into a show, to such a point that in children's games "the game of throat-cutting came to hold an honored place," according to Juan Agustín García in *Sombras que pasan* (Buenos Aires, Andrecta y Rey, 1925), quoted in Clotilde Gaña and Ada R. M. Donato, "Símbolos, signos e imágenes del rosismo: El rosismo como tema de impacto popular," in *Proyección del rosismo en la literatura argentina*, Seminario del Instituto de Letras (Rosario: Facultad de Filosofía y Letras, 1959). Lucio V. Mansilla writes, "Federalists cut throats, unitarists castrate; there are desertions and betrayals on all sides" (*Rozas* [Buenos Aires, Editorial Bragado, 1967], 80).

27. Rosas's military alliance with his gaucho soldiers is different from the alliance of the military professionals like Lavalle (or with the civilized wing of the unitarists) who have no economic base or political fortune and who live off of politics and their public func-

tion. The economic, military, and juridical alliance of Rosas with the gauchos synthesizes the gaucho genre in a single type of action: "So from then onwards I thought it very important to gain a decisive influence over this class in order to control it and direct it; and I was determined to acquire this influence at all costs. I had to work at it relentlessly, sacrificing my comfort and fortune, in order to become a gaucho like them, to speak like them, to do everything they did. I had to protect them, represent them, guard their interests. In short I had to spare no effort, neglect no means to secure their allegiance." Rosas says in "Nota confidencial de Santiago Vázquez . . . relatando una conversación mantenida en la noche del 9 de diciembre de 1829 con el gobernador de la provincia de Buenos Aires Juan Manuel de Rosas," reprinted in Lynch, *Rosas*, 109, n. 42.

But Pérez's *Biografía de Rosas*, which narrates one of the moments in which Rosas needed to mobilize the peons against the enemy armies, combines the history of Rosas's life with a theme later reiterated in Ascasubi: the levy and the gaucho's suffering in the enemy army are arguments to desert and join Rosas's own army. Between 1828 and 1829 Rosas deliberately raised the popular forces to oppose the unitarist rebellion. According to the British minister Ouseley (Lynch, *Rosas*, 112), the gauchos were rounded up violently for military service, while *La Gaceta* maintained that it was an enthusiastic uprising of the people against the savage unitarists.

Thus, in Pérez and Ascasubi the negative facts about the soldiers' treatment are proof of the cruelty of the enemy army; the other sector is the one that despoils, deceives, and impoverishes the gaucho, and not, as in "Cielito" and in *La ida,* the army in its totality. The narration of these evils that were suffered always precedes the decision to desert and to join the opposing army, and the suffering and lament of the soldier serve to fortify one's own military alliance. See what Ascasubi's minstrels sing in "Los payadores" (subtitle: "Seated in a circle around a campfire at the bottom of the trenches of Montevideo, singing the following verses, three young Argentine minstrels lamented, on the same day in which, abandoning the ranks of the Rosist army beseiging Montevideo on the orders of General Oribe (alias Alderete), they moved to the ranks of the Defenders of the Plaza"):

NATIVE OF ENTRE RÍOS:
Ay, in the name of the Lord!...
this Entrerriano is going to sing,
there, tongue, don't get flustered
in such a magnificent attempt
—in such a magnificent attempt;
I abandoned the tyrant,
and now I'm with the Orientals,
and a free gaucho I'll be.

NATIVE OF BUENOS AIRES
Ay, on this occasion...
my sorrows loose in the wind,

I too come unhappy
yonder from Buenos Aires—
—yonder from Buenos Aires;
I was a boy who was well off,
but now I see myself
cursed by the tyrant

NATIVE OF CORRIENTES
Ay! I see myself in such misfortune...
A sad Correntino is singing
dragged from his homeland
to follow a destiny—
—to follow a destiny
against my will,
to put us at last
in a sad situation—

Ay! I hear the bugle
proclaiming the fame of Lavalle
the Liberator;
as I pronounce his name
my heart calls me—
—my heart calls me;
I ask my good listener's pardon
I'm Lavalle's subordinate,
I'm a notorious Argentine—.

This excerpt is an example of the kind of lament that corresponds to the challenge of "La refalosa." Ascasubi clearly separates the tones: the division between challenge and lament reproduces the division of the gauchos themselves. The minstrel soldiers who are singing the lament are soldiers of Rosas who desert for Lavalle's army to be his "subordinates"; here the use of the lament to constitute the military alliance is obvious. The minstrels lament their loss of liberty and indefinite economic losses ("I was a boy who was well off"), rather than losses in and of bodies as in "Cielito of the Retired Blandengue" and in *La ida.* The lowest challenges in Ascasubi correspond in the lament to the highest levels of loss, which form a nearly infinite scale in *La ida,* between Fierro and Cruz.

A Note on the Politics of Desire of the 1960s in the Latest Fiesta of the Monster

The Politics of the Ascent to Extremes and to War
The heard never-written voices before Osvaldo Lamborghini's *El fiord* (Buenos Aires: Chinatown, 1969) are the extreme point of the literature born with the genre: its lowest and most violent edge. The "Motherland or Death" universe (p. 22) of the fiestas of the monster occupy the entire space of the basement in which the action occurs, a strategic

series of indissociably sexual and political alliances between sectors that fight over one of the houses of the motherland, the CGT (*Confederación General de Trabajo*). The text plays with the extreme margins, between the lowest margin of language, of bodies, of space (the southernmost point of the south that is the basement), and the northern fiord of the title, which has the other language or face of eighteenth-century English poets. Between the two poles is the entire space of the motherland and the sonorous crowd of Peronist demonstrations with the latest father of the motherland of the genre. The politics of an ascent-descent to extremes allows the reading of the extreme case of confrontation of discourses that leads to war and the reading of the nature of this war: the assumption of the countervalue of the Other as a value and an affirmation. Verbal challenges, moral scandals; this is the savage, nameless horde of Peronism in action.

Between the poles of north and south, and also between those of right and left: the logical space of *El fiord* coincides with the political, narrative, and verbal space. The voices, letters, and words that surround Perón, the mottos, emblems, and flags, are those of the extreme right and revolutionary extreme left. The text refers constantly to the tradition of Peronism's extreme right and connects it, by contiguity and opposition, to the revolutionary tendency of the guerrilla. And the autobiographical story it narrates traces a political history of the Montoneros, from the Guardia Restauradora Nacionalista to Marxism. [The nineteenth-century Montoneros were groups of gauchos on horseback who practiced a specific type of warfare (attack and withdrawal) similar to guerrilla warfare. The first of these groups were those of Güemes, a caudillo of the north of Argentina in the wars of independence. These Montoneros are not to be confused with those of the 1960s and 1970s, who were Marxist guerrillas on the Cuban model. *Trans.*] It recounts its history between two wars, between the war of extremes and the war of politics, and the desire for those extremes. And it recounts the rise and fall of the language. And those other extremes, beginning and end: between the birth of the son and the death of the father the story takes place, with incest at its center.

As if it only wanted to speak of the relations between the two poles of the divided motherland.

Literary Politics: The Fusion of Transgression and Revolution
El fiord is an exercise with all the challenges of the genre's war, condensed: political, literary, sexual, verbal, cultural, familial. The challenge works the matrices of verbal transgression with the obscene voice, the narrative with the accumulation of forbidden actions and the accumulation of genres and tones. Everything is simultaneously challenge and lament, farce and holy rite, history and tale at the edge of the equivocal, translation and reproduction. It is an act of subversion in which the only thing that matters is to cross frontiers, boundaries, margins. The lowest voices heard, the violent bottom of the language, are connected with the ritualized words of politics and pass through the entire volume of the literature translated and read at that time: Sade, Freud (of whose name the title is an anagram, but in orality rather than in writing), Bataille, Artaud, Nietzsche, Fanon, Marx. Theory, politics, the aesthetics of transgression as revolution or of revolution as transgression. The aesthetics of liberation.

The book narrates a ritual orgy between extreme borders: childbirth, sodomy, incest, the killing of the father-lover, dismemberment and cannibalism. It's a "fiestonga" or huge party which contains the alliances of the genre and the uses of bodies. Pornography serves to describe transactions between depersonalized "organs" or between depersonalized "characters": letters, initials of names, positions of the playing cards of the genre. Pornography multiplies the possibilities of the story's interchange and action, of possible and impossible figures in never-written positions.

The category of transgression articulates the relations between the different universes of the political and literary revolutions of the 1960s. The literary revolution is transgression and the transgression is political revolution. Writing is the continuation of politics by other means and vice versa; it is the theater and the dream of the revolution's politics of desire.

El fiord is a text in code, dated, with all the effects of the genre's conjuncture; it was written during the military dictatorship of Onganía when Perón was in exile: during the preparation for war. It was published by a nonexistent publisher and all the postures of semiclandestinity in an oppressed and tenacious country with all its hero-traitors may be read in it. The play with the initials of names and their positions (*the symbolic politics of the letter*) constructs each time the positions of the sectors in struggle and of all the cards played in the genre: a play among letters-names-bodies, which is also the confrontation between, for example, Timoteo Vandor and Andrés Framini or between the two Confederacións General de Trabajo (CGT). The circumstantial alliances and the treasons and denunciations (the "lows" of politics) are represented in the conjunctions, disjunctions, and bodily and sexual violences, and *also* in the conjunctions, disjunctions, violences, and cuts of the letter-names. It all culminates in the transgression and insurrection against the one who commands and in his assassination, which is at the same time the disintegration of his name and the beginning of liberation.

The Politics of the Double Use of Power and Knowledge

El fiord takes place in the paradise-hell of the double uses of bodies, voices, meanings, letters, and spaces. And the uses are the two powers that the narrative distributes between perverse sexual alliances (the corporeal use of power as force and violence), and verbal alliances (the use of violent words or ideas about power as knowledge).

The narrator is used and uses his body to establish political alliances and this use is always double, in both meanings-sexes-directions. The narrative pursues the occupation or "capture" of the CGT and the elimination of its leader. The narrator is simultaneously he "who has been a father and a husband," a toady, a servant or dependent in the house of the father of the motherland, an outlaw gaucho, a traitor and a hero of justice, and also an ex-seminarist (with the other Father). Double use of bodies and of sexual, verbal, political, familial, and religious violences. The horror of the double use of the genre is, in *El fiord,* the sexual enjoyment of power. The text's central alliance is that of the narrator with the one who knows, with Sebas, who is excluded from the use of the body: he is Saint Sebastian or the martyr of his faith, the oppressed-repressed, *and he is also the courageous gaucho:* "and only from sheer bad-tempered gaucho and guerrilla he took it into his head to pull the trigger" (23). Sebastian raises the flag at the end of the text, when they all ascend to the other space: as it always happens in the genre, the one who knows connects the space above with the space below at their outer limits. And at the extreme of nonuse is the amputated woman without feet or hands (the ex-wife of the narrator), who descends from the other space into the basement: for the first time in the genre the figure leaps over the boundary of the genre.

The alliance between the narrator and the one who knows (which is a sexual no-alliance) is that of voices and words that define *El fiord* as a text of the genre. It is an alliance of low voices, heard voices, other voices, and the high words of the other, written, universe. The verbal scandal consists of this alliance, which is also an impossible translation or treason ("my ally and comrade, the inimitable Sebas" [7], and "the untranslatable Sebas" [14]). The one who knows, who is quoted constantly, gives the narrator the double language of the text, a violent condensation or alliance between the common written register and another register that is low, dirty, bad. Sebas, who is knowledge and the very site of the code (the power of knowledge without use of the body), does violence to the language in order to harbor two levels and introduce the typical hierarchical difference of the challenge, while the narrator translates this alliance into a story, or narrates the action of this condensation (for example, between "object" [*"objeto"*] and "asshole" [*"ojete"*]), which is the series of political alliances of violence and power, with a double sexual use of bodies. The narrator moves from theory into practice and recounts this movement.

These two powers, force and knowledge, the double use, and the sexual and verbal alliances, are the materials of *El fiord*'s politics of transgression.

The Symbolic Politics of the Identity of Opposites or Political Ambivalence
The double use, the violent alliances, and the poles of the spaces are accompanied by a massive double façade that is *El fiord*'s real architecture. Each space—that of the orgy below and that of the sea, the fjord, and the fiesta of the leader above—is incomplete without the other, and each action and figure is incomplete without the other. The division between opposite poles implies alliances, wars, and two-sidedness. The two spaces, and also the extremes of right and left, mutually refer to each other in a pulsating movement that culminates in the negation of one by the other, in the transformation of one into the other, and in the affirmation that both of them are both true and false at the same time. The movement from quantity to quality, the story's intensive accumulation of actions, completes the system. This is the word of Hegel, Freud, Bataille, Artaud, and Marx in alliance in literature and politics.

The master (father and Loco [Crazy]) who is killed and eaten below is the same as, and at the same time the Other of, the leader from above: the false teeth of the doll assassinated in the fiesta below are the same as the false teeth, likewise orthopedic, of the image of the aging Perón in the fiesta above. Below, the master is eaten, and above, he eats them: "And handles, moreover, disconnected eternally or momentarily from their hammers, and fragments of crude tarred swastikas: God Motherland Home; and a sonorous multitude—within which I can distinguish with absolute clarity the face of each one of us—penetrating Perón's orthopedic smile with flags" (17).

Contiguities are opposites and also the same: one turns around within the other. Masculine and feminine genders turn into each other (the metaphors of pregnancy and labor are applied to Sebastian), and extremes become related through contiguity: "Onward comrade Sebastian, bosom friend, dirty dog" (9). It is impossible to differentiate between executioners and those executed, between fathers and hated masters, and between leaders and loved fathers. It is a practical and totalizing lesson in dialectics. The logic of the symbolic is founded in the political logic of the real in order to transform it into the impossible. This central code that *El fiord* articulates is the infinitesimal point where the fiestas of the monster lose themselves.

It is the structure itself of the fiestas of the monster that may be clearly read in *El fiord:*

–   *the boundary of the voice of the Other:* the impossible voices of the lowest level of the language, or the representation of the violence of evil in the language;
–   the movement into the horror of the double use of bodies with the direct attack on the body of the one who is above (Ascasubi's Cielo [heaven] or Lamborghini's Amo [master]);
–   and at the same time the veneration of the one who is above (Perón in *El fiord,* the poets of the north: high literature) by the one who identifies himself as *the one who writes.*

This structure is that of the play, in politics, with the poles of reason or of language. It leads to what is unsayable because it confronts two monsters: the one who writes it and the one who says it, the Other. Or the one who writes what the Other says. Words have a double use and the fiestas of the monster occur between the monster of the voice and that of the written word.

The fiestas of the monsters scan the genre each time an ascent of the masses to power occurs or is announced: each time the impossible voices, heard and never before written, occupy the entire space of the motherland. Between the first, that of Ascasubi (and also the second, of Borges-Bioy), and the last, the difference is double: the first and second are written from the heavens and wish to coincide with the present; the last is written from the basement and wishes to coincide with the literature of the future, the barbarous or utopian future.

And a Personal Note
I would like to tell you one of the things that I did with Osvaldo Lamborghini during a brief time in the days of fiesta of 1973 [Ludmer refers to Campora's brief government in 1973 after the end of the military dictatorship (1966–1973), which were lived as a fiesta. *Trans.*]. Together, playing at a mutual exchange of words, we wrote a note on Macedonio Fernández, "Elena Bellamuerte," and the lost object. Since this had to do with a secret and unconfessable practice (that neither of us, I believe, had ever engaged in with another of the other sex), it was immediately socialized, and appeared anonymously in *Literal 2/3.* To write this anonymous work we worked many nights, with a kind of script that each of us made during the day and that swallowed up the days, because we asked

Two More Challenges with Throat-Cutting

That of the Indian

The first challenge in *La ida* is presented by the Indian at the border. Apparently this challenge also has to do with a fiesta: "And to make every-thin' just perfect, / when things were goin' the worst for us, / up came an Indian frothin' at the mouth, / with a spear in his hand, / shoutin' 'Fin-ished, Christian, / I put spear in you up to feather'" (ll. 577–582). The other genre or the genre in reverse that segregates the barbarous language of the savage is the grammatical gender/genre of his words "spear" and "feather,"

---

ourselves what language to use to speak from the other side of language. An antihallu-cinatory (meaning antirealist) and antiprogressive diatribe emerged: the two terms al-ways go together even though they change places. We quickly discarded the novel even though we weren't thinking in terms of genre because we ourselves were all genres, every gen(d)re: we were he and she, *El*ena B*ella*muerte. The novel, a realistic genre according to Anonymous (and the climate of writing was one of a little fiesta), offers a landscape to tourism and places an anatomical drawing in this landscape, which it writes about. Only poetry, strange body in the *corpus* of the language, is a space where hallucination is im-possible because there the story has no clue and the only thing attempted is to play a dirty game with the internal body (of the language). In defining poetry as the place where hal-lucination is impossible, Osvaldo defined his own aesthetic: he wanted to reduce all "lit-erature" to that impossible, counterhallucinatory poetry, so that the theater of the word could be seen.

Since Anonymous was antiprogressive he/she maintained that meaning and its mas-querades insist on not progressing and also maintained that poetry erases death, because death can only be killed by the word and what a word does is always to transform another word. Thus our styles joined together and we killed Elena's and Macedonio's death. With Anonymous we wanted to do what we did and what continues to be for me (and I'm sure for him too) the only criticism that can be written, and perhaps also the only literature: lampoon, that is, aesthetics, mixed with microscopic analysis and theory, where we put the poem into practice and use it in a brutally direct way in our writing. Now he is dead and so is the poem.

I would like to say something about his voice. In Osvaldo the draft coincided with the final text: he was one of those writers who would sit down and write, without much theater and without vacillating, a page that could not be doubted. And his literature couldn't be doubted because he himself never submitted to doubt. He put doubt into ac-tion and he did it with the tone of his voice, an oral tone that was picaresque and gauch-esque. With this tone he laughed at himself, at the violence of his word, and also tried to read something else besides what it was saying, because if the written could be erased by another word, he was sure, there would be a poem rather than death.

which have been transformed into masculine nouns.[28] Next God and the saints appear: "God forgive that savage / for wantin' so much to kill me" (ll. 595–596), says Fierro, *and cuts his throat*, and this is a holy deed: "Right away I jumped down to the ground / and planted my feet on his shoulder blades; / he began to screw up his face / and did all he could to cover his throat... / but I performed the holy deed / of finishin' him off" (ll. 607–612). This is exactly the same as the fiesta of the monster, but in reverse, toward the bottom, with another difference in code and in the army at the border, where the gaucho soldiers don't have firearms (l. 461). *And here too the horror of the double use of the body appears,* gauchos used as soldiers and as peons, without pay: "First I sowed wheat / and then I built a corral, / I cut adobe for a wall, / made a frame for it, and cut straw..., / those bastards! You'd work and work / and you wouldn' get a cent for it!" (ll. 421–426).

In *La ida* the route of the double use is the route of horror and loss. In the army they don't give him clothes, they don't pay him, they call him an animal, they take away his horse and they put his body in the stocks. In that moment he decides to desert, and afterward, in his own space, he discovers total loss; from then on he will be the one who has lost everything. He cries "like a woman" (l. 1018), and is transformed into a bad gaucho who challenges everyone. Here ends the history of throat-cuttings, double uses, and losses in *La ida,* recounted from below. All that's missing are the challenges of the outlaw gaucho without a use, the confrontation with the representatives of the law, and the loss of the motherland. The inverse "Motherland or Death" of Ascasubi.

That of the Amputee

Cielito of the Retired Blandengue[29]
Anonymous

Don't come to me with your runaround
about the Motherland or guerrilla fighters

---

28. [The feminine nouns (*la lanza, la pluma*) have in the Indian's speech become masculine (*el lanza, el pluma*). *Trans.*]

29. [The Blandengues were a cavalry corps created in 1750 to maintain order in the countryside and prevent Indian incursions. After the May Revolution they were known as the

we all have plenty of time
to kill ourselves for nothing.

Cielito, cielo, yes,
cielito of Cat-o'-nine-tails
what Motherland or buzzard
loves a thief?

Go to the devil, I tell 'em,
with your verses and gazettes,
which are only lies
to rob us of our few coins.

Cielito, cielo, yes,
cielito of the god Cupid
I never ask permission
for telling the truth.

They've tricked me twice
like a black from Guinea
and for so little... sheeucks!
They don't sell me by the pound.

There goes the cielo good sirs,
go cielito and more cielo
this time they're not getting me
even if they lasso me.

Sarratea finished me off,[30]
I was a sergeant with Artigas,

"Cavalry of the Motherland." In Uruguay, the Veteran Corps of Blandengues, to which Artigas belonged, was occupied in defending the borders against Portuguese smugglers. See Rivera, *La primitiva literatura gauchesca* (Buenos Aires: Jorge Alvarez, 1968), 92–98. *Trans.*]

30. [Manuel de Sarratea (1774–1849), a member of the first triumvirate government in Buenos Aires (1811), was sent in 1812 to reorganize patriot troops in the Siege of Montevideo; he made the mistake of confronting Artigas rather than being conciliatory, and his own troops overthrew him, largely because of his lack of military experience. See ibid., 96, and Wright and Nekhom, *Historical Dictionary*, 884. *Trans.*]

the first gave me one hundred blows,
and the second gave me a hundred.

Cielito, cielo, yes,
cielito of the heart
the wages were good
for something that didn't pay a salary.

I've met Blasito
and Encarnación too,[31]
who were both commanders ripe
for a throat-cutting.

Cielito, cielo, yes,
look at me, any sky whatsoever
when they grabbed the stick
Damn! what a brawl.

Tired of suffering
I retired from the service
with many more lice
and one job less.

Cielito, cielo, yes,
cielito of the Blandengues
I'm also missing a leg
and I have plenty of pennies.

By the sweat of my brow,
I've managed to collect four cows,
and now that they're getting fat,
they already want to steal them.

Cielito, cielo, yes,
cielo, listen to my reasons
these regolutions are enough
to get even idiots bent out of shape.

---

31. [Blasito and Encarnación were lieutenants of Artigas. *Trans.*]

I know the Puebleros
the movers behind the whole mess—
they're sons of bitches,
thieves who try to scare us.

Cielito, cielo, yes,
here goes a cielo for everyone
look what nice patriots
the Portuguese and the stinking Spaniards are.

Last time they marched
through God's country
shouting peace and rest,
Don Lorenzo and Don Muñoz.[32]

Cielito, cielo, yes,
Ah cielito of my land
if they were calling for peace then,
why are they calling for war now?

Ever since the siege I've been
hankering to play the violin
for Vasquez the commissary
Juan Benito, and Antolin.[33]

Cielito, cielo, yes,
here goes a cielo, good sirs
if you want to see them happy
make them Provisioners.[34]

I hope they leave the country,
the whole pack of them,

32. [Lorenzo Batlle was minister of war and finance during the Siege of Montevideo; Francisco Muñoz was an official in the besieging army. *Trans.*]
33. [Vasquez here may be the commander Ventura Vázquez who sided with Sarratea against Artigas. See Ascasubi's "The Slippery One" for another reference to "playing the violin," or cutting their throats. *Trans.*]
34. [A reference to the widespread abuses perpetrated by those in charge of provisioning the troops. *Trans.*]

or I'll have to teach them
a remedy for killing moths.

Cielito, cielo, yes,
as sure as pissing
these are the informers
of Don Carlitos Alviar.[35]

That's enough cielo good sirs
the morning's gone
and I'm getting kind of tired
of singing for such a long time.

Cielito, cielo, yes,
here comes a kick in the pants
I've known three motherlands
and I don't want to know any more.
(Rivera, *Primitiva literatura gauchesca*)

In this anonymous "Cielito of the Retired Blandengue," written between 1821 and 1823, it becomes obvious why Hidalgo's Bald Indian can't
have a voice. For the first time in the genre, the massive "I" is that of an ex-
soldier without a leg. And from then on the genre struggles, confronting Hidalgo and the motherland from a double economy: that of the
countryside and that of bodies. It is antimilitary (all the commanders
and all the factions are victims of its insults), anticity, and antipatriotic,
and it speaks in the name of the truth against the lies of the poems and
gazettes—against the genre. Like Martín Fierro in *La ida* or like Cruz, the
soldier of the anonymous cielito only recounts his personal misfortune:
the soldier's economic and bodily suffering, or the horror of the use of the
body without pay by those who command. *The service* removed his occu-

---

35. [Carlos María de Alvear, who as the commander of patriot forces received the surrender of Montevideo from royalists in 1814, as director of the government of Buenos
Aires, created policies that favored British and Portuguese diplomatic interests at the expense of Uruguay and Argentina. These policies "only helped to create a barrier of re-
sentment that resulted in the definitive segregation of Uruguay and in the subsequent
paralysis of the ideals of a constitutionalist federation that the caudillos obscurely proposed" (Rivera, *Primitiva literatura gauchesca*, 98). *Trans.*]

pation and his leg, and for the first time in the genre verbal violence leads the singer to *the justice of throat-cutting:* justice for the commanders who do not pay and who give beatings ("they were commanders ripe / for a throat-cutting"), and for the commissary and others ("Ever since the siege I've been / hankering to play [them] the violin"). It's 1821–1823.

The voice of the cielito emerges when the one who sings is the same as the one who has fought the war (and not Hidalgo's pure singer), *and the singer has lost almost everything;* all he has left are a few cows, which they also want to steal from him. The articulation of the I, plus the negation (and the lexically negative verbs: steal, lose, take away), sustains the writing and is its frame. The center of the text is a contradiction: the same body can't serve two purposes. And the codes of the challenge are at their extremes: above, the god of the amputees *in which the truth is placed,* and below, the black slave *in which deception and lying are placed:* "Cielito, cielo, yes, / cielito of the god Cupid / I never ask permission / for telling the truth." And "They've tricked me twice / like a black from Guinea / and for so little... sheeucks! / They don't sell me by the pound." *Certainty* only exists in bodily function: "as sure as pissing." Between Cupid, the black slaves, and bodily functions: the genre's system of hierarchical differentials and codes, from above and from below, always functions in the voice that challenges.

The text could have been written by a Spanish sympathizer, by a free, poor rural laborer like Fierro ("By the sweat of my brow / I've managed to collect four cows"), or by a rural landowner in need of field hands; the choice is between one or another of the coercions applied against the gaucho's body: work or the army.[36] Throughout the history of the genre *the*

36. When the peons were being rounded up for military service, field hands also became dramatically scarce, because, for fear of the levy, the natives of Santiago del Estero, Cordoba, and San Luis "didn't go out to work." See Rodríguez Molas, *Historia social del gaucho,* 185 and following. Around 1820, however, the demilitarization of the gauchos and the fortification of the political power of the countryside, linked to the "ranchers' expansion," occurred (Halperin-Donghi, *Revolución y guerra,* 366). The gauchos were needed for peacetime jobs and the workforce was disciplined yet again, with penalties for abandoning jobs and the obligation of a written contract for the peons of the countryside, from whom was required a ticket and a certificate of good conduct (ibid., 370). Moreover: "the spokespeople of the landowning class wished to speak in the name of the entire population of the countryside," says Halperin-Donghi in the prologue to *Pro-*

incompatibility between war and productive activity has been presented, and this debate constitutes one of its nuclei. Any emphasis in the economy (which is connected to the I and the story of its life and its losses) implies a parallel antimilitary emphasis; the economic alliance of the rural land-owner with the gaucho always appears at the base of the texts of rupture or of placement at the border of the genre. The soldier-peon oscillation sustains it. It's a military alliance (in which the singer directs the antago-nism of his tone against the enemy of the one who writes, and this is the value of motherland and liberty) or an economic alliance (in which the singer speaks his antagonism against the army and the motherland and tells of his losses). *And the fundamental mark of the economic alliance is that,* when it is not accompanied by a military alliance (as in the unique case in the genre of Luis Pérez with Rosas), *it appears at degree zero in the texts:* the word/voice (of the) "gaucho" seems to speak alone, for itself, with its own rationale, against the army (and against the law, as in *La ida*), and also against the texts of the genre. The genre turns against the genre. The antipatriotic voice of "Cielito" (perhaps the first anarchist text of the Rio de la Plata: it's Uruguayan, like Hidalgo) is a peasant voice, like Pérez's, without excessive gauchesque inflections but with insults and corporeal functions into which the truth is placed.

The only goal of this series of challenges is to examine the relations be-tween the double use of the body of the gauchos and throat-cutting. As has

---

yecto y construcción de una Nación (Argentina 1846 – 1880) (Caracas: Biblioteca Ayacucho, 1980), lxxxv.

With respect to the "beatings" of the cielito, Mansilla says in *Rozas:* "In our day we have seen, after having proclaimed when Rozas was overthrown everything that his downfall ought to have prepared, in honor of human dignity, the following order carried out in the barracks: 'let them be given two thousand strokes!'

"To whom?

"To some gauchos headed into military service.

"For what crime?

"It wasn't enough already to have dragged them violently and arbitrarily from their homes, abandoning even hope, because God alone could know if they would ever return to their poor ranches; it was still necessary to humiliate them by torturing them.

"In the name of what?

"It's shameful to say it; in the name of this abominable slogan: 'So that they may learn to love serving in the army'" (48).

been seen, throat-cutting is always about an economic problem, about the genre's economic alliances. From Ascasubi on, the double (economic and political) use of the gauchos' body is linked with the horror of throat-cutting and with the loss of the motherland. In "Cielito," which writes, from below, the threat of throat-cutting to the military leaders, the use of the body in the army, without pay, leads to the loss of a job (economic loss), and also to loss within the body. In *La ida*, the double (unpaid) use of the body of the soldier on the frontier to cut the throats of Indians and to do vile work, and not on horseback, leads him finally to desertion and from there to the horror of total loss, and then to the loss of the motherland.

The Challenges of the Thug

In the prelude to *La ida*, the challenges and laments are inextricable from the chains of identities or definitions of the word/voice (of the) "gaucho," on the part of each of the two codes. The same thing happens in the text in its totality, which is organized around a central canto, a kind of black hole with a void: Fierro's challenge to the black man and woman. This seventh canto is at the very center of the text (six cantos on one side and six on the other), and this is the place where the text turns on itself. To its left, in the first part, are the singer's challenges to his rivals, and the challenges of the Indian enemy to the soldier and of the soldier to the immigrant recruit on sentry duty: here Fierro translates and parodies the heard voice of the foreigner, which is simultaneously the voice of command and the password of the army. To the right of the seventh canto, in the second part, are the challenges of Fierro as a deserter, without use, without place, without woman or sons: the language of the one who has lost everything and who confronts other gauchos.

Each of these challenges is supported by a definition of "gaucho," by a game with what belongs to oneself and what belongs to the other, and by a specified use of the body. Different genres and codes are contested, and logics are traced: a logic of identity and a logic of difference as a negativity, with hierarchies and prestige, domains and protections. As always, at the center there is a conflict between meanings.

The challenges of *La ida* are founded in verbal lies and duplicity, but in the heard voice rather than in the written word. The same words mean at least two things, one trivial, the other containing the body of the Other and its uses, linked to an animal or to the female sex organ. The same voice says one thing and another, and it shows, in its work with intonation and in its means of articulation, that meaning is not single, that the common language may also be the Other, that unities may come apart and scan in some other way, and that an expression may have at least two uses. In the challenge and the taunts, everything revolves around the heard voice, its virtualities and rhetoric, and everything means in two different places. The heard duplicity appears as a weapon against difference and it also signifies this difference. The duel and the death that follow it thus constitute a war between subaltern rivals over an issue of identity and over a difference of voices or of oral code. In each meeting, representatives of the gaucho's "Others" or of other gauchos meet, and each time the voice of the challenges represents the difference of a code. With the Indian it's the difference between savage and Christian in the difference of grammatical gen(d)re in the Indian's voice; with the immigrant guard it's the difference in pronunciation in his voice, parodied by Fierro with snakes and lizards (animals that creep and crawl); with the black it's a difference in scansion in Fierro's voice, which signals the differences in sex and color; with the bully it's the differences between brothers-in-law and between bulls and calves in relation to the heard voice of prestige or fame; with the military squad it's the difference between oral and written laws. The languages of the challenge and of war, moreover, oscillate between showing off and issuing condemnation, and this double meaning of the intonation is associated with the tragic, as in Oedipus's oracle. The Other is thrown into a hermeneutic situation in a determinate space, that which is occupied by the one who challenges.

The encounter with the bully or favorite of the commandant goes like this:

> Another time, in a barroom,
> I was drinkin' away the afternoon,
> when a gaucho dropped in who bragged
> of being real tough and a fighter;
> as he rode in, he brought
> his horse up to the porch;
> without sayin' nothing to him
> I stayed at the counter.

He was a local bully
that nobody wanted to take on,
because he had connections
with the Commandant;
and since he was protected
he went around very cocky,
and any unlucky guy in his way
would get shoved aside. (Ll. 1265–1280)

The challenge happens like this:

He hopped off his horse, came in
and pushed a Basque aside;
shovin' half a jug at me,
he said: "Drink up, brother-in-law."
"It's for your sister," I answered,
"since I'm not worried about mine."

"Eh, gaucho!" he answered,
"where're you from?
A grave must be lookin' for you;
you must have a thick hide,
since where this bull bellows,
no calf is gonna bellow." (Ll. 1289–1300)

This is a canto with a formal novelty. It opens with three eight-line stanzas describing the bully, and then suddenly the sextina emerges; it seems to be born from a stanza and a half, with a cut and a leap that represent each other ("He hopped off his horse, came in"). In this encounter the two men seem only to be talking about the genre and the two meanings of "brother-in-law."[37] The Other arrives when Fierro is there, but the space (that of fame, or the prestige of "courage") is that of the local area or small town. The rule of the encounters through challenge and death is this: he who enters or invades the space where the Other is, loses and dies. There are two spaces here that are being fought over, like sisters. The one

37. ["Brother-in-law" here suggests an intimate relationship with the sister of the person addressed; Fierro turns the insinuation back on the speaker. *Trans.*]

protected by the commandant is the inverse figure of Fierro in relation to the army and to those who command. There is a rivalry of protections and of uses on the part of the army (or of nonprotections and nonuses).

The bully is the one who calls himself a bull, courageous, and who appears as a sexual rival, a rival in a space, and a rival for the protection of the commandant. This last rivalry is the one that marks the alliance itself in *La ida:* the use of the body and courage of the gaucho requires the protection of the superior in exchange. In this way the paternalistic alliance is constituted. As Fierro says, "I'm an *ignernt* one, / and I know I don't count for much: / I'm either the hare or the hound / 'cording to how things go; / but I think those who rule us / should look after us some" (ll. 979–984), and "since everybody's his master / and nobody's on his side" (ll. 1351–1352). One who is protected by the army confronts an army deserter, or a subaltern with protection confronts a subaltern without protection. The protected one makes his challenge with the double meaning of "brother-in-law," and Fierro's challenge asks whose is the sister in question: it's another conflict between meanings and directions. The one protected by the commandant will be killed twice in the text, both times because of problems with women; when Cruz kills the other toady, it's over his own woman.[38] Each time there's a repetition or the number two emerges, there's a textual affirmation. There's a struggle over who protects the gauchos, with whom they should ally themselves, with the military officer who commands or with the boss. And the gauchos who kill those who are protected by the commandant are the ones who have been cheated by the army, and moreover cheated of their women by the army: they have lost everything. In the game with one's own space and that of the Other, between equals, there thus emerges a rivalry for use and protection and also a sexual rivalry.

Following this crime, the encounter with the army represents the maximum proof of courage between equals: one against many. This is the final

---

38. Cruz likewise aims at the commandant an enunciation with a double meaning: "Careful you don't get your ass in a jam; / you better get help to get out of this fix" (ll. 1823–1824), but Cruz confronts the flunky rather than the commandant: "And since anyone in command / always has a few flunkies, / one of them / who happened to be around / came in gritting his teeth / like a puppy on a teat" (ll. 1831–1836), and kills him.

point, when the difference of laws and crimes is fought over: one's own laws and crimes or those of the judge and his representatives in the army. On one hand there's the law of courage, and on the other, the differential law; once again, the choice is that of use, and Cruz deserts. The two gauchos who have killed the ones protected by the army and who have lost their women meet and form an alliance: *the first horizontal alliance, or alliance between equals, in the genre.* With the pact between Fierro and Cruz, the spiral of challenge with the black hole of canto VII at its center closes:

> Then, more than ever before,
> booze made me want to fight
> and I picked one with a black
> who came riding in with his woman.
>
> As she came in I saw
> she wasn't looking at nobody,
> so being drunk I said,
> "*Cow...* ming to the dance?"
>
> She got the point
> and answered me right back,
> lookin' me over like I was a dog:
> "A bigger cow is your mother."

It goes on:

> "Black beauty"... I said,
> "I'd like to have you... for my mattress,"
> and I began hummin'
> this nasty little tune:
>
> "God made the whites;
> St. Peter, the mulattoes;
> but the devil made the blacks
> as coal for hell's fires."

The black comes in:

> I knew he was boilin' mad
> and went over to him and said, real fast:

"No matter how fuzzy-headed a man is
he never gets mad over something like this."

He came back fast,
like he felt sure of himself:
"You must be fuzzier,
you gaucho bum, you," he said. (Ll. 1147–1182)

And then:

I ducked and cleared a space,
sayin' to the people: "Folks,
let that bull make his charge;
alone I was born... and alone I'll die."

After I crocked him, the black
slipped his poncho over his arm
and said: "You'll find out
If you die alone... or with my knife." (Ll. 1191–1198)

The fight follows, in which Fierro kills the black, whom they bury without prayer or mourning.

This canto is the only one in four-line stanzas, and it seems to be the most primitive canto of the text, together with cantos XXVII and XXVIII of *La vuelta*.[39] This is the only moment in the genre in which a gaucho challenges and kills his lower Other, and it is the place in which the text and possibly the genre turn around. This moment needs a future supplement in *La vuelta*. It recounts only one event and it is the only section in which any of the gaucho superstitions are mentioned (bad light, soul in pain).[40] It is also the only direct challenge Fierro makes that doesn't involve the army or the law, and the only challenge in which a woman speaks in the text: to abuse Fierro's mother. Here the gaucho thug and his first

39. On the problem of the stanzaic irregularities, see Martínez Estrada, *Muerte y transfiguración de* Martín Fierro, 1:121, "The irregular stanzas."
40. [Bad light, soul in pain (*luz mala, alma en pena*) refers to the phenomenon of animal bones shining or glowing in the countryside at night (a chemical effect). Gauchos believed it was the souls of the dead "*en pena*" who could not find peace, because of their sins or for some other reason. *Trans.*]

crime are presented: a possible whorehouse, alcohol, sex, and death. This is a mortal encounter between two Others, in their own space of fiesta and entertainment. This is a monster fiesta as in Ascasubi, but completely inverted: depoliticized, demilitarized, and written from the fiesta of nonuse. Or from the law of vagrants and bad amusements.

This song of difference and exception can be clearly read only from the minstrel song of *La vuelta* (and from Borges's "The End"), in which the brother of the murdered black wants to avenge him and challenges Fierro to sing. Canto VII, then, is not only the center of the text; it also opens a frame that is only closed in canto XXX of *La vuelta,* three cantos from the end. It may therefore be said that this is the canto that links the two texts in a specific continuity, that of the relations between gauchos and blacks in their own spaces of leisure.

The voice of the one who has lost everything, who has no use, who is drunk ("Other"), challenges the other subaltern of a different color and sex. The position of the challenge in *La ida* (always directed at equals or toward the bottom) says that in the oral code, the dynamic of identity and of difference is resolved into the equation difference = negativity. In the presence of the black woman and the black man sexism and racism emerge as "natural" (just as "natural" xenophobia emerges in the presence of immigrants).

They fight over the woman, and Fierro is the one who calls himself a bull. As in the literature of the Brazilian cordel, a literature by and for the poor, the black is defined negatively, and his representation follows stereotyped formulas: in the stanza Fierro sings, he is linked with the color of the devil, the sign of maximum negativity.[41] This has to do once again with the play between one's own and that of the Other, in the nonuse of the body of Fierro and in the sexual use of the bodies of blacks. The death of the black signifies an expulsion from the community of the gauchos (the same meaning that the Indian's death, the burlesque challenge of

41. See Rita Desti, "Letteratura ed ideologia: Il personaggio del 'negro' nella letteratura 'de cordel' Brasiliana," in Stegagno Picchio, *Letteratura popolare brasiliana e tradizione europea.* The black is defined negatively in the literature of the cordel; this racism is attributed to the fact that freed blacks began to compete with the workers of the northern Brazilian plains, who were white.

the immigrants, and the death of the bully and the other members of the army had). In the presence of the woman and the ex-slave or the one who comes from somewhere else, the thug assumes his values of freedom and virility. And he directs at his others the same degradation and despoliation that he himself has received from those who condemn him for his differ- ence. Those who have been excluded repeat the strategies of exclusion and those from below fight among themselves, over their differences and rivalries.

Sexism, racism, xenophobia: in these challenges the antithesis of the ra- tionale of the universal values of equality, liberty, and fraternity may be heard. *La ida* says that the murdering voice of the gaucho who has lost everything reproduces, in his own space and with his other subaltern ri- vals, the difference of the differential law. This is where Hernández has placed future barbarity; faced with a lower margin, the gaucho's logic of identity emerges as the logic of racism and sexism. In *La ida*'s chain of definitions and challenges, a racist, sexist, xenophobic nationalism was able to found itself. The classic not only gave us the oral biography and the text of justice and the tones of the motherland, all signs of Argentineness; it also founded the challenges of the outlaw gaucho in the rationale of the noncitizens, those excluded from liberty, equality, and fraternity, who are also the enemies of these principles.

There is a void in this canto. What's missing is the economic use of and rivalry between the gaucho and the black for work in the countryside, which can only be read from within the minstrel song of *La vuelta*. And here is where the text and the genre turn around. If we start with the con- frontation between Fierro and the Indian, and the throat-cutting of the Indian, and end with Fierro and Cruz's exile to the Indians, the enemies of the enemy, this turning of the text on itself may be clearly seen. For the first time in the genre the same gaucho is "bad" and "good"; for the first time the constitutive division of the genre is placed within the very subject who is singing. In canto VII the horror of the body without use appears, located in the one who dictated the differential law: "I felt like an odd card / and didn't know what to do with myself; / but they called me a bum / and they began to chase me" (ll. 1123–1126). The confusion and fright of this scene, the most primitive of the text, seems to suggest that Hernández started to write it from his lowest border.

The Laments (on the Side of the Gift)

La ida, Technical Details and Notes

Sextinas

They follow two more or less fixed formulas:

(1) A singular theme or subject and a line of successive generalization or amplification; for example, "Sufferin' doesn't bother me / as long as I'm in one piece; / let the sun come in summer / and the frost in the winter. / If this world is hell, / why should a Christian worry about it?" (ll. 1711–1716). Me–in one piece–a Christian–summer–winter–this world–hell (this formula may be seen in the dedication to *Don Segunda Sombra*).

The amplifications may end with a definition, with *to be:* "He's always on the run, / always poor, always hounded; / he hasn't a cave or a nest, / it's like he had a curse on him; / because to be a gaucho... damn it all! / to be a gaucho is a crime" (ll. 1319–1324). The processes of generalization in sextinas and cantos always culminate in a nonabstract, living universe: a collective or cosmic all.

(2) A theme or subject and the rival or enemy (which may be impersonal, like the sun and the frost in the example above, or personal), or else the ally, who helps and gives: "Why that warn't work, / it was more like [a show], / and after a good throw, / after you'd showed your stuff, / you'd get a swig of likker / when the boss called you over" (ll. 223–228).

These two formulas may also be combined.

It is possible to conceive of the entire genre through the forms of *La ida'*s sextinas. The categories of enemy and ally would be there, and also the order or rationale that is constituted in the movement of generalization. This would be a generative focus.

The generalizations, however, that constitute *types* or genres (the gaucho, the gringo, the storekeeper, the toady) may belong simultaneously to the oral code and to the other code, that of nineteenth-century literary realism ("Hernández is realism's maturity," writes Angel Rama in the prologue to *Poesía gauchesca* [Caracas: Biblioteca Ayacucho, 1977]; see, also by the same author, *Los gauchipolíticos rioplatenses: Literatura y sociedad* [Buenos Aires: Calicanto, 1976], for the difference between political and social poetry).

Cantos

The same formulas as in the sextinas. In each canto there is an intro-duction, a general description, and/or a type or collective (the gringo, the Indian, etc.), and a confrontation with one of these types. The confron-tations or duels are always horizontal or toward the bottom, and the confrontation with authority is symbolic. All the dialogues end in duel or desertion.

The formula of the challenge: entry into a space, dialogue with chal-lenge, fight, the death of the Other, the departure of Fierro or Cruz (a la-ment may follow). This is the formula of the war of discourses without a solution. If the words or countervalues that the opponents speculatively hurl at each other are added, we have a tableau of elements for analyzing the formula of challenges that leads to war. Those killed by Fierro and Cruz are those whom, according to the text, the gaucho wants to expel from his community. *La ida*'s series of stereotyped confrontations has a precise meaning: out with blacks, outlaws, "decent" gauchos, and also In-dians and immigrants.

Descriptions

They take the form of cycles: the day (work on the ranch, canto II), life (of the gaucho from birth to death, canto VIII). They are the places in which to analyze the constitution of "all-ones." Paradise lost is placed in the first cycle, the horror of the gaucho's present life in the second. In both cases, they are about *life and justice,* the values that govern the text. (In the poem of gifts of canto XIII, everything alive is read through God, and the code of justice is enunciated.)

Numeric Code

It is ruled by the number 2. Two gauchos, two events in each canto, two taunting couplets of challenge (Fierro to the blacks and the singer to Cruz), two dead outlaws, Fierro's and Cruz's two women who go to other men. The 2 can be conceived as a unity composed of two halves, or as a two-sided unity: Fierro and Cruz, one half and the other half of "the gau-cho." Usually, after two actions or events, comes the all or totality. Two de-sertions (Fierro from the army and Cruz from the military squad), which lead to the desertion of "civilization," to exile. Or Fierro's two crimes (the black and the bully), which lead to the confrontation with the whole of the squad composed of the representatives of the law.

A two-sided unity, or a unity divided into two halves. This is one of the theoretical options for conceiving of the text and the genre. *La ida* presents this option. The two halves of Fierro and Cruz are and are not the same. In fact, this has to do with two different roles: that of the deserter and that of the amputee (metaphorically speaking). But both roles end in that of the innocent outlaw. And Cruz is also a deserter of his house occupied by the army (he found his woman there with the commandant), and Fierro, deserter from the army, was amputated from his house (woman, sons, ranch). In *La vuelta* the 2 constitutes the typical system of binary oppositions: Vizcacha and his delinquent advice, Fierro and his legal advice. But the 2 of *La ida* is affirmation, division, and double-sidedness; it constitutes polar opposition only in the functioning of certain frames.

Frames

(1) The letter to Zoilo Miguens on the one hand, and "El camino transandino" on the other. This is the written frame, with the literate word of Hernández.

(2) The prelude on the one hand, and the tuning of the guitar on the other. This is the oral frame, that of the voice of the gaucho.

(3) The prelude on the one hand, and the closing of the text with the narrator's voice on the other hand. This is the typical frame of the dialogues of the genre, that of the oral-written alliance. The final narrator recounts the crossing of a border, affirms the truth of what is told, generalizes, establishes another addressee, and directs the final meaning of the text.

(4) The prelude on one hand (with the challenge to the other singers), canto VII (the center of the text, with the murder of the black), and the minstrel song of *La vuelta* (with the black's younger brother's challenge, and his intent to avenge his brother). The same natural and cosmic topics that appear in the prelude appear in the minstrel song with the lament: sea, sky, earth, night, love, law. This is the problem of *La vuelta* as the supplement of *La ida*. It is the problem of what is missing or of what gets said in another way. *La ida* is the hermeneutic text par excellence (a condition

of a classic?); it requires another text, by the same author, to read it and give it meaning. Another text that perhaps belies it. In *La vuelta,* the place of the one who knows appears, massively occupied by Fierro; the minstrel song, moreover, is the text's proof of knowledge. Here is the supplement of knowledge to *La ida,* which unveils the enigma of canto VII: the Other, of another code or color, is a sexual and economic rival. The entire problem of *La ida* is that of work in the countryside.

(5) The text is also framed by two inverse utopias (heaven and hell): that of canto II and that of canto XIII. The former is that of the perpetual fiesta of work in the countryside and of the rural alliance with the boss. The work is "a show," and the uses of the pleasures of bodies appear: drinking, eating, love, games, songs, and stories. Here "his woman slept / all snug in her poncho" (ll. 149–150). These are the days of fiesta on the ranch, the breaking in and the branding, but they are narrated as if the fiesta were eternal, because time is removed from time: by the cycle of the day that is all days. This is the retrospective utopia of the subaltern, or the model of paradise, which is always formulated as a loss in a present of dislocation. It is here that Hernández places the economic alliance with the boss of the ranch.

The utopia of canto XIII, on a future life among the Indians, is its inversion: no-use, no-work, "you can spend your time lyin' around / watchin' the sun go 'round" (ll. 2249–2250), the possibility of intervening in the Indian raids, and this: "Maybe there'll even be a woman / who'll take pity on us!" (ll. 2243–2244). These utopias indicate past and future; the first is lost and the second will never happen. It is the barbarous future. This is another reason *La vuelta* was written: to transform this future into hell.

The fact of framing the story with two utopias that are diametrically opposed in their view of work once more states the center of *La ida.*

Narrative Scheme

It's the stereotype of oral autobiography: being accused of a crime that one didn't commit, or that according to one's own code isn't a crime; confrontation with the representatives of the law; and death or exile. In the soldier-peon debate, the biographies of *La ida* produce the most extreme antimilitarist text of the genre.

With the scheme of oral autobiography, for the first time in the genre the history narrated is also oral and popular; the song and what is sung are identified with each other, and the division between register, tone, and story is erased. The central axis is the division of codes according to languages, or differential law.

La ida's biographies have two borders that define them and along which they converge: to confront the law or to represent it. The elevation of the rebel as illegal, or his transformation into a representative of the law. The culminating moment of *La ida* occurs when Cruz recognizes Fierro as a "courageous one" (possessor of the maximum virtue of the oral code) and deserts in order to unite with him. The axis of confrontation is the category of crime, which turns around. The moment of alliance between equals is the point of greatest violence in *La ida*. In oral biographies the transgression of the law appears as an individual one; now, with the association of Fierro and Cruz, the character of the confrontation changes, directing itself at the totality of "civilization."

In *La ida*, biographies are narrated as autobiographies; the deserter and the amputee are each one-half of the gaucho. There is also a third biography, a generic one, in canto VIII (ll. 1315–1384), whose center is the definition of the law: "to be a gaucho is a crime" (l. 1324). Here the system of the double reading of each action, or of the double meaning of each enunciation, or of two positions on a situation, according to each of the codes, may be read. The Other, written, code contains marks of writing: quotation marks. This impersonal biography, which goes from birth to death, manifests the radical double-bind to which the gaucho is submitted: "If he takes it, they say he's a fool; / if he doesn't, he's a bad gaucho. / Lash him, give him a clubbin' / since that's what he needs! / For anybody born a gaucho / this is his damned fate" (ll. 1379–1384). The center of the oral biography is this double-bind: on the one hand the subject belongs to an order or code that constitutes him as a member of a community (and the "bandit" for the state is protected by local opinion), and on the other hand there's the code to which he must submit himself if he doesn't want to be illegal. Crime, like the "gaucho" voice, has two meanings. Therefore the confrontation with the army is the visible manifestation of the arbitrary division into legal and illegal: to turn them against each other is the function of the apparatus of justice that functions in *La ida* as an apparatus of the state. (According to Hobsbawm, rural politics in the regions of structural duality foments and multiplies the bandits on the one hand, and on the other hand, it integrates them into the political system.)

The double-bind that generates the differential law may only be read from within the oral code: the foundation of the investigation of the "southern delinquency" in Italy is the popular juridical conception with its codes, such as the "vendetta": the first article establishes that the offense must be avenged if honor is not to be lost. In Cerdeña, stealing animals does not constitute an offense or crime but is normal. See Mariano Meligrana, "Il 'delinquente' nella cultura e nella concezione popolare del diritto al Sud" (in *Classe,* no. 10 [1975]): "bandit" is a concept foreign to popular culture; it is the external, authoritarian translation of a recognition of the community through fidelity to its own juridical order. Official justice is perceived as an illogical external mechanism; this creates the need for a defense that takes form in silence and lies (silence, exile, cunning), as an affirmation of one's own truth and one's own faithfulness to history. The recognition of the existence of an oral law that is organic and relatively autonomous (and therefore of a "plurality of juridical orders") is as subversive as the alliance between Fierro and Cruz. (See Lombardi Satriani and Meligrana, *Diritto egemone e diritto popolare.* In Italy, capitalism was introduced into the countryside around 1862–1865. At the same moment two movements resisting the legislation of the state or official juridical unification appeared: banditism and resistance to the compulsory draft, especially in Sicily. These are political phenomena that were not recognized as such but reduced to episodes of common delinquency. From a naturalistic and racist perspective, or from the perspective of psychiatric pathology, they were treated as bandits: literature presented them as heroic figures.)

The biographies (*La ida*'s three biographies: of Fierro, Cruz, and the gaucho as everyman) may be read within this frame. See Carlos Albarracín Sarmiento, *Estructura del* Martín Fierro (Amsterdam: John Benjamins, 1981), which mentions the "autobiographical cantos" as connected with the ballad collection and the *corríos* (*corridos*) and *jácaras:*[42] folkloric inspiration in narrative structure. See also Alejandro Losada Guido's prologue to *Martín Fierro* (Barcelona: Nauta, 1968), 35. Olga Fernández

---

42. [*Corridos* and *jácaras* are light romances that relate the events of a picaresque, open-air life. *Trans.*]

Latour de Botas, in *Prehistoria de* Martín Fierro (Buenos Aires: Platero, 1977), has studied the creole *argumentos* or *corridos* of the oral tradition and their derivation from the Spanish romance. In the *matonescos, corridos* about fighting, the protagonists are innocents who fall into disgrace in the eyes of justice or political prisoners or deserters driven by desperation and misery. There's a difference between the Spanish fighter and the Argentine: the latter is an unfortunate persecuted by fate, a misunderstood innocent. Certain narrative techniques of Hernández would fall into this category of plot.

Domingo Faustino Sarmiento and Lucio Mansilla worked in the same field as Hernández. For Sarmiento, as for the previous genre, whether the gaucho is legal or illegal depends entirely on his alliance or integration with civilized institutions, especially the army and the family (from this point may be read that of the prelude, "who has been a father and a husband"). In Sarmiento's biographies the moment of abandoning these institutions marks the division of lives and stories: Facundo deserts the Arribeños regiment, Aldao leaves the army of the Andes, el Chacho rises up against the national power that has recognized him as a general. These men's acts of rebellion transform them into barbarians. The legal gauchos, by contrast, are Sandes, Navarro, and Lamadrid: "the civilized spirit, dedicated to liberty." Political alliances decide the glorification of Sandes and the vilification of Aldao (see Adriana Rodríguez Pérsico, "Sarmiento y la biografía de la barbarie," *Cuadernos Hispanoamericanos,* no. 456 [1988]).

In the *Excursión,* Mansilla narrates his biographies from the opposite perspective. The gauchos hiding out among the Indians tarry in the liberating motifs of confrontation with the law (and there is always a judge and a military squad in his narratives) and in misfortune, which is inevitable in his narrative. And like the stories of Fierro and Cruz, Mansilla's biographies only differ in whether they are about family histories and love (Macario, vol. 1, p. 111; Crisóstomo, vol. 1, p. 156; Miguelito, vol. 2, p. 32) or about soldiers who desert (Rufino, vol. 2, p. 120; the spy of Calfucurá, vol. 2, p. 224, which contains the desertion, the murder in a country store, and the flight to the Indians).

With *La ida* the gaucho's register is, for the first time, identified with his code, the law of oral culture. Hernández's project was to universalize a local case through writing, to make it part of the minstrel song and of a tradition, and through this operation he made the drama of the greater and lesser (or hegemonic and subaltern) codes one of the emblems of modernity. This is the drama of the differential laws. Beginning with *La ida*, the genre may be conceived as the space in which the division, the confrontation, and also the passage between two cultures and legalities is written.

The text was read as written, transcribed autobiography, and, as in Mansilla, as a paternalistic and liberal-democratic defense of the gaucho, and also as a defense of the interests of the ranchers who wanted to protect their field hands from indiscriminate levies: peon against soldier. These readings have their frames in the text. But the reading that oralized and folkloricized the poem (and which wanted to forget its construction as literate transcription) is centered in the turning of the text on itself, in the encounter of the two gauchos beginning with the confrontation between the two codes, and the constitution of the horizontal alliance, the alliance between equals. One gaucho tells the other his life story, and the two are the same. Autobiographical stories not only convey a memory— they are also the place in which a way of life, and a collective identity, is elaborated and reproduced.

Conjuncture

Written in circumstances of crisis and of an ascent to extremes, hegemony affirms itself through repression. A direct attack on the law of levies and on the border patrol. The previous exile of Hernández with López Jordán; Sarmiento put a price on their heads. Written in the Hotel Argentino; Hernández alone, visited only by his brother and Antonio Lussich, who dedicated *Los tres gauchos orientales* to him. Hernández's connection to the white Uruguayans who had financed *El Río de la Plata* (see T. Halperin Donghi, *Hernández y sus mundos* [Buenos Aires: Sudamericana, 1985]). Dedicated to and placed under the protection of Zoilo Miguens, rancher from Buenos Aires, and accompanied by "El camino trasandino," an article on the crossing of another border. It appears as a pamphlet, a hybrid form, linked with journalism and not "literary."

The Logic of War

This is the logic of the genre: all differences are transformed into insoluble antagonisms. The war against the common enemy is transformed into a war against one's own gaucho-soldier (the genre produces his antithesis). There is no alliance between soldiers and military leaders. The enemy (Indians) is transformed into a potential friend, becoming the enemy of the enemy, a double negation. The gaucho is not delinquent when he joins the army; rather, he becomes delinquent when he leaves. He is not integrated into civilization but rather barbarized and exiled. This is the war against war and also the schema of the confrontation of discourses without any possible solution. Sarmiento's "civilized" laws and armies transform their subjects into barbarians.

Polemical Discourse

This centers on the word "gaucho," which has two interpretations according to the codes. It narratively constitutes a chain of definitions and postures of the gaucho: singer, worker, soldier, Christian, deserter, outlaw, murderer, courageous one, amputee, according to the uses of bodies (his double use in the army, his double fiesta at work, his nonuse as an outlaw). (In Cruz, the double use is placed in his woman, whose name in *La vuelta* is Innocence: the innocence of Cruz.)

The Double Face

This figure governs the text—the two-sidedness of the hero and of the crime; the two-sidedness of the Indian enemies; two meanings to the dialogues. Everything has a double reading: words, actions, characters, lives. The logic of the war and the polemic on double meaning, the double code and the double face: *La ida* as the genre itself in a conjuncture of crisis.

Transformations

The work with the codes and with double-sidedness constitutes the text as a field of transformations, of the passing of each thing into its opposite. The center of the transformations is the hero himself, who becomes an infamous hero, a condemned saint, an illegal legal, a traitor hero of justice. The story recounts this metamorphosis of the reversible figure. The transformations follow the line of contiguity: each detail turns into its opposite in the space that follows it (the "spaces" being of various sizes: the text in its entirety, a canto, and sometimes a sextina and the one that follows it). Challenge and lament follow each other.

Cards

La ida appears to contain all the cards of the gaucho genre or of the treatise on the motherland: the gaucho's Others (Indian, immigrant, black, and woman), the gaucho soldier, the ex-soldier, the workers, the amputee, the outlaw, the toady or accommodator, the singer, the commander of the military squad. And the authorities, who command in the army and in the law: here the judges and majors "speak" for the first time in the genre.

But the card of the one who knows, who has crossed to the other side of the frontier, is missing. He is inverted in the text, in Fierro's not-knowing of the written word, which is associated with those who command and which represents his criminal sentence. No alliance between the gaucho and the written word is possible. The word "list" represents the written and at the same time the criminal sentence in the two central spaces of the text: the political and juridical space, and the military space.

The lists of voters send Fierro to the border: "The Judge has a grudge against me / from the last election; / I went lazy on him / and didn't show up to vote that day, / and he said I was on the side of the *exposition.* // And that's how I got punished, / maybe for somethin' somebody else did; / whether they have good or bad / people to vote on, I always stay away; / I'm a gaucho through and through / and I don't give a damn about those things" (ll. 343–354).

The lists of those receiving payment send him into silence, cunning, and desertion. Says Fierro when they don't call him up to get paid in the army:

> To spill my guts
> I saw the Major and went over to talk.
> I edged up to him
> and still actin' casual,
> I said, "Maybe tomorrow
> they'll finish payin'."
>
> "Whaddaya mean t'morrow, or any other day,"
> he snapped back at me.
> "The paying's already over with;
> you animals'll never learn."

> I laughed and said: "Me... I
> ain't even got so much as a penny yet."
>
> His eyes looked
> like they were going to pop out,
> and then he said with
> a look fit to kill,
> "And whaddaya expect to get
> if you ain't even on the lists?"
>
> "This is the last straw,"
> I said to myself.
> "It's two years I've been here
> and even now I ain't seen one red cent;
> I get in on all the fighting
> but I never get on the lists." (Ll. 739–762)

It continues:

> But how could I fight them?
> I was just a babe in the woods.
> I might as well give myself up for dead
> to keep from gettin' in any deeper,
> and pretend I'm half asleep,
> though I'm really wide awake. (Ll. 793–798)

See Picardía in *La vuelta*, 3350: Picardía becomes a quote from *La ida* within *La vuelta*.

Silence, Exile, Cunning = Resistance?

In *La ida*, there's something more than challenge, lament, and autobiography. There's a kind of production of meaning that consists of the division of the subject, silence, and the contradictory relation between being and seeming. This universe of dissimulation, cunning, and desertion has been called resistance.

In a historical process, there is resistance when two or more codes confront each other, one of which is hegemonic, identified with reason, truth, universality, law, and the center, and places the other code outside of law and reason. The lesser, the subaltern, the Other, is excluded from the political channels of confrontation, in the impossibility of occupying a position of power; it must survive inside the dominant law, which it knows but does not recognize, calling on a kind of production of meaning that consists of the construction of duplicities and divisions: each time it unites the two codes, that of the other and one's own, and constructs the masquerade of an alliance of subordination, but the codes don't converge or complement each other according to the figure of alliance but rather contradict and negate each other. There is an absolute asymmetry in the relations between the two voices and cultures. That of the dominant code does not recognize the nature of the other's code or culture, and it reads the other's production of meaning as irrationality, chaos, lie, and ignorance. From below there are two codes, one's own and that of the other, and from above there is only one's own. Here it is the oral code confronting the written code, but it could also be codes of sexes, nationalities, different languages, religions, or ethnicities, and each time the figure traces distinct designs. With the goal of maintaining oneself in the legality of the Other, which is reality, and of surviving, the voice of oral culture separates what is united, links what is separated, displaces spaces and reorganizes and transforms everything it touches in order to construct duplicities and divisions that feign the univocality of the Other. Underneath, beside, or within each *yes* is a *no* (which is another yes); the schism may appear between word and action, word and interior discourse, appearance and reality, in one space and another, one time and another. Beyond every acceptance is the rebellion of contaminating the other's code and law with one's own. Each enunciation, and each gesture, contains another part that accompanies and follows it, like its shadow: action, joke, or secret discourse that passes in silence. And each enunciation and action have two readings, meanings, and interpretations according to the codes. For this voice, only the proliferation of division and duplicity is possible. In *La ida* it is Cruz who says, directly: "I have my share of troubles / and misfortunes, you better know; / I also have my sorrows, / though it doesn't bother me much: / I know how to look like a lame pig / when the situation calls for it. // And with a few tricks / I go on livin', in spite of my rags; / sometimes I act one way / when I feel another way, / but I go for the booze / like a fat man goes for popcorn" (ll. 1699–1710). In *La vuelta,* Picardía says (in the four-line stanzas, the "archaic" part): "I know the only thing to do / if you want to make the best of things / is to say Amen to the lot of it / and laugh at the whole affair" (ll. 3729–3732).

The duplicity of resistance serves as a weapon in confrontations with others (immigrants and blacks, and, in Cruz's narrative, bullies and commandants): the double language is hurled at the Other, shouted as double. The secret of the resistance will for a moment reveal its truth. See what Picardía says to the praying aunts, or really to the black woman, in canto XXI (ll. 3031–3072) of *La vuelta*. (See Antonio Melis, "Figure del revesciamento e figure dell 'alteritá," in P. Clemente et al., *Il Linguaggio Il corpo La festa: Per un ripensamento della tematica di Michail Bachtin*. Metamorfosi 7. [Milano: Franco Angeli Editore, 1983], 153. Resistance appears as an antidote to the contradictions that emerge from a rectilinear application of the category of carnival. It is a practice of long duration that enables the preservation of cultural identity, even if disguised, over a long period of time. A simulation and alterity imply interaction between cultures and create a space for unedited forms of syncretism.)

Resistance appears as the obverse of the alliance.

From which position should *La ida* be considered? From justice, language, and universal grammar, or from the histories, archaeologies, and contrivances of knowledges and powers. Certainly Chomsky and Foucault were climbing the mountain from opposite sides. On one side is the political function of popular illegalities, the popular solidarity with the illegal. From the introduction of anarchism forward, the hero became the memory of popular fights and confrontations. On the other side it has to do with the classic, with a specific relation between this text and the motherland: a world of untranslatables and of intonations of fields and spaces.

The Intonations of the Motherland

There exists in literature and culture a zone that often transcends enunciation: it's the intonation of the voice, certain enunciative postures, a way of creating rhythms and making the language resonate and of suturing these rhythms, postures, and gestures with a series of relations between subjects and themselves and between subjects and Others. When these representations declare themselves untranslatable and untransferable, when they serve as identification and as a form of recognition among those that transmit them, when they condense nostalgia for those who are at a distance, when they resound with the same quality as the language itself, they can become hypostasized and found a range of nationalisms. The tones of the heard voice that the genre took from the minstrels in order to constitute itself became the basis of the construction of a series of representations that were identified with the representations of the national. The tradition of the genre worked and contested oral material, a musical tradition solidified it into certain movements, and from then on they were available to any symbolic project that wanted to postulate itself as Argentine. Challenge and lament are verbal actions, postures, and they are accompanied by stories; moreover, they constitute a system of cultural and social integrations and exclusions. They gave their rhythmic and dramatic matter to the tango, which laments the rupture of the pact with the woman or the friend, and to the milonga, which sets the challenge between rival men or rival sexes to music. The grotesque combined or alternated them to represent another contradictory pact with a new Other, the immigrant. They were repeatedly depoliticized, politicized, aestheticized. The lament emerged in the popular representation of the people, and it reappeared in social realism's aesthetic of suffering, and the challenge was read as an antipopular representation of the people. In Borges, the challenge for the name and violence against the literate possessor of European culture are installed as founding nuclei of his fiction.

They accompanied a certain linguistic nationalism, against other intonations and against the threat of the corruption of the language by immigrants; a political nationalism, as central nuclei of the community against foreigners; a popular nationalism, against the oligarchy allied with the foreign; a racist nationalism, against Indians, blacks, immigrants. And on top of this base of universal values linked to intonations, an essentialist nationalism may also emerge, in which the gaucho incarnates the essence of the Argentine man who fights for freedom and justice.

Within the genre and its intonations the nucleus of nationalism may be conceived through the alliance that constitutes it, through the state function that it assumed, through the system of inclusions and exclusions that it erected, and through the fusion of the poetic and the political. These intonations and verbal actions from the oral tradition, the matter of the genre's alliance, mark two traditions or matrixes of our culture, which insisted each time that the passions of the motherland wanted to be written.

Intonations and Codes in Borges

The Separation of Intonations in *Evaristo Carriego*

When writers write about other writers, they found their own space and work their own material; the written body of the other allows them to look for themselves. On the subject of the intonations of the genre, I would like to show this use of a writer by another writer in the only book of criticism Borges wrote, which was also his only book written as a whole, as a book: *Evaristo Carriego*.

Borges and Carriego had a space and a man in common: Carriego was a friend of his father's and lived in Palermo, as he himself did. Within this minor poet, who wrote for the people, Borges searched out another common space—the literary. The text identifies the physical space (the neighborhood of Palermo) and the space of literature, and the question that sustains the exploration and confusion of spaces is where Argentine literature exists—in what place and in what intonation.

Carriego's Palermo is for Borges a zone of mixing, provisional and double, countryside and street. And to this spatial mixture is added the mixture of men: in Palermo live both those on the fringe and those whom Borges calls "the decent and unhappy little business," the progressive, mate-drinking Palermo. Palermo's mixture of spaces and men sustains Carriego's literary mix. Carriego's literature contains two literatures, and within one of them, the creole, two creolisms are mixed: the romanticism of Entre Rios and the bitterness of the suburbs. Palermo and Carriego are made out of two things; they are a mixture, and each part of the mix is also mixed; this figure will become familiar in Borges's stories. Borges will cut the mixture of Carriego and Palermo and their literature to obtain one part: between the little seamstress and the roughneck he chooses the roughneck, separating lament and challenge.

The part of Carriego's literature that Borges annihilates is that which contains sentiments and tears or that which works with the intonation of the lament. Borges writes against the writer who is venerated for his humanitarianism, decency, and melodrama. And the attack on Carriego's pious literature becomes confused with the attack on the literary institution that consecrated it. In "Declaración" from 1930, which begins the book, Borges states it directly: Carriego belongs to the visible church of our letters, whose pious institutions (courses in declamation, anthologies, histories of national literature) rely on him. But he also belongs to another, invisible, church, and this inclusion does not owe itself to the weeping part of his word. Borges identifies and confounds a kind of poetry with a way of reading, a teaching, an institution. Piety, poverty, and tears—this part of Carriego's poetry—has its criticism, anthologies, and histories, all of them melancholy.

In reality, Borges initiates two attacks. In the zone of Carriego's literature, the literature of the previous poet (which is also a zone of Palermo and of a class of men), he confronts his own contemporaries. He says of Carriego: "His need to move people led him to a lachrymose socialist aesthetic, whose unconscious reduction to absurdity accomplished much in the manner of Boedo."[43] *And against his contemporaries* he links the literature of the lament with the representation of daily, domestic life, with its gossips, knick-knacks, and low blows. This is Carriego and social realism and the aesthetic of tears. To put it another way, in half of Palermo, the progressive half, and in the half that corresponds to Carriego's literature, is Boedo, against whom the book of criticism is written. And this literary alliance of poverty, neighborhood, daily life, and tears, this representation and this politics, is what Borges liquidated in Argentine literature.

Argentine literature is linked to the people and their life. But not to this life, says Borges, and not in this literature for the people. And not in the rhetorical imposture of the literature of the people when literature is desired. This is the other bad part of Carriego: the verbiage, abstract terms, and sentimentalities, Borges says, are the stigmas of the versification of the outskirts. And once again he conflates this literature with its institution, and in such a way that it's impossible to tell, when reading Borges, if he

43. ["Boedo" refers to both a street and a literary movement: a group of social realist writers who met in the working-class Boedo neighborhood of the Palermo section of Buenos Aires. There is a well-known opposition in Argentine literature of the 1920s between "Boedo" and "Florida" (the latter an elegant street in the center of Buenos Aires and a more avant-garde, playful, formalist group of writers). See Jorge Luis Borges, *Evaristo Corriego* (Buenos Aires: Emecé, 1955). *Trans.*]

is writing about poetry, teaching methodology, or criticism: they are "stylists," "acoustic souls," poetry as a vehicle for rhyme, along with texts with variants, critical apparatuses, and the authorities. In short, neither the lachrymose representation of the life of the people nor the rhetorical imposture of the people in the making of poetry. And also not this poetry or its respective academies, which are conflated.

There are three temporalities in Borges's text: his own time, which confronts him with the aesthetic of social realism; Carriego's time, which is like his father and his space and which contains tears that are precursors of those other tears; and, finally, the past time of Carriego and of his father, the time of the other precursors: the gaucho tradition that appears as a fundamental reference in Carriego and in Borges. These three times, which are superimposed, like the spaces, speak of signifieds in the past and of meanings in the present. The tradition may change each time: meanings are given to it or taken away, it is politicized or depoliticized, it is deflected; the tradition is historical and it functions as a soft, workable literary material.

Gaucho poetry has been such an event in the history of our culture that it has brought us to where we are, to the death of Borges, to repeat and to choose one intonation or fragment or another to signify that we are Argentine, and also to reflect on political literature and on the politics of literature. Moreover, it has convinced us that the only possible sanction of a literary work is absolute popularity, its fusion with spoken language, its unconscious quotation in conversation. Gaucho literature gave us two intonations: the challenge of violent language and of war, and the lament over despoliation, injustice, and inequality before the law. But in the genre there is no separation between the poetic and the political or any category of realism: this appears afterward and it may be that it has retroactively transformed the reading of the genre. In *Martín Fierro*, challenge, war, tears, and laments are all together, alternating and linking themselves into a specific syntax. Both intonations are political, both become representations of the people, and both come to signify Argentineness. History dismembers them, reformulates and transforms them, and the lament, the loss and social complaint that always precedes a political decision (to desert, to confront, to go into exile, to resist), becomes reduced in the Carriego of Borges against Boedo to individual piety through the misfortune of the other, of the little seamstress and the maiden aunt: *it becomes femi-*

nized, depoliticized, and quotidianized. And because Borges knows that in order to write Argentine literature in this moment it is necessary to work with its signs, with the signs of the classic tradition, he chooses the other intonation and the other representation: the challenge, Ascasubi's fiesta-war and card game, Eduardo Gutiérrez's novels, and Cruz's gesture when he cuts the strings of the guitar and kills the singer: all of this is in *Evaristo Carriego*—against the politics of the lament, against Carriego, and against his own present. And if tears are founded in domesticity, the challenge and war take on the representation of counterdomesticity, of the other life in which Borges places literature. *With Borges the separation of the classic intonations is completed; from now on they appear as enemies, as two enemy aesthetics.*

Now the other half of Carriego, in the other half of Palermo, may appear, and on the subject of *La canción del barrio* Borges writes about gauchos, little brothers, milongas, and *trucos*.[44] In Carriego's "El casamiento" and "El velorio," Borges encounters his material, which is "the intonation of the talkative lower class." The milonga is one of the great conversations of Buenos Aires, the fistfight the other, and death provides the wake, a general space of conversation that doesn't shut its door to anyone. This is the fundamental gesture of Borges's criticism and possibly the foundation of his literature. The material of Argentine literature may be found in certain spoken moments of the culture of those who don't have a literature: in the *heard moments* that escape daily life and cut time and space: in the fistfight and its conversation composed of challenges, in which the idiom is suddenly, strikingly Other, in the rhythm of war and the spoken fiesta of the milonga, in the narrations of duels and retaliations that the poor tell among themselves, and in the inscriptions that they put on their carts. These speeches outside of language take men out of their daily life and make it unreal, so that it can return to its happiness and plenitude: they are the functional equivalents of the book.

In Borges, therefore, it is not that truth may be found in crude men or in elemental lives. *Rather, it's their heard stories,* and the transformations in the language that they effect, that occupy the hours outside the life of a culture without literature—without institutions or realism. There is no opposition between literature and life but rather between various modes

44. [A creole card game. *Trans.*]

of literature and language and various ways of life. This is what Borges takes from the Palermo of Carriego, and when he writes it, it is impossible to know if he is speaking of himself or of another writer; of his material or that of the other. The other, bad, Carriego, is conflated with literary institutions; when he writes about this Carriego, that of the shared space, he simply writes: he uses him to make his own literature. Carriego's creole half helps him write the texts that accompany, complement, and form the book of criticism: the texts of Palermo, the fistfight, the inscriptions on carts.

And now, the alliance. If Palermo and Carriego's literature are places of mixing, Borges's Palermo and literature are constructed from Carriego's good half, that of the conversationalists and challenges, and the other half of Borges, the English books. The literary material is, for Borges, a mixture that produces collision and confrontation. And when he writes about Palermo and arrives at the most wild extreme, at Tierra del Fuego and Juan Muraña, the written language and the quotation of literature in another language rise higher and higher, to Browning. And again in the summary, and again in the prologue of 1950, beside the roughneck, he quotes in German. The literature written in another language is directly invoked, quoted. Carriego and his Palermo invented for Borges *the external space* that he needed in order to form the alliance with the internal library. In 1955, he states it directly, when he no longer needs to fight with social realism for life and for institutions: Carriego uncovered for him what was beyond the library of innumerable English books and beyond the spiked iron grille of his garden. And if half of Carriego is the other life of the Others, the other life of Borges, which he removed from daily life, is in the library, which gives him quotations from other languages. Those outside the life of both of them, which are both outside of the language, of spoken Argentine and its intonations, and outside of the written. The construction of this alliance, which is a collision (because taking something outside of life may in many of Borges's stories be transformed into taking life), is literary material in Borges: language, technique, narrative. And the collision that produces the alliance and the confrontation of two other languages and two other lives leads to the end, to death, to the closing of the figure and of texts.

Borges's book of criticism is a mosaic, with aggregates and fragments: a nonorganic book. This and the attack on institutions, the impulse to search for literature where it is not called literature, the definition of the literary as what is outside of life, the mixture of high and popular literature are the historical marks of the vanguard and of Borges's longing for modernity. In the confrontation with Carriego, with piety and realism, in the confrontation of registers, in the telling of confrontations and violences, Borges found his own literary intonation. This is the Borges who wrote *Evaristo Carriego* at the age of thirty to separate the intonations of the gaucho tradition. Thirty or forty years after his passage through Carriego, others would pass through Borges to read and write in confrontation and violence; they would politicize and recuperate his challenges in order to direct them, once again, against the pious representation of the daily life of the people.

Borges before the Law

The construction of a language-law equation: this could be the most general, universal definition of literature. In literature, this equation becomes clear, precise, visible, in the relation between literature and the people. In literature for the people, and in the literature of the people. In the former the construction is evident because the literature recounts it. Literature for the people would be that which uses, as a theme, the form of the most general equation of literature. The operation consists of identifying the law with justice, in reciting the law, and in representing its inexorable triumph in the verbal register or with the intonation of the voice of those to whom it wishes to address itself. Literature for the people *confuses law with justice and translates this fusion into the language of the people,* in the way in which the people tell themselves stories: in the way in which the world is represented.

The literature of the people, for its part, may accept this translated fusion or not. It may appropriate and transform it, and it may also offer it another fusion, contrary as a mirror: then the literature of the people clearly separates justice from law, *identifies justice* with its own voice, register, history, representations (*with its own language*), and hurls this fusion at the law.

Borges would have liked his stories (of confrontations and retaliations, of confessions and spells, of those who await justice and those who administer it to them) to be read as popular literature. He organized many of his fictions around the idea of justice and administered justice in his fictions. He used two literary justices: one below, the oral, national, that of the people's bible of the gaucho tradition; and one higher up, that of the English Bible of the Old Testament God and of retaliation, which is also that of the literary tradition of writing. Sometimes he fused them, as he linked the high literature, whose language is necessary to translate that of orality, with the low, which needs the translation of orality into the written. He fused them in order to direct them against the law. In "The Secret Miracle" God suspends time (imposing his law, eternity) so that the Jewish Christ executed by the Nazis may end his work; in "Death and the Compass" the familiar justice of the delinquent Jew triumphs, and it is simultaneously the infamous justice of the underworld against the justice of the law; in "Emma Zunz" the justice of the Jewish worker triumphs as he avenges his father, alone, in his own law. Moreover, Borges fused the moment in which justice is carried out with the moment of the truth of a subject's fate ("Conjectural Poem," "Death and the Compass," "The South").

In Argentine literature, Borges went backward and downward; to José Hernández, to a few of Carriego's poems and a few of Eduardo Gutiérrez's melodramas. It was the Argentines who inspired him and made him write: they were the places in which Borges felt the language as his own. He read, used, and worried them because their justice lacked respect and obedience. Today it is possible to place him next to Hernández and see how he imposed and imparted his justice to the other, who wrote only about the relation among language, justice, and the law. One in each century, they changed literature: Hernández turned the gaucho genre around and ended it, and Borges turned Hernández's La vuelta around and made "The End" to it.

He wrote two stories, one for La ida and one for La vuelta. He was fair. His construction of the language-law equation consisted of taking the key moment of each one and at the same time taking away its key. In "A Biography of Tadeo Isidoro Cruz (1829–1874)" (The Aleph, 1949), he used Martín Fierro's encounter with the army and Cruz's desertion. It is necessary to go further back and further down to read his gesture and place it on top of that of Hernández.

The gaucho's confrontation with the army forms part of a major story, that of oral biography. This is a story related to a rural bandit, a deserter, or a vagabond, which was sung in any region with large landed estates that was going through a period of transition and modernization: southern Italy, Andalusia, Brazil; in Argentine folklore this story is found as a "*relación*" or "*argumento*." It narrates a series of actions in which a gaucho, in this case, is accused of a crime he did not commit or that *according to his code* (that of customary oral justice) *is not a crime,* and confronts the representatives of the law. Oral autobiography is a juridical tale, constituted wholly by the play of the law: its center is the subject who is guilty according to one law, modern, written, and hegemonic, but innocent according to the other, his own. It describes nothing more than the tragedy of a subject between two juridical orders (between two bibles), at the precise point at which if he accepts one he ceases to belong to the other. Obviously, this is a collective biography; it is the fiction of a divided society, prior to the political and juridical unification of the state, and also after it, when the codes that collided keep stirring up one's consciousness. But what made oral biography an exemplary story in Argentine literature (and culture) is that its meaning changes according to whether it is written as biography or written (and sung) as autobiography. According to the code (the language and the law) that is chosen, the voice comes from outside (from above) or from below and from inside the subject. The writing of this life is divided into its use as biography by Sarmiento and its use as autobiography by Mansilla and Hernández. The biographical use served to attack the subject and make him an example of criminal barbarousness (as a delinquent); the autobiographical use served to defend the subject and attack the political enemies of the one who was writing.

When Sarmiento recounts Facundo's childhood and youth, as he himself says, he uses oral testimonials, but these stories repeat a biography constructed after his death, a retroactive biography meant to erect Facundo as a popular hero. From the confrontations with parents and teachers and the murder of the judge who asked him for his papers, to the desertion from the army and the encounter with the military squad (that is, from his confrontation, one by one, with the representatives of the law at each stage of his life), Facundo's entire life prior to his political power did nothing more than repeat the stereotyped schema of oral biography. But the injustice, innocence, and voice of the subject are missing (the two codes are missing: his language and his law), and therefore Facundo seems to be not only a mystery, an enigma, an Other but also a delinquent without a rationale, by nature (by his own nature), by pure barbarian insanity.

Twenty-five years later, Mansilla transcribes (translating his language) or constructs stories told by those who took refuge among the Indians, and his is the opposite gesture: the narrators linger within the linked motifs of confrontation with the law and "misfortune," inevitable for them. Mansilla uses these autobiographies to denounce the arbitrariness of justice and the inequality in which the popular classes, who need to be protected and educated, find themselves. Like Hernández, he uses autobiography to attack institutions: both of them maintain that the gauchos are illegals and rebels because a determinate type of politics and law (that of their enemies) has transformed them into illegals and rebels.

In Martín Fierro's *La ida,* the autobiographies of Fierro and Cruz are violently antijuridical tales (against the law of levies, which is enforced in the countryside; against those without land and not in the city: the law that denies equality before the law and also takes laborers away from the landowners). And they are violently antimilitary tales: induction into the army is what dispossesses Martín Fierro and turns him into a bad gaucho; the army commandant is the one who takes away Cruz's woman and opens his chain of crimes. In both cases, the judge decides arbitrarily, each time in an opposite way: he applies the law of levies to Martín Fierro because he didn't vote (and this was not viewed as a crime by the law), and he condemns Cruz (who was a delinquent fleeing from justice for having killed the commandant's toady and the singer who made fun of him) to confront those who confronted the law of vagrants and levies, that is, "delinquents." Cruz says that the judge said (and he says it *without using his tongue,* in indirect discourse), "He handed me a *placamation* / that said I was brave, / that I was a decent man, / and that right then and there / he was making me a sergeant / so I could be put in charge of people" (ll. 2053–2058). Courage, the supreme value of the oral code (its law for surviving and defending oneself in an implacable world), may be "decency" or "delinquency" according to who is using it. Like the gaucho and his biography, it has two uses. That is why Cruz and Fierro, in the moment of confrontation, the crucial moment of *La ida,* one on one side and the other on the other side, represent the two codes: Fierro is delinquent in the eyes of the written law and courageous in the eyes of his own justice (his law) and the code of his literary language; Cruz is courageous and "decent" according to the code of the judge. The operation consists of making equals confront each other: the agents of one code collide with those of the other in a battle whose frame and context is the community of those who contemplate them (those to whom it is directed), and which is always offered to them as fiction. And, as with courage and biography, the moment has two meanings, two interpretations, and two uses: it is fiction for the people or the fiction of the people according to Cruz's position, according to his identification with the justice of the law of the army, the no-language of the judge, or his identification with Fierro's justice, the justice of his equal: the one who shares his language. When Cruz recognizes Fierro as courageous, he inverts the category of crime (he inverts the judge): "Cruz will have no part / in this crime / of killing a brave man" (ll. 1624–1626).[45] Hernández wrote, and hurled at his political enemies, the most radical text of oral autobiography: it shows the existence of two juridical orders and how one of them, used in a differential way, according to different languages, places the other order outside the law. The law makes delinquents.

Borges took this moment of *La ida* and narrated it as itself, from within, on the side of the justice of autobiography, *but without Cruz's language* and in indirect discourse, as Cruz did with the judge. And he constructed a parallel with another autobiographical moment: Cruz refuses to go to the city, to the place of the written code, and he kills the traitor peon who surrendered to the city, the one who made fun of his refusal to share the code. Afterward, already criminal, he confronts the army and is trapped. The two autobiographical moments, which in Borges's story are the two moments in which Cruz crosses into illegality because he takes on his code, unite and are superimposed on each other *by a word that takes the word away from him:* "He realized (beyond words and even beyond understanding) that the city had nothing to do with him." And at the end: "As Cruz was fighting in the darkness (as his body was fighting in the darkness), he began to understand. He realized that one destiny is no better than the next and that every man must accept the destiny he bears inside himself. He realized that his sergeant's epaulets and uniform were hampering him. He realized his deep-rooted destiny as a wolf, not a gregarious dog; he realized that the other man was he himself. Day began to dawn on the lawless plain: Cruz threw his cap to the ground, cried that he was not going to be a party to [the crime of] killing a brave man, and began to fight

45. [My translation. The Carrino, Carlos, and Mangouni translation did not include the "crime" that Ludmer is discussing. *Trans.*]

against the soldiers, alongside the deserter Martín Fierro" (Borges, *Collected Fictions,* trans. Andrew Hurley (New York: Viking, 1998), 213–214; bracketed material added). This is how Borges's story ends, without Cruz's voice and in indirect discourse, without language (without words, without understanding, only with a body or animal destiny as he fights), but with his law. The void of Cruz's language is covered by Borges's literary language. The other void, that of the rest of the biography, which is biography and not autobiography, is covered by Sarmiento's narrative schema, Sarmiento's code of biographies of decent gauchos. With Sarmiento's code and writing—that is, with Hernández's political enemy in the very moment in which he wrote *La ida*—Borges confronts the autobiography of Hernández.

Borges's biography of Cruz is like Sarmiento's biographies—in its narrative system, in its opposition of city and country, because it omits judges, because it has an epigraph (from Yeats) in English (although it is not translated as Sarmiento's are), and because Cruz's passage through the army civilizes him: when he comes out, he reappears "married or domesticated, the father of a son, the owner of a parcel of land. In 1869 he was made sergeant of the rural police. He had set his past right; at that point in his life, he should have considered himself a happy man, though deep down he wasn't." Here, in the moment of Cruz's entrance into the law, Borges enters to refute Sarmiento and to pass to the side of Hernández: when there exists something profound within Cruz. Cruz, the uselessly civilized gaucho, carries one of Borges's names, Isidoro; the names of his ancestors are distributed among those who command the troops, on the side of Sarmiento.

In "The End" [1944] (*Ficciones,* trans. Anthony Kerrigan [New York: Grove Press, 1962]), Borges confronts Hernández with himself; he confronts *La vuelta* with the logic of *La ida*. There the black who lost the minstrel contest kills the hero Martín Fierro and justice is done once more, this time from below the gaucho. In Hernández's text, in the didactic book of Argentine culture, of modernization and the pact, Martín Fierro enunciates (in an impersonal and almost anonymous language, a language of transition between the gaucho and the judge) the new law of the juridical unification of the state. This implies that the gauchos must abandon their code of justice (but not necessarily their language) in order to integrate themselves into the one universal law. Now justice and law coincide with the language of the gaucho, and that justice is also God's justice. And moreover, Fierro says, "The law is that we have to work" (l. 4649). When the black loses the minstrel contest (because his teacher was a friar and because he didn't know the work of the countryside, which is therefore what is now in play within the law) and reveals that he is the younger brother of the black that Fierro murdered in *La ida,* the challenge is no longer for knowledge, for the competition for knowledge, but rather for the other justice. *It is at this moment that those who are present separate them.* Confrontation was the key moment in *La ida;* the separation of bodies is the key moment in *La vuelta:* differences are now resolved through dialogue, through the word.

In "The End," Borges sets oral and familiar justice against the law once more, and now Martín Fierro is the representative of the law. In opposition to Sarmiento's text, for the masses, in his language, Borges raises *La ida,* the text of confrontation, like a mirror. The other mirror that he constructs reiterates, in an inverted way, the fight between Fierro and the black in *La ida:* in "The End," Martín Fierro marks the black and the black lays him out in a final knife fight. This is an inversion of the place of the language; Borges gives Martín Fierro and the black a voice, because in the dialogue Martín Fierro separates himself from the words of the law, from his own advice, and takes on the ancient justice. He is given a voice so that he can renounce himself and so that justice is carried out with his code and also with his body. Borges describes the black: "His righteous task accomplished, he was nobody. More accurately, he became the [Other]: he had no further mission on earth, but he had killed a man."[46] The literary language of Borges was also specular. The two stories about the classic form a mirror image: in "Biography," Cruz finds his destiny, while in "The End," the black loses his.

Borges gave language to these bodies in a struggle for the final justice. And to do this he had to make another body—that of the one who sees— mute and empty. The storekeeper, Recabarren the Basque, is left speechless and paralyzed in the right arm after the minstrel contest. This is a pure gaze without time, a body without language, voice, or writing; a gaze con-

46. [I have substituted "Other" for Kerrigan's translation, "stranger"; the Spanish reads, "Era el otro. . . ." *Trans.*]

flated with that of the plain: it is the representation of God. And in this word of the mute is the word of the one who writes: "There is an hour of the afternoon when the plain is on the verge of saying something. It never says it, or perhaps it says it infinitely [and] we do not understand it, or perhaps we understand it and it is as untranslatable as music... From his cot, Recabarren saw the end" ("The End," 162). Eternity contemplates the death of the body to whom Borges gave voice and justice. Or, because he gave bodies in struggle a voice and justice, he had to make the representation of God mute: to take away God's tongue and put himself in God's hands. And to represent him in the name—with many r's—of the English Bible of the Jewish God. Within the void of the language of God's law he constructed his literary language. And he also constructed his utopia, which is untranslatable language, the plain's music without a code.

In his stories on the classic, Borges used the schema of the literature of the people, of the confrontation between law and justice, and he removed the tongue of someone and stuck out his tongue at them. In the "Biography," in order to leave them—that is, those he was representing as the people in the decade of the 1940s—with justice and remove their tongue, he gave them the body, a body in war, that understands. A language may be contradicted and robbed, but a body can't. In "The End," to leave the people language, body, and justice, he had to kill the popular hero and remove the language of other bodies, putting into them the law of God, the law of eternity. Inside this verbal void and corporeal fullness he constructed his literature: his particular equation of language and law. He accomplished this whole operation by confronting literature for the people, that is, the literature that constructs the equation identifying justice with law and places this fusion within the people's language. In the decade of the 1940s, his enemy was this literature that translates law as justice. He disagreed with this translation.

A classic is that which can be used as present by many presents: we can't read or use Borges in any other way now. He himself wrote, with his literature, the literary code (the language and the law) with which we read him. What I mean is that for us he was and continues to be literature. When Borges's language-law equation can be worried by another justice, Argentine history and literature will have changed. Then there will be another book, in which the equation of Borges will be what that of Hernández was for Borges, one of his two bibles: "The adventure is composed of an illustrious book; that is, of a book whose material can be everything to everyone (I Corinthians 9:22), because it is capable of almost inexhaustible repetitions, versions, and perversions" ("Biography of Tadeo Isidoro Cruz [1829–1874]").

Chapter Three

In the Inferno's Paradise

The Argentine *Fausto*

A Pastiche of Literary Criticism

I

Argentine literature before the definitive establishment of the state in 1880 (that is, before the autonomization of the political and its constitution as a separate sphere from the cultural and literary space) may be read according to the construction of representations, and therefore according to the positions of subjects, in the following order: (a) Others: Indians-blacks-immigrants-gauchos and their relations with one another; (b) those who command and who know: military officials-politicians-ranchers-priests-doctors and their relations with one another and with Others; and (c) spaces: the desert, the border, the countryside, the interior, the city, exile, Europe: their relations and their various linkages with Others and with those who are competing for power. Outline of representation: the drawing of the map constructs the state every time.

But if one more look were desired (if we wanted to add mass to a set of grids that can make the paths between subordinates, those in power, and the unfolding of spaces excessively flat), the point of departure would be identification and the play of minimum distances between that which is postulated as political and that which is postulated as literary. The political is the already said: the state function of the written as instance of unification, with the integration of some and the exclusion of others, and, moreover, the position that is referential or derived from the written in the political conjuncture, which is always a moment of relation between the sectors that are competing for hegemony. The literary is the specific, ever-changing articulation between language (understood as register and culture) and law (containing not only the idea of justice but also the idea of a general and abstract norm, "rational" and "universal"). This language-law articulation takes the form of a relation among various "irrationalities"-particularisms (passion, enigma, disorder, violence) and the postulated universal values (freedom, progress, justice, unity, civilization). Starting from this relation, from the multiple forms and modes that it can assume, various narrations and textualities are defined, and the place of writers is once again delimited: their work consists in producing an entire lace of different kinds of conjunctions, filiations, exclusions in the interior of the links between specificities and elements of cohesion. The writer, according to the circuits of interlocution in which he is situated, according to the genres he uses, and according to political circumstances, distributes forces in the language and in the map of the state: with the same gesture he undifferentiates politics and literature. Before 1880, cultural and political conflicts are identified with each other: the two are one and this is one of the nuclei of our culture.

In order to divide the gaucho genre into periods according to its internal history (and not according to the political stages to which it linearly refers), a first cut may be postulated—that of the parody of *Fausto,* the first text of the genre that clearly separates literature and politics. It defines the former through exclusion of the latter and introduces a typically modern sequence that may be enunciated in the following way: depoliticization, autonomization of the literary, problematization of the representational constructions of the genre, and an opening of a new debate among writers, or a reformulation of writers' specific functions.

Everything may be synthesized in a cut or a change of location; the cut is the leap produced by the progressive depoliticization of one of the lines of the genre, the stories of the gaucho's visit to the city on the occasion of a political celebration. The change of location is, in reality, a metaphor and a displacement of the section of the newspaper that marks the boundaries of the written: the chronicle of the fiesta is no longer "civic" and political but rather purely cultural, that of a performance at the Colón Theater. *Fausto* depoliticizes the relation between language and law (registers and codes) because it distances itself from the representations of the genre and because the universal laws and conventions are precisely those of representation.

The dialogues and stories of the gaucho's visit to the city may be read as the exact counterpart of the cielitos and moldings celebrating military victory in the countryside: in these the writer "went" to the countryside (to the battle and the ranch) to use the oral register and culture of the gauchos in order to politicize-militarize them and to unite and celebrate. In the visit to the city, the gaucho goes to the political, now civil, festivities and contemplates and uses (with difficulty and sometimes with fear) the culture of the city. The visit thus appears as the necessary complement to the paternalist equilibrium of the alliance, and, at the same time, it is constituted from the start by its secondary, derivative, and, as such, problematic, character.[1]

This line of the genre is, in reality, a treatise on *civil relations* (political, commercial, juridical, cultural) between the city and the country; it constructs and measures these relations and therefore the alliances that transcend war and work, the two spaces of the gaucho's subordination (soldier, peon) that found the genre: his two basic pacts. The history of the dialogues of the visit to the city is the history of representation, and therefore of postulation, of unnecessary relations, strictly festive relations. The chain of the dialogues tells this history, which is also one of the histories of the genre, the most literary one.

The visit lays it bare and says directly that there is no gaucho genre without some type of alliance or contract. In the political logic of the genre each link between characters, words, enunciations, spaces, and actions passes through the strategic categories "ally" or "enemy" and takes the form of the pact and alliance or the form of confrontation and war, respectively. But in the visit to the city a type of contract appears in the middle of the road, where the Other of whom it speaks finds himself *between* the ally and the enemy: it is commercial transaction, the place where money appears, and therefore contains the possibility of a swindle ("story"). In the city, moreover, there exists the danger of being tricked by

---

1. See Amaro Villanueva, *Crítica y pico* (1945; reprint, Buenos Aires: Plus Ultra, 1972), chap. 4, "El ingenioso Hidalgo." Writes Villanueva, "to arrive at the *Relación* is to appreciate how that civil impulse, that spirit of militancy that is the incontrovertible stamp of his earlier creations, declines. Here the reader sees that awakened *revolutionary smile* of old become tarnished and disoriented, by a coarseness no less subtle than that which Heine distinguished in Byron. In the *Relación,* this smile can be seen gradually turning against the very protagonist of the story, who is the gaucho of the Monte Guard and the apparent composer of its most notable cielitos, to the rhythm of the events through which his festive wanderings through the city take place. And this constitutes a strange and unforeseen spiritual conversion of Hidalgo's popular muse, which is not to say a self-betrayal" (167).

   If the founding mechanism of parody is inversion (of spaces, of procedures), the visit to the city, insofar as it inverts the "departure" of the writer for the countryside, may already be read as parody. A story, development, or attrition of forms would not have to be invented; just the secondary in the form of the inversion and its consciousness.

something similar to money, of the same substance: the written word.[2] If the series of dialogues of the gaucho visit to the city is read as a single story, the history of the genre as a history of depoliticization that succeeds in transforming the pact into a story can be clearly seen to appear. The circuit goes from Hidalgo to del Campo: from the political pact of the unity of the city and the countryside, the duty of going to celebrate the motherland on its anniversary, to the pact of the buying and selling of souls between Faust and the devil.

This history, the condition of the modern and autonomous fiction of *Fausto,* locates itself in two series of specific narrative events: in the complications, obstacles, and collisions of the gauchos who participate in commercial agreements and pacts, and in adventures in the city. The series of these two orders of obstacles draws another map, which culminates in *Fausto* and which appears as the most radical critique of the representation of the genre's alliances.

Bartolomé Hidalgo's "Relación de las fiestas mayas" (1822) begins the series. Here a pact is inserted into the interior of an Other, and the story, the tale, is literal. The one who went to the city, Contreras, narrates what he saw of leisure and celebration, the spectacle of the city's culture on the occasion of the political anniversary. He describes this to Chano, who couldn't go because of the wound he got in a knife-fight with a horse-tamer who *did not fulfill the commercial pact.*[3] This accident, the first col-

---

2. In Luis Pérez there is a text without dialogue, "Carta de Lucho Olivares al Editor," in *El Torito de los muchachos—1830* (Buenos Aires: Antonio Zinny Bibliographic Institute, Buenos Aires, 1978) (Olga Fernández Latour de Botas's "Estudio preliminar"). It appears in nos. 7 (p. 26), 9 (p. 35), 11 (p. 43), and 16 (p. 57). It narrates Lucho's visit to the city and his problems with the storekeeper over a confusion about papers (money and political newspapers). The text opens like this: "On the day of San Bartolo / Since the devil's running loose / On the same ground level / I ran into some rolled up trash." Lucho thinks it's money, and he gives it to the storekeeper to pay for his drink, but the storekeeper tells him that they are newspapers, and after a fight, he makes him leave his poncho as payment. Outside, he asks a "schoolboy" from la Recoleta to read them to him, believing that it's the *Torito,* but they are unitarist opposition newspapers from Córdoba. The wrapped up "trash" of the city articulates, identifies, and conflates letter, economy, politics, and obstacles.

3. Bartolomé Hidalgo, "Relación que hace el gaucho Ramón Contreras a Jacinto Chano de todo lo que vio en las fiestas mayas de Buenos Aires, en el año 1822," in *Poetas.* Says Chano, "On the twenty-fourth, Sayavedra / the horse-tamer came to me / to buy some

lision of the series, serves as a justification and excuse for *not having fulfilled a political obligation* by going to celebrate the national pact, the union of the city and the country against the enemies of the revolution. In a moment of crisis, which holds the danger of treason to the revolution, Hidalgo tries to re-create the patriotic fervor that accompanied the first celebrations.[4] Chano was wounded and couldn't fulfill the political pact *because* Sayavedra the tamer didn't fulfill the commercial pact; alcohol had transformed him into an Other, and any Other implies fighting and the danger of breaking the pact. The incident takes place in the country, between equals; it is private, and it is subordinated to the political pact as that which impedes its fulfillment.

Beginning with this figure, the chain in movement and the play of the genre's syntax are reconstituted. History frees the scene from its dependence on the political pact and transfers it to the city; the excuse for not going becomes a motive for going; it is in the city that transactions are accomplished. Through the pressure of the genre's poetics, which can't conceive of a motif that doesn't reproduce the constitutive link between two cultures, selling thus appears as another face of the relation between city and country. The other takes on the mask of the "live one" that intends to cheat: the rich person or gringo only accepts the payment under the threat of the knife. Every transaction is marked by complications and therefore the dangerous weight of the city prevails: it is the very place of the swindle.

There's a double context and a double reference, characteristic of the

---

horses; / I set the price at eighteen rials, / which was to his liking / so not another word was said / and we closed the bargaining / with signs, so the deal was made / with cane liquor and bitter mate." Sayavedra, "with the liquor under his belt," wants to undo the contract and they get into a fight: "He left and I was still steaming, / not feeling the knife-cut so much / as its keeping me from going / to see the May functions: / honoring that day for which / they gave me a gunshot wound / and I will fight until he lies / on the ground, in pieces. / If you were there, Contreras, / tell me what happened" (ll. 15–54).
4. See Halperin-Donghi, *Revolución y guerra*, 182–183: "The festivities of the 25th of May, in early development parallel to the traditional devotional festivities, came to rival the latter in success" (he is talking about 1811 and 1812). Halperin-Donghi points out that the fiestas measured "the political mood of the city toward its leaders through the enthusiasm with which its multitudes celebrated." In those festivities "the city was celebrating itself; drunk on its own glory, the 'immortal' Buenos Aires presented itself as the liberator of a world."

phenomena of the genre: on one hand, in Hidalgo, there is a synthetic scene constituted through a *topos* (commercial contract–violation of the contract) that functions in subordination to the political pact, and on the other hand there is its autonomization and variation, which depend on the contemporary contexts (circumstances) of the writers of the genre and on their ways of constructing the representations-relations. What the series tells, once again, is the process of depoliticizing the representation of the gaucho in the genre; the more the pacts and contracts lose their public character, the more important and autonomous the commercial becomes. Or rather: the commercial occupies the public space that the political leaves vacant. The moments of this chain are marked by the texts of Luis Pérez, Manuel de Araucho, and Estanislao del Campo:[5] in *Fausto* one participates in a generalized depoliticization that leaves the commercial and the cultural alone, like autonomous spheres of relation between city and country, incarnated in the two protagonists of the dialogue: La-

5. *Luis Pérez:* in the incomplete dialogue, "Dialogue between Señor Chuche Gestos and Antuco Gramajo, on the subject of the fiestas in celebration of the ascent to power of the illustrious restorer of the Laws, Brigadier General D. Juan Manuel de Rosas, dedicated by its author to S. E." (1835), in Rivera, *La primitiva literatura gauchesca*, 173. Chuche says that he couldn't go to the city because he fell off his horse and "his shoulders hurt" (the accident is literal, unconnected to an economic contract). The other tells how the prolonging of Rosas's command was celebrated with the pinnacle of public power. In Pérez, the political visit preserves and repeats Hidalgo's tradition.

Manuel de Araucho: in "Dialogue between Two Gauchos, Trejo and Lucero" (1835), in ibid., 163, Lucero says: "Where was I? In the town / where they almost wore me out, / friend, the devil's running loose. / I went to see an old money-bags / who owed me a hundred grullos / for a part of some cattle / because he had a slaughterhouse. . . ." The man doesn't want to pay him because "the price has gone down"; "I don't have a cent" (he told me) / "because I'm broke" . . . / "I put my hand on my knife, / telling him, 'thief, / fork over the dough, son of an itch, / or I'll cut out your guano.'"

Estanislao del Campo: in *Fausto* (Tiscornia, *Poetas gauchescas*), Laguna says: "It's been about a week / since I went down to the city, / because I needed / to see if I could sell some wool; / but they come at me with tomorrow, / and there's no money, and come back later: / just today I almost hit / —in the forehead, with the coil of a whip— / a gringo, who may be a liar, / but I already spoiled his game" (ll. 111–120).

Notice, too, the transformation of the Other, who tries to break the pact: from Sayavedra the horse-tamer, to the "old money-bags," and finally to the "gringo."

guna and his sale of *wool* with its obstacles, and Pollo and his eventful visit to the theater where he attends the representation of another pact, the sale of the *soul.*

And as the function of the gaucho changes, the function of the writer changes: this correlation is the basis of the genre.

The constitutive alliance of the genre postulates a multiple *us.* On one hand it alludes to the two sectors, the city and the country, which together confront the political and military enemy: this is the strict *us* of the political alliance. But at the same time, insofar as the verbal register is solely that of the country, this *us* refers to "those who speak this way" confronting a literate or city *them* (and moreover, and on the other hand to "those who sing and write": the poets of the two cultures who unite the modulations of their registers). And the verbal and cultural alliance, *which only the genre accomplishes,* is constituted by the union of the body of a popular oral enunciation, intonation, and register with an enunciated and a body of written, learned, political, and juridical ideas. When the gaucho goes to the city, he encounters those who speak in another way, or rather, he encounters the enunciated of the letter, the other culture. In Hidalgo, Contreras tells Chano how the fireworks riddled his poncho full of holes, how he climbed the soaped-up tree trunk and "threw it into the inferno,"[6] how he lost his money in the game, how he couldn't see the plays, once because he was tired and another time because a vase was blazing and he fled in fear of fire. But these obstacles, always subordinate to and alternating with the political festivities, linked with the tradition of the rustic in the city, with the possible production of laughter in the listener (reader), with the fact that the gaucho, when he is alone, always narrates suffering and difficulty, are transformed once again, according to the degree of depoliticization, and accentuate the cultural difference. The "fires" that bother Contreras proliferate, the difficulties multiply, and in Ascasubi the incarnation of the astute townsperson, the doctor, appears. Fires and doctors are linked with the inferno, the devil, and the possibility of being cheated in pacts and lawsuits; the conclusion is the identification among

6. See lines 14, 38, 161, 193, and 215, in which the nuclei "inferno" and "devil" are reiterated.

city-doctors-story-devil, that is, *city, inferno, letter, law.*[7] For the one who
writes, the attack on doctors implies the correlative exaltation of military

7. In Ascasubi's first dialogue from Uruguay, "Jacinto Amores, Uruguayan gaucho, on
the coast of Queguay, telling his countryman Simón Peñalva a complete version of the
civic festivities put on in Montevideo in July 1833 to celebrate the anniversary of the
swearing in of the Uruguayan Constitution," Simón says: "But, friend, who got you into
/ playing games with the city? / Don't you know that the city folk / could confuse / the
proudest gaucho?" (Ascasubi, *Paulino Lucero,* 27, 31, and 39).

In this dialogue, obstacles proliferate (he lost the game, he fought with the storekeeper, he fell off his horse, women insulted him), and, as in Hidalgo's "Relación," a social map of the city, that is, of those who share the power, is drawn. Compare Hidalgo's
description with Ascasubi's. In *Hidalgo:* "Later on the soldiery / went on into the plaza /
and from the fort to the church, / the whole stretch got occupied. / The goverment came
out at eleven, / with an escort on horseback, / with honchos and commandants /and a lot
of other guests, / doctors, scribers, / justices on the other side, / behind all the officials /
the brass snaking around; / the soldiery made way / and they all went on / till they got to
the church" (ll. 130–144). In *Ascasubi* it's clothing (or appearance) that is foregrounded:
"And the soldiery? Ah, what a thing! / I was enchanted / seeing them so decked out / shining in formation, / when the musicking / suddenly resounded, / while from the church /
the goverment appeared / with all the officials / leaving the function. / What well-
trimmed uniforms! / what colored plumes! / what curved swords and knives / radiant like
the sun! / Then mingled with the military men / a dark herd came out, / dressed in great-
coats / and a sight of fancy crests; / because they wore their pants only to the ankle; / and
a rapier and a cane, / and shoes with buckles, / and a big bowler hat... / the singular outfit
/ this whole pack uses / —mayers and scribers, / and doctors, all of them / for the regu-
lar: / people, friend, who can / make intrigue / and suck out the heart / of the devil himself, if he takes a fancy / to put himself to litigating."

Each degradation of learned people is accompanied by a correlative exaltation of the
military (see Halperin-Donghi, *Revolución y guerra;* he writes that in revolutionary festivities, military glory is exalted into the first term: "The political utilization of military
prestige presupposes the existence of a consensus of opinion recognizing this prestige as
eminent over political and administrative talents" (212; see also 222). Ascasubi does not
recognize—he does not represent—the gaucho's other relations, only those that pass
through militarization. In this dialogue, Jacinto is detained at the entrance of the theater
because he wears a poncho, and it is a military official who allows him to enter: "Then a
don Chutipea / dressed as a military man, / accepted my explanations, / and waved me
in, / even with only my poncho... / Now there's a liberal man!" The alliance between the
military man and the "good gaucho" is the fundamental nucleus of Ascasubi's texts: "Between a gaucho and a city man / there's no inequality / when the former is honorable /
and knows how to behave" (*Paulino Lucero,* 39). In Ascasubi, the depoliticization of popular culture, its exclusive militarization, and the division of gauchos into good and bad
constitute the nucleus of oligarchic populism.

officials or landowners, as occurs in Ascasubi and Pérez respectively; the dialogue of the visit to the city may depoliticize the gaucho (may depoliticize the representation of the alliance with the gaucho), but it always politicizes the voice of the writer as a representative of one of the opposing sectors. If the visit to the city is, like all narration, the crossing of a border, the gaucho's entry into the other world implies his depoliticization and the clear politicization of the other party to the pact, the writers. The latter thus confront each other as *representatives* of one of the groups in power who are fighting for hegemony, or, as in *Fausto*, as *makers of representations,* that is, they are *without representation* and about it, speaking of themselves.

What Hidalgo links up in one way (the commercial pact and its drawbacks, the collisions in the city, everything subordinate to the political pact, the foundation of meaning) undergoes a process of disintegration and autonomization of spheres; the scenario of the city makes this separation possible. Between the political festivities in the plaza and the gathering at the Colón Theater, this process is synthesized. There are two opposing places of public life (and of newspapers): the popular space par excellence, in which the two cultures mix, and the exclusive space of the literate culture and the city: the place in which European culture is represented.[8]

II

In short, *Fausto* is constituted through the exclusion of the political. It definitively transforms the political fiesta into something purely cultural and thus changes the representation of the system of relations between the

8. The visit to the city ends with iconography: there is an illustration in the almanac *Alpargatas* from May 1946, drawn by Luis Medrano. It is entitled "A Week in May," and three creoles with bulging eyes, rich (darker faces, mustaches, boots, and cravats), are walking guided by a "bright" little boy who carries their suitcases, to the "Confidence" Hotel. Beyond the cupola of the congress, and in the Avenida de Mayo appear other, clearer faces. I know no better representation of the gaucho tradition of dialogues of visits to the city: the representation of the men's childlike position (it is a child who guides and cheats them), their domination by ignorance of the code. The irony of the name of the hotel, in the foreground, directs the scene and anticipates the complication. It is possible that the decade of the 1940s includes the end of the gaucho tradition.

gaucho and the city, and, therefore, the link and the alliance of the two cultures in the genre. The effects of this depoliticization are multiple: the text is autonomized and its relation with circumstances, context, and the set of the system of references is transformed. For the first time, a gaucho poem appears, disconnected from journalism and purely "literary," which cuts the genre into two parts: *Fausto* is not only a necessary avatar of *Martín Fierro*'s history and a consequence of its logic but also one of the founding conditions of the other text.

The first effect of depoliticization is the mutation of the event and, simultaneously, of the relation between the frame and what is narrated. The genre constituted itself through the institution of a specific type of relation between the enunciative frame (the mise-en-scène of the speaker, his register and the situation in which he finds himself: popular and familiar orality) and the enunciated-narrated (the political event and cultured ideas translated into gauchesque orality). In *Fausto* the gaucho friends do not meet in the country (there is no visit from one to another); rather, they converge in an intermediate place that is between city and country— El Bajo, between the two cultures. The space from which the text is enunciated, and the space of the subject of the writing, is placed in this between, in the neutral. And what is told is not a political or military event or a visit to the city for a civic fiesta but rather another type of dated and circumstantial "news": a stage performance at the Colón Theater. The gaucho enunciator and the modality of the enunciated are preserved: the event actually occurred and is "true" (and the text may be read as a journalistic cultural note on that which occurred, but in another part of the newspaper and the public space). But that which occurred—and this is the second transformation of the statute of the event—is not, for the narrator, merely the event of the performance, but also *that which the performance represents:* a fantastic story. In this double transformation of the event (from politicocultural to artistic-cultural and from a performance to that which it represents as having happened) the text arises.

The relation between the occurrence of the event and its statute of truth passes through beliefs. El Pollo, the narrator of the opera "just as it occurred," *believes because he sees:* he has witnessed the appearance of the devil in person. This is a story of appearances, hard to believe but certain. The gaucho believes because he sees, because he believes in the real existence of the devil, and because he lacks the category of representation and the convention of verisimilitude. From the beginning, art and superstition appear linked by belief: "religious" belief and "artistic" belief unfold their relations of substitution. And the modern contract between seeing and believing (the "rational" contract that challenged beliefs, asserting that only what is seen is real and true) supports these relations. Gauchos believe in simulacra (theater and devil) because they see them: the two cultures now embrace in their stories and beliefs. And another circle emerges from this one: that of belief in what is said, since Pollo *narrates* what he saw to Laguna. Laguna believes, with some vacillations at the beginning ("do you realize what you're telling me?"), but Pollo resorts to consensus: "half the city saw it." Laguna believes because he too believes in apparitions, but also because Pollo, the old man telling the story, is an authority and has called on the objectivity of his vision.

The links between superstition (religion), art, and now politics may be explored in the stories of *Fausto*. In the constitution of the liberal pact as consensus the important thing is *to know how to make them believe it*. To persuade, to convince, to cause to believe: therein appears the meaning of the gaucho genre in one of its directions, toward the rural masses. To represent the patriotic gaucho in such a way that he is persuaded to join the army against the coercion of the levy. The genre before *Fausto* is manifestly a producer of political and military consensus. But the knowledge of how to make somebody believe something may also be used to trick or to make a story. And in *Fausto*, which only speaks of knowing, seeing, and telling, beliefs pass through the artistic category of representation. *Fausto* produces not only a displacement of public space but also a change in the place of the discourse of truth in the gaucho genre.

The encounter of the two gauchos is narrated in turn by a voice that is sustained by irony: the inverse of Pollo, for whom everything seen is true and real, this first narrator divides "see" and "believe" with the help of another excision of truth, between "be" and "seem." He uses the topoi of the earlier genre (the encounter between gauchos, greetings, sublime references to horses, the offering of drinks) as a spectacle and says, "what a good rider the young man is! Lord! / I *believe* there's none better" (ll. 7–8); "Ah, creole! he *appeared* / stuck to the animal" (ll. 11–12); "what luck that *he believed himself* / to be more than just an animal" (ll. 15–16); "Wow!... *it seemed to me,* / even his bolas were made of silver!" (ll. 29–30); "their two souls *almost* / melted into one" (ll. 63–64) (emphasis mine). He relies on subjectivity (appearance is what makes someone believe), while Pollo relies on objectivity and on others. This is an ironic narrator: he refers to the enunciateds of the genre but at the same time invites unbelief, or rather, a belief that is like the belief in a fiction or representation through the suspension of disbelief. He tells of the encounter of the friends that opens the gauchesque dialogues of visits to the city as if he read or saw a simulacrum or representation with unreal gauchos. He reads from within the Colón Theater. If Pollo narrates the representation as something that occurred in reality (thus generating an excision in the event, to which is applied a different gaze and verbal register from those that frame it), the first narrator, through an ironic modality, separates the cultured gaze from the verbal register—he separates the eye from language—and he splits himself between what he sees (or what it seems to him that he sees) and what he believes. He divides enunciation from what is enunciated: what the former says is contrary to what the latter says. As a result, the encounter between the gauchos appears just as fictitious and theatrical as the opera. The learned and poetic reading of the genre resumes within irony as antiphrasis and duplication of the word of the other (just as in Pollo's narrative the popular reading of representation resumes): this has to do with a representative fiction, a convention, that is unable to pass as reality (and this above all is what Hernández will say about *Fausto* in the letter-prologue to *La ida*). But irony produces ambiguity and paradox, and at times it is undetermined and capable of generating a double-bind. For its recipients there is a literal or ironic (antiphrastic) decodification, and this is what has occurred in the commentaries citing del Campo's errors and his lack of knowledge of the country.[9]

9. The critical judgments on *Fausto* in the moment of its appearance clearly show that it was Hernández, in the letter-prologue of *La ida*, who introduced the debate and changed the readings. Both José Mármol and Juan Carlos Gómez see that what del Campo made is a mixture; Gómez writes, "In this importation of the legend of the Middle Ages, in this nationalization of the metaphysical poem" (these judges encounter each other in Villanueva, "Juicios críticos sobre *Fausto* de Estanislao del Campo," in *Crítica y pico,* 201). And Ricardo Gutiérrez laments that in order to understand the text completely it would be necessary to be familiar with Goethe's text and with "the sublime score of the French genius" (217). [the musical score of Gounod's opera "Faust"—*trans.*]. Carlos Guido y Spano speaks of parody directly: "His parody is full of grace and humor, of novelty and

The text therefore operates on the two poles of the genre and the two cultures: each part sustained by a narrator is told from the modality, the mode of representation and the belief that corresponds to the other culture. Each part, and each narrator, is based on a type of text and a type of literary and cultural convention and tradition, and the common trait or

---

freshness" and criticizes urban society as full of an artificial finery that has resulted from adopting exotic customs (219).

No one questions the verisimilitude of the text, no one speaks of a joke at the gaucho's expense, and no one makes a political critique. All this changes with Hernández, who directly confronts, from within the genre, the representation of the gaucho in *Fausto:* "Perhaps my task would have been easier and more successful if I had merely tried to make readers laugh at the expense of the gaucho's ignorance, as has been endorsed by prior practice in this genre of composition." And later, "Moreover, my friend, I hope that you will judge my work with benevolence, even if only because Martín Fierro doesn't go to the city to tell his comrades what he saw and marvelled at on some May 25th or other such occasion. Some of these references, as in the Fausto and other works, certainly have much merit, but Fierro tells instead of his work, his trials and misfortunes, and the unforeseen catastrophes in his gaucho life, and you are not ignorant of the fact that this task is more difficult than many imagine" (J. Hernández, prologue of *La ida*).

From then on the commonplace that "Fausto makes fun of the gaucho" has been repeated, appearing especially in Leopoldo Lugones and in Ezequiel Martínez Estrada. Lugones writes, "His well-known composition is a parody, *sui generis,* transitory and low. It undertook to laugh at itself and at the expense of a certain impossible gaucho, who comments on a transcendental opera whose plot is a philosophical poem. Indeed, there is nothing more preposterous than that invention. Not only would a gaucho not have understood a word of the opera, nor managed to stand it without falling asleep or leaving, such music being atrocious to him; it is also inconceivable that it would occur to a gaucho on his own to enter a lyric theater" (*El Payador*, chap. 7, in *Obras en prosa* [Madrid: Aguilar, 1962]). Evidently, Lugones reads according to the rules of realistic verisimilitude and not according to those of parody, despite having recognized parody when he saw it. Martínez Estrada writes (*Muerte y transfiguración de* Martín Fierro, 1:294), "Del Campo ridicules the gaucho, making him describe and interpret what he saw in the city—that is Hidalgo's game—." Further on, he presents the other commonplace, "the picturesque": "Del Campo insisted on an execution similar to that of Hidalgo's dialogues, accentuating the picturesque in the ignorance of the gaucho, but without the political intention of his precursor."

As for del Campo's lack of knowledge of the countryside and its customs, all the commonplaces (on the "piebald horse" and the gauchos' embrace, among others) originate with Rafael Hernández (*Pehuajó: Nomenclatura de las calles* [Intendencia Municipal de Pehuajó, Secretaría de Cultura, Educación y Difusión, 1967]). In his discussion of del

point from which the alliance may be constructed is that both, to put it plainly, are half-breeds: the gaucho genre, the writing of the oral, made from the embrace of popular and learned culture, and the opera, a learned text in an oral version, a song based on the written, oralized literature based on a cultured text that is constructed in turn from a popular oral legend (del Campo would have worked from the written libretto, just as Hidalgo based his "Relación" on the journalistic chronicle, which appeared in *El Argos,* no. 39, the first Saturday in June 1822, which narrates the events of the civic fiestas of May, 1822).

Campo, Rafael Hernández says (after conflating the one who's going to sell wool with the one who's going to the theater, Laguna with Pollo) that the piebald horse is "tame, *gallops like a dog,* and is suitable for women to ride" (48). About the lines, "Able to carry a colt / And to rein him in at the moon," he says that a bit, and not reins, are placed on colts, and that "reining a horse belongs not to the creole horseman but to the rabid gringo" (49). Finally, of the friends who embrace: "Who ever saw two gauchos embrace? —Not even when they dance" (49).

For Borges the meaning doesn't come from particulars or circumstances but rather from universal values: "More important than the coat of the much-maligned *piebald horse,* who is not permitted to be a racehorse, and than a few comparisons that lack verisimilitude, is the splendid spectacle of friendship that *Fausto* proposes. What is valuable is the happy and open friendship that the dialogue of the peons reveals" (in *El Martín Fierro* [Buenos Aires: Columba, 1953], 17).

Only E. Anderson Imbert (*Análisis de* Fausto [Buenos Aires: Centro Editor de América Latina, 1968]) leaves these readings aside and extends the irony to the fact that "the bourgeois of Buenos Aires who attended the premiere of *Fausto* at the Colón Theater fancied themselves quite European, but they were as backward with respect to Paris as the gauchos were with respect to the Colón Theater" (29). He speaks as well of the "simulated earnestness of the gauchos" and the "artistic lie," and analyzes the forms of the text. He also writes, "To exalt the *Martín Fierro,* the injustice of lowering the *Fausto* has been committed" (47).

For Eduardo Romano, a parody does not imply an intention of ridiculing the gaucho (*Sobre poesía popular argentina* [Buenos Aires: Centro Editor de América Latina, 1983], 25), and for Leónidas Lamborghini ("El gauchesco como arte bufo" in *Tiempo Argentino,* June 23, 1985) the text parodies the opera more than anything else, creating the "demolition of the [European] Model," the "Authority-Model." Lamborghini reads the entire gaucho genre as parodic and comic, as making fun of the system and the civilizing project. He reads it from within the resistance.

[There is also an unintentional play on words here, which Ludmer takes advantage of: the name of del Campo, whose knowledge of the countryside is being questioned, means, "of the countryside." *Trans.*]

The first effect of the depoliticization then consists of the transformation of the event, the frames and the narrators, and in the filling of the narration with two types of story whose modes of representation and readings are constitutive of the two cultures, in a ringlet that braids them: these crossed beliefs sustain the text. Art appears as an equivalent of popular superstition; the genre as a fictional construction and a spectacle; the consensus is artistic.

In *Fausto*'s internal debate over the genre's law of verisimilitude, the artistic codes, and their readings, parody also means that *these forms are impossible.* Here *Fausto* effectively closes the genre's line of visits to the city, and possibly also the set of the theatrical and operatic ("El gauchesco como arte bufo") gauchesque dialogues. (The parody had already been prepared by the "written" frames, the parts and letters of Pérez's and Ascasubi's gauchos, and by the grotesque exaggerations of Aniceto el Gallo.) In *Fausto,* the dialogue between two cultures occurs between the gaucho genre and cultured poetry; the two meet and parody each other. The reading produces laughter through the contact and biassociation of two apparently incompatible models. But the parody is inscribed in a conception of literature as an autonomous system and it plays in the interior of this conception *at reading one sector* (genre, text, convention, register) *from within the other,* opposite and alternative, sector, which appears as its complement in the system. Parody thus represents *a purely cultural conflict,* and its pragmatic strategy stimulates the reader to participate in this conflict: instead of the opposition of two political, economic, and military sectors, here it is two literary spaces that confront each other—the cultured and the popular. This conflict is the same as that of the gaucho in the city, represented in the form of obstacles. In *Fausto,* the confrontation between the two cultural sectors takes the form of parody, an intermediate mode between war and alliance, an ambiguous and double relationship: the transformation of the pact into a story. And, in the parody of the gaucho genre, in the reading of it from within cultured poetry and with its laws, the genre is constituted, in that very moment and also retroactively, as a literary genre.

In other words, parody depoliticizes, or, rather, decontextualizes the genre in its relation to politics, because it questions the referentiality of representation and carries this questioning into the literature itself. And the struggles, alliances, and sectors confronting each other are massively translated into culture, with its two opposing, but at the same time mingled, positions. Each cultural sector contains a theory of the original and a theory of the system: in the aesthetic of the earlier gaucho genre (and also, in part, in that of Hernández), the literary discourse duplicates, reproduces, and refers directly to reality. The texts appear as parts (or as derivatives, as secondary) that must be complemented from outside in order to constitute the heterogeneous totality "sign plus reality" that deserves to be placed in the category of "truth." Literature is a branch of the other, political and original. By contrast, in parody, as in all processes that autonomize literature and exhibit it as an institution, the totality or system is incarnated in the homogeneous relation between discourses (genres, "styles," conventions): the totality is literary, cultural, and semiotic. It is a net of texts in chains of affiliation, a series of alliances-confrontations between writers and between names: Aniceto el Gallo and Anastasio el Pollo. Parody transforms everything that it touches into convention, cuts off referential relations with the world, installs a place from which it is read, and installs the written within a family: parody is the son's aesthetic.

The strongest mark of autonomization is the emergence, in *Fausto,* of a discourse on gauchesque literature in the interior of the genre itself. But this discourse may now only be enunciated from within the other literature, from within the Colón Theater. Through parody, the change in original, contextual closing, and autonomization, the genre literaturizes or aestheticizes itself, within its very subject; not only because it breaks the link with the political chronicle and installs itself in the cultural chronicle but also because it demonstrates, by revealing the conventions, that the genre is pure artifice and that it works in the same way that contemporary cultured poetry does.

In *Fausto,* the genre fictionalizes itself through the parodic inversion of certain *topoi* and the parodic exaggeration of others. The axes of the earlier gaucho genre are belied or shown to be stories: encounters, the theme of the horses, the war, the gaucho's poverty, the tone of the lament. The encounter between friends contains Laguna's story about the horse's faithfulness, which Pollo *doesn't believe* (identifying himself with the first narrator in his ironic division): "One time, during the provisioning, / my brother-in-law passed out; / three days later he recovered / from the insult, and, believe this, friend, / look out what I tell you; / the stallion hadn't even budged" (ll. 85–90). Pollo replies, "—You've done well, gaucho fibber! / Did you know that I didn't expect / a lie that big / to jump out of you, sharecropper?" (ll. 91–94).

Laguna has money, he has won at gambling (in the earlier texts, the gauchos were always cleaned out), and yet he still complains of poverty. Says Pollo, "—With *this war story* / pennies have turned into thugs," and Laguna replies, "—We, the peasants of the earth, / are going to die poor. / I've almost reached the point / of sheer desperation... " But this too is a story that Pollo quickly unmasks: "— Oh, go on with your *lamentation*! Lord!... / You're talking for the sake of talking, sharecropper; / the cow of good fortune / has made you her beloved. / Don't cry, Don Laguna, / don't complain to God on me; / or else, let's compare / my snack with your banquet, / and then straight away we'll see who comes out / the poorer of the two of us" (ll. 131–140). Laguna's complaint as a story is confirmed by the text itself: at the end, he takes out "the bankroll" and pays for both their food. The stories that the "live ones" in the city might tell are, in *Fausto*, the themes and conventions of the tradition of the genre, which the gaucho friends now tell each other, without believing each other.

War, one of the founding conditions of the genre, not only appears here as a story but is also the present reality of Paraguay (Valentín, of the opera, was there, says Pollo, ll. 490–494), but seen and lived in the narrative of the opera—not from the battlefield and the army, but from the city. This inversion of war's perspective and space clearly defines the text in its relation to the genre: in *Fausto,* what happens to those who don't go to war (to women and doctors), to those who remain in the city while soldiers and gauchos fight, will be told.

In *Fausto,* the gaucho recites in his register the nuclei, themes, and forms of contemporary cultured poetry (del Campo was also a cultured poet): love, the woman, the landscape, and time, which appear, when read from within the genre, as antigauchesque,[10] to the degree that they are not

10. From now on, the genre incorporates love and the woman, although with different meanings. In Antonio Lussich's *Los tres gauchos orientales* (1872; reprint, Montevideo: Biblioteca de Marcha, 1972), Centurión elaborates on these topics (ll. 590–669), but Julián stops him, pointing out that this is not the point of the dialogue: "Leave the babes out of it, / This mate's finished already / So save the rest / And tell us something about this

linked with war and political processes. Cultured poetry in *Fausto* introduces a universalizing gesture (another change in location, this time of
universals) that distances the genre from the conjuncture and event of the
moment: it's about some man, love, and woman. In the very constitution
of the genre the learned word imposed the universal dimension in Hidalgo's verses and in the paeans to freedom and equality. The learned word,
general and abstract, may be read in the discussion of the gaucho's integration within the law, and in Ascasubi in the appellations to the freedom
for which the gauchos must fight, against tyranny. That universal word
came from political ideology. Now the universal dimension of the other
side of humanity emerges: the subject, the body, and desire are born; private space is outlined against the public and correlative space of universal
man. The category of universality is contemporaneous with two movements: in the interior of learned culture, with the establishment of subjectivity and the intimate sphere, which literature does not stop working,
and in the popular culture of the emergence of resistance and double
meaning, which questions this universality and particularizes it: this is the
matter of *La ida*. The transfer of political universals to the subject, which
Fausto produces in the genre, leads directly to the song of *La ida:* "a man
who's kept awake / by a heavy sorrow" (ll. 3–4).

   Pollo speaks not only of love and the landscape; in *Fausto*, the *topos* of
the complaint for happy days gone by and the misfortune of the present
time, which in earlier gaucho poems alluded to the political conjuncture,
refers to the biological time of the subject. Pollo is old, and complains
of it: "Isn't that el Pollo [the Chicken]?" says Laguna, and Pollo replies,
"—The Chicken, no; that time is over, / now I'm an old cock, brother, /
with teeth like a fish-hook, / the soil itself is denied me, / to the very last
grain" (ll. 53–60). In the modernization of the genre that *Fausto* introduces from within high culture through the parody of its conventions,
there is a true promotion of the subjective and the individual. This sub-
jectivization is one of the central procedures of the distancing from the
social context and of the break with the political conjuncture.[11] In other

---

peace!" (ll. 762–765). In *La ida,* love has a different meaning: it appears in the negative
(the loss of the woman) as one more aspect of gaucho oppression.

11. See Predrag Matvejevitch, *Pour une poétique de l'évenement* (Paris: 10/18, Union
générale d'Editions, 1979), 96.

words, universalization of the private and autonomization are almost synonymous; to universalize is to make literature significant outside of the
space in which it emerges and, at the same time, to produce a meaning that
distances the interpreters from its space. For the first time, the voice of the
gaucho, which, through the opera, speaks of a cultural tradition that begins with *carpe diem,* is heard as the voice of man.

To the depoliticization of representation, the autonomization, the parody
of the genre's conventions and the revealing of them as fictions, and to
the universalization of the subject, del Campo adds a fundamental gesture: his donation of the taxes collected from the sale of *Fausto,* printed as
a pamphlet, to the military hospitals that tended the wounded from the
Paraguayan war. Here are the political conjuncture, the war, and the gaucho soldiers, foundations of the genre. This is another displacement of
space, this time to a space outside the text. The gesture is outside of *Fausto,*
in another public space, but within the genre, and it serves to redefine the
genre, insofar as it situates the excluded and fictionalized in another zone,
confirms the break, and gives it another frame (a text is not a miniature of
the genre; the genre occupies the common interior and exterior space of
many texts). The exclusion of the founding data and conditions of the
genre appears again as text and gesture in *La ida,* together with and accompanying it: the learned voice and modernizing politics, present at all
times in *Fausto* but absent from the words of Fierro and Cruz (or included
in order to reject and negate them) make themselves felt in "El camino
trasandino." Del Campo and Hernández, in identical and inverse gestures, confirm the lack in their poems of the genre's traditions: they confirm that they are changing the genre, reorganizing its space, and that they
are excluding from the texts what they put into the genre, but outside, at
the same time.

Fausto creates an innovation in the construction of the frame of gaucho
dialogues. Prior texts open with the "direct" voice of the gaucho and close
with the voice of the one who writes the dialogue and who also sometimes
speaks it; thus they constitute a half-breed frame, half "oral," half "written," that reproduces the alliance. But now the frame (and the dashes that
introduce the voices, replacing the names of characters) belong completely to the order of writing; the same narrator who "witnessed" the

meeting between the friends also closes the text. This is a homogeneous, closed frame that contains another frame within itself, that of the second, "oral" narrator. The transformation of the frame, the installation of a double frame (the underlining of that which for some constitutes the very property of art), and the change in the system of references simultaneously affect two levels in *Fausto:* each culture contemplates itself from within the other, and the parodic effects of the mutual readings produce transformations in the genre (the separation from the political context, literary autonomy) and also in cultured poetry, which Argentinizes a European *corpus* and opens a line that clearly continues in Borges and Macedonio Fernández. But moreover, and more important, the frame produces a formal autonomy: the text, isolated by the frame of the other thing that isn't it, turns on itself, refers to itself, and generates internal division, specular relations, paradoxes, and effects of self-engenderment. It opens the reading of the series autonomy-frame-self-referentiality-fiction-doubles-isomorphisms.

The repetitions, doubles, symmetries, and parallelisms underscore the internal duplication, in such a way that, in each of the cultural spaces, the themes and forms of the other are encountered:

– The gringo's intention to cheat ("tell a story to") Laguna (in the commercial pact, the sale of wool). Laguna doesn't let himself be tricked: "I've already spoiled his game" (l. 120).

– Faust's pact with the devil (a "story") (the sale of the soul). Says Laguna, "—Wasn't he a learned doctor? / How did he let himself be cheated?" (ll. 319–320).

– Pollo's lament over poverty and old age.

– Faust's lament over old age and love.

– The ornaments (jewels) of Laguna's horse.

– The doctor and the devil's gift of jewels to Margarita.

– The two gauchos mingle their souls in an embrace.

– Faust sells his soul to the devil.

– The theft of Pollo's knife at the theater. Says Laguna, "Some gringo like a light / it must of been for the nail / —And how could I not have noticed! / So I

– Valentín puts the saber in front of the devil: "I presented him / with the cross of the hilt" (ll. 555–556).

made the sign of the cross"
(ll. 233–236).

– Pollo goes to the paradise of the Colón Theater (with its 100 steps).	– Margarita dies and goes to paradise.
– The gauchos knew, and Laguna "served with," Fausto Aguilar, the colonel "of the other band" (ll. 256–264) who is also "in heaven" (l. 265).	– The devil "serves" Doctor Faust: "I'm here at your command, / count on me as your servant," the devil tells the doctor, who is half "stupefied" (ll. 313–316).

These reiterations and correspondences between the situation of enunciation and what is narrated (the opera) establish a series of identifications: gringo with devil (both tell "stories" and steal; they are also linked through the cross of the knife/spade); gaucho with doctor (this is a negative identification: Laguna doesn't let himself be tricked and the doctor does); gaucho with Faust (in this case Pollo: both lament old age); gaucho with devil (both serve their respective Fausts); bejewelled horse with woman (Margarita); gaucho with woman (Pollo and Margarita, the "good ones," go to paradise, where the military Fausto is already). The identifications are linked with symmetries, synonyms, repetitions, and parallelisms[12] to constitute a closed discourse, which can be heard to say: with symbolic consciousness. Self-referentiality is the common element of the symbolic systems, and it appears in the text in the form of isomorphisms ("the same thing" on different levels: a part reproduces the whole, one level reproduces another level: to be, to make, and to say are the same), and in the form of effects of self-engenderment and doubles.

It is apparent that what has been defined as "specifically literary" is no more than an avatar of the closure-autonomization of the written and of a

12. The specular symmetry of the *décima*, a verse form, may also be included (abbaa / ccddc), as well as the use of homonyms, which is connected with the figure of the double. There is also a whole aesthetic of hues (pink, ruddy, sea, Laguna [lake], etc.), and the play of signifiers and their almost generative relationship: Mar-garita, mar [sea], mañana [tomorrow] [III, ll. 433], and the woman-flower (Margarita [daisy]). Some of these aspects are lucidly analyzed in Noemí Susana García and Jorge Panesi's "Estudio preliminar" in the edition of *Fausto* published by Colihue (Buenos Aires: 1981).

place of reading. And self-referentiality also produces the typical paradoxes that make the relation of the symbolic system to truth and meaning
indeterminate and create dispersion. In order to resolve the paradoxes it
becomes necessary to pass to another, verbal or narrative, level; but if the
text is in play precisely in the oscillation between two (narrators, situations, spaces, Fausts, cultures, paradises) or four, two's duplication, and
then ends the game, the indeterminacy installs itself and produces fiction
with two of its basic traits: a transcendence of truth-falsehood and an
identification between saying and doing (or between the constative and
the realizative). In a circle typical of these systems, the doubles, isomorphisms, and self-engenderments represent in turn the fictional and indeterminate character of the text. Again, the paradoxes and deferrals *exclude
all authority,* each superior level or instance that can resolve them in terms
of meaning and truth. In *Fausto,* the referential directions function at the
same time (they are superimposed) and on a double level. In the first place
there's the reference to the opera, which is already a representation. In the
second place there are the crossed references of each culture to the other,
with the use of parody and with irony, that is, with a schism (also indeterminate) between enunciated and enunciation, with a double word and an
oscillation around belief. In the third place are self-referentiality and closure, which produce self-engenderments, doubles, paradoxes, and recur-
sivity; this self-referentiality seems to constitute a hierarchical system (it
is not flat, like the idea of obverse/reverse), but the new level, rather than
resolving the paradoxes of the first, reiterates or inverts them: the chains
may proliferate in series that close themselves at their starting point. In
Fausto, the story functions as an element of scansion and of textual
organization:

> "with the story of the war" (l. 121)
> "the story which I offered him" (l. 284)
> "Do you know that you're telling me a story?" (l. 362)
> "And now the story is told." (l. 1258)

The story appears in both cultures, in the enunciated and the enunciation, in the narrators and the narrated:

– The first narrator and his story: "it would be believed"
  – the story Laguna tells Pollo (about the horse; he doesn't believe it);

- the story the gringo tells Laguna (which Laguna tells Pollo: it has to do with the economic pact regarding wool; Laguna doesn't believe it).

- The second narrator (Pollo to Laguna: he believes that the opera really happened)
  - the story the devil tells Faust (the pact of the soul; he believes it);
  - the story Faust tells Margarita (trickery, seduction; she believes it).

A narrator tells a story (in the gaucho genre) within which another narrator tells another story, which itself contains various stories. The only stories that are believed are the ones connected with superstitions and art: these are the true stories. The text explores the difference between "stories" (lies, exaggerations, swindles, tricks) and beliefs in the two cultures, told both literally and ironically, and some encased within others: the frame of the first narrator and his ironic story of the genre includes the stories told by and to Laguna (about the horse and about the gringo's money), which the gauchos, Pollo and Laguna respectively, do not believe; the frame of the second narrator, Pollo, and his ironic story of the opera from within the genre, includes the stories the devil tells Faust and Faust tells Margarita, which everyone believes.

This is how the mutation of the genre through the transformation of the pact into the story is accomplished.

In the construction of the military alliance, the earlier gaucho genre represented the rural masses' antagonism toward the enemies of the motherland and freedom, and the masses' subordination to the figure of the one who commands. It integrated the gaucho's culture and oral tone with the other reason; it connected with its most visible elements of aggression (or that which was thought to be popular aggression) and directed them against the enemy: it used the gaucho's language as a weapon. In the construction of the political alliance, the earlier genre also represented the figure and register of the gaucho as a critique of the enemy in the form of a lament over injustice. The center of many gaucho dialogues is occupied by the juridical code, the liberal law (and its reciter, the one who knows) that must be inculcated in the gauchos: it used the gaucho's language as law. Politicization and integration into the law are identified, forming a political and juridical unification in the map of the state.

But the depoliticization and fictionalization of the representations of the genre's alliances that *Fausto* accomplishes, closing the history of the dialogues of the visit to the city, carry a series of consequences. The most immediate of these is the appearance of a zone of oral culture with no political function or possible use: beliefs, stories, and gazes. And, correlatively, the appearance of another function of the writers of the genre: the function is no longer the construction of alliances and the recitation of the law but rather the search for another way of making believe and for true stories. Evidently, the functions function reciprocally.

To depoliticize the juridical code and to exclude it are the same in *Fausto*. And if the juridical code ceases to be in force:

a) The artistic code of credible representations occupies the totality of the text and sets up a space absent of either allies or enemies of the gaucho: absent of compulsion or reprisals. A code, with fiction and parody, in which it is possible to kill without blame, and also a fluctuation of meaning that excludes all authority or tribunal that might stabilize it.

b) The text is expanded into a multiplicity of codes, rules, and pacts: narrative pacts and codes, treaties of buying and selling, rules of the game, pacts of service. *Fausto* tells the story of the play of the plurality of the play of laws when the Law has fallen.

c) The first level of the text, that of the scene, is occupied by the lawyer Faust and his perverse pact, which is legal and illegal at the same time.

d) And *for the first time in the gaucho genre,* a popular code of customary justice, opposed and confronted by the learned law, can appear. Justice for its own sake, vengeance, and the protection and solidarity of equals arise; that is to say, *another justice, another alliance, another consensus:* "When a man offends you, / quick, without looking back, / you slip out the knife and snick! snack! / you stab him twice. / And when the authorities / send out their squad, / you're off on your piebald / drinking the winds. / None of them can unseat you, / because he'd come to misfortune, / and you're the guest of honor / at any ranch you come to" (ll. 921–932).

In other words, the elements of popular culture that are not integrated into alliances, that learned culture has no use for, establish another gaze, legality, and consensus that particularize the dominant legality. And therefore, in an ambiguous or double way, as in parody, the two cultures now confront each other as two particularisms or specificities and no longer as center and periphery. Two parallel and relative spaces raise the two symmetrical pillars that hold up the text.

The fundamental cut that *Fausto* produces in the gaucho tradition is the attack on the two sectors that constituted the founding alliance of the genre's representations: the doctor (the one who knows and the master of the law) is cheated in a pact by someone more astute, the devil; the devil also kills Margarita's brother, the military man.

In Araucho's and Ascasubi's dialogues, the devil is linked with the city (the place of the fiesta, disorder, and cheating), and in Ascasubi's dialogues, moreover, doctors can "suck out the heart / of the devil himself, if he takes a fancy / to put himself to litigating." In del Campo, according to the parodic procedure of generalized inversion, it is the devil who cheats the doctor and appears as the most astute of them all.

Autonomy and self-referentiality produce duplications, identifications, and equivalences. *There are two Fausts:* the *doctor* of the opera and the *colonel* of the other band: "He's a doctor, you say? He's a colonel / of the other band, my friend; / I know that creole / because I *served* with him," says Laguna (ll. 257–260). And Pollo says, "Forget the one who's in heaven, / because it's another Faust I'm talking about; / there can be two burros of the same color, my friend" (ll. 265–267). This equivalence (an identification that is at the same time an opposition) is reinforced because both Fausts have people who serve them (*militare* means not only to fight but also to serve): gaucho soldiers for one Faust and the devil for the other: "My dear doctor, please don't be scared of me, / for I come to *serve* you; / ask whatever there is to ask for / and order me to do as you please" (ll. 317–320). The gauchos are linked to the devil through the parallelism of the two pacts of servitude. And the narrative of the opera shows that the devil (the gauchos?) undermines the power of the one who knows and commands. In the generalized duplication, another military official appears (there are two Fausts and two military officials), Margarita's brother, "the good-looking captain / who was going to Paraguay" (ll. 491–492), who, rather than dying on the battlefield, is killed by the devil on his own ground, that of the struggle. The devil thus vanquishes each in his own field: he vanquishes the doctor by transforming himself into a lawyer in the text, in a legal contract or pact: "And if he bumped into this lawyer / with the shoe-tree for his own shoe?" (ll. 395–396).

There are also two devils. The first appears in Laguna's story about the gambling, in which he won: "first I won his bridle / with reins and halter, / and in a few more games / the man lost everything that wasn't attached to him. / And you know what he said / when he saw he was in trouble? / The one who's skinned me alive / must have witchcraft. / *In short, they thought / the Devil and I...* " (ll. 145–155). And this prompts Pollo's intervention: he saw the devil in person. The one who gambles thinks the devil's helping Laguna, that Laguna has an *alliance* with him; *the devil, then, can be an ally,* a beneficent force. But Pollo immediately introduces his negative meaning[13] as an enemy. The devil is an ambiguous, double-sided character, ally and enemy, who has the same relationship with the doctor that anyone who enters into an unequal pact, a pact of servitude, may have: he can help and attack. And what Pollo witnesses in the city, in his scene, and tells Laguna with relish on the bay, is how the devil, sent by European culture, makes the doctors of the city ridiculous, like idiots who believe every story they hear. The devil is to the doctor as the doctor is to the gauchos.

At the same time, the gaucho's narrative tells how the doctor, taking advantage of the military official's absence due to the war (the doctor as master of the city and the law, with no opposition), *allies himself with the devil in order to trick the military official's sister.* While the one who knows and the one who commands, represented by the voice of the writers of the genre, are visiting the countryside in order to propose alliances with the gauchos, the gaucho in the city witnesses the spectacle of their struggle: in reality, *they fight among themselves,* each one with his servants. And in this dispute the writer, who is now devising the construction of believable representations (how to tell stories) and the Argentinization of European cul-

---

13. See Jacques Le Goff, "Cultura clerical y tradiciones folclóricas en la civilización merovingia," in *Niveles de cultura y grupos sociales* (Mexico City: Siglo Veintiuno, 1977). He contrasts the ambiguous and equivocal character of folkloric culture (beliefs in forces that are good and bad at the same time, the use of a "double-edged cultural instrument") with the rationalism of the other culture, which separates good and evil, true and false, into polar opposites.

ture, distances himself like the gaucho, placing himself in the fluctuation, in the in-between: in the tracing of superimpositions of the two cultures and the two literary languages.

Ambivalence invades the text and the double game never ends: military officials, devils, gauchos, good ones/bad ones, allies/enemies. Because meaning responds not only to words but also to actions: a burlesque judgment of the genre in a poem that has been read as a joke at the gaucho's expense. The narrative of the opera presents a symbolic vengeance, and popular symbolism may function as aggression, vengeance, and death if it remains veiled and ambivalent,[14] ambiguous enough to be able to attack doctors and military officials and to exalt and kill them at the same time. The seam is now the gaucho who—in alliance with the devil?—laughs at the genre, at the doctor of the story. The gaucho in the city has encountered the letter once again, this time in the form of a performance-representation, whose telling or duplication undoes the genre and at the same time definitively integrates it into literature.

A text without alliances, in which gauchos can speak without reprisals. This also occurs in "Gobierno gaucho," the other del Campo poem in which the gaucho, transformed into an Other by alcohol, takes power and commands and legislates against the levy, against the land-grabbers, against the commandant, the judge, the country storekeeper, *the work papers.*

14. On the elements of resistance in popular culture, see especially Michel de Certeau, *L'invention du quotidien,* vol. 1 *Arts de faire* (Paris: 10/18, Union générale d'Editions, 1980), chap. 2 and 3. And especially Darnton, *The Great Cat Massacre.* In analyzing the episode of the "Cat Massacre," Darnton writes that the one who is weak but tricky transforms the oppressor into an idiot and releases laughter. "Tricks" allow the poor to gain a marginal advantage by playing with the vanity and stupidity of their superiors. And, moreover, Darnton writes that popular symbolism disguises the insult so that it has no consequences; it plays with actions and ambiguities that hide its meaning. Popular protests in France, up until the rise of the proletariat at the end of the nineteenth century, had a powerful symbolic dimension.

Chapter Four

Pact and Motherland

The Trickery of Hernández's Professor's *Curandera*

The Book of the Pact

La vuelta, the text of the state (the very institution of the genre, its theorem and condition), distributes voices, words, and stories in a precise way. It represents juridical and political unification in the fiesta of the encounter, and at the same time a pact between things known and things said. In the word/voice (of the) "gaucho," to say is to do and to be is to have to be; in *La vuelta,* the play of saying-doing-having-to-be is universalized by knowledge: to know how to say what has to be done. Turning the genre into a thing of the state is identified with the didactic and familial alliance; the gaucho father is the master and he provides the title for the future novel, that of the second master.[1] For the first time, a text of the genre names itself as a book (of national art and industry) and takes the form of the book of the state in the genre.[2]

To know how to say what has to be done.[3] The text of the state is a school and it may be read with the family of words belonging to schools:

1. [Ricardo Güiraldes's *Don Segundo Sombra* (1926): *Don Segundo,* the "second master." *Trans.*]

2. The stories of the motherland tell of encounters, fiestas and sacrifices of bodies, pacts of justices and laws, with a truth value. At each turn of the white and sky blue ribbon, the stories of the motherland of the genre may be encountered: they tell of encounters between gauchos, who make or tell about fiestas and the services or sacrifices of bodies, and who also make or tell about pacts of justices and laws. At the end, in the farewell, there's the truth value. Each story of the genre may be read from within this basic schema.

3. In the use of the voice, *La vuelta* represents the functioning itself of the state; in each moment the work of the representation of and by the state may be read in the representation and position of the word. It is organized according to a hierarchical scale of voices (ways of saying) that coincide with the very hierarchies of reason (the state's reason): the upper margin, at the port, is the learned word of the "liberati," and the lower margin, at the desert, the no-word of the Indians. Between these borders, the institution of knowledge speaks in the word/voice (of the) "gaucho." And this institution, in turn, welcomes all: there are familial, juridical, political, economic, artistic, religious knowledges of saying. The word and the voice pass through classifications, divisions, and autonomizations: to cure by the word, to correct the word, to be converted by a word, to condemn with the word or impose the no-word, to name, judge, promise, confess, translate, bless or curse, bet.

lessons, examples, tasks, mistakes and equivocations, inquiries and tests, presences and absences, grades (good and bad), confessions and penances, prohibitions and impossibilities, warnings and expulsions. And also paradises and hells.

The texts of the pact with the state or of the recitation of the law are second in the genre. They presuppose another, prior, text or time, and another voice and another alliance that were disputed. There is political and juridical unification because earlier there was division and differential law. Martín Fierro exists as the master and hero of knowledge because earlier, in *La ida,* he was the hero of confrontation who challenged the differential law with his own oral law. The texts of the pact with the state are second, and between them and those texts that precede them the diptych of the motherland of the genre, its double façade, is constituted. The prior text remains excluded/included in the margins of the later text; the didactic alliance carries to its borders what it excludes as violence, evil, and threat, and also as sacrifice and loss (these were the two nonvoices of the extremes of Hidalgo's "Nuevo diálogo patriótico": that of the outlaw gauchos and that of the amputee). The pact with the state is constituted on an exclusion and a loss; it also constitutes them as it constitutes itself in order to define its interior space.

The end of the genre's process of institutionalization is read at the end of *La vuelta,* after the transmission of the law of counsels: after the starry sky and the moral conscience. The narrator says in canto XXXIII that Fierro and his sons changed their name. Here the genre stops; this is its border, and the narrator constitutes the before as evil or guilt: "They had no bad intentions / in doing it, I've no doubt; / but the naked truth is, / it always is the case / that if a person changes his name / he's got something guilty to hide" (ll. 4793–4798). They give themselves names, forming the alliance of the secret of the new name, and they expand into the entire space of the motherland in order to expand the new voice.

La vuelta allows the relation between the pact and the motherland to be read. It not only reproduces and prefigures the debates or verbal wars of the motherland as state (one of the first of which is who does the educating) but also, in each state text, reproduces in its interior the signs of the genre's motherland, the prior motherland, in its margins.

The margins of the pact are the borders of the voice and of the gaucho's name, and they appear as uncorrectable in the stories of the minors. Here the genre reiterates its own relation with external space: that of a difference of voice and name toward the lower margin. And in this reiteration the genre constitutes the signs of its internal motherland, which are those of the literature and reading of the future.

Penitence in the Margins: Two Incorrigibles

A National Language Lesson and a Game with Institutions

As we have said, institutions are the place of a border, the point where a process is detained. And they constitute their object at this border. (For example, the institution of meaning would be displaced indefinitely from sign to interpretant if it didn't pause each time for a moment to form signifieds and references: to assign names and titles.) In this margin of space and time, institutions also establish their exclusions. Institutions, which only exist through their representatives and places,

> are the place of the impersonals, the nobodies, who refer to the founders or all-fathers;

> are also the place of a pact or alliance which constitutes them;

> are the place in which a name or title is assigned;

> are the place of beliefs and at the same time they identify themselves with a particular reason, with the law of reason;

> are the place of transmission of this reason: of appointments, commentaries, and readings of testaments and their wars.

External Inclusions

Suddenly, in the exact center of the text of the state, the didactic scene of the correction of the gaucho's voice erupts: a national language lesson.

> *Canto XVI*
>
> When the old man fell ill
> and I saw he was getting worse,
> and he looked as if there wasn't even a hope
> of his getting any better,

I brought a *culandera* along to him
to see if she could make him well.

As soon as she saw him, she said to me,
"This one [can't stand the whipping].
I don't give him much time to go—
he's going to show us something strange,
because there's a Tabernacle
come out under his arm."

As the saying goes, there's always in any herd
one ox with a missing horn...
Sure enough, someone standing by the door
[belted out a shout] straight away,
"*Tabernacle,* indeed! what a [dumb beast]—
a *tubercule,* you mean."

At this interruption
the singer answered right back,
"If you ask me, this is not the time
for outsiders to butt in....
A *tabernacle,* mister,
was what the *culandera* said."

The stranger had another go
and lashed out at him again,
"There goes the second shot you've missed—
I'll see you, and I win hands down—
cu-ran-de-ras is the proper name
for women who make cures."

"Too many fingers in one pie
won't work," the singer replied,
"and I'll tell the busybody
who's stuck his nose in this business
that I didn't think I'd come here
to talk among such [liberati]."

"And if I'm to go on telling you
the story of my guardian,

I'll ask this *Professor* here
to let me stay in my ignorance—
because when you're weaving, you'll always find
another weaver who is better at it."
(Ll. 2439–2480)[4]

This is the final verbal confrontation, the border moment in which words are fought over. If the learned word is imposed, the genre ceases to exist as a space of the word/voice (of the) "gaucho." This is therefore the border of the genre in its historical stage, that which defines it until the constitution of the state. Henceforth, in future genres, the learned word cohabits or is in dialogue with the voice of the gaucho: each register assumes a precise place and returns to trace through contiguity the alliances, and also the wars, between the two cultures. The learned word—"Here!" —separates from itself another, lower, register, which has a lesser code: it generates a verbal, narrative, spatial subalterity or subalternity and continues to travel the chain or ribbon of the genre's motherland. But in this moment of *La vuelta,* the two words/voices confront each other in order to argue over words and ways of saying. The lesser voice of the gaucho must resist correction (rather than giving the perfect example of a complete correction with no forgetting, as in *Don Segundo Sombra*), because without that voice, up until this moment, there would be no genre. The didactic alliance rejected, the lesser resists the state's linguistic unification.

A border of the institution of the genre: the professor is at the border of the door of the country store, which is now the place of the genre, its house. He erupts into the small motherland of the genre and stays at the door, between two public spaces (and between two publics and two opposing aspects of the politicoliterary institution). From this position he challenges the singer to a verbal duel on the subject of the curandera. He challenges from above with "what a [dumb beast]"; he constitutes the speech of the minor as other, evil, guilt, error, ignorance. And between the curandera (mentioned by the minor) and the professor (mentioned by

---

4. [I have made several changes to Ward's translation, indicated in brackets, to highlight certain features of the language of the original that are central to Ludmer's reading. She discusses the metaphorical language of blows and whipping; the hierarchization of the human and animal realms; and the speaker's conflation of "literati" and "liberals" (*liberatos* in the original). *Trans.*]

the narrator), a detachable sequence is constituted, with an opening and a closing, that could contain the entire text of the pact as a border of the genre because it confronts two different knowledges about language. The war for the knowledge of how to say it that is the nucleus of the language law is installed here.

The "ox with a missing horn" or maverick at the door represents the state institution of learned language; the absence of this institution defines the genre. The scene couldn't be more violent, because the representatives of two institutions of saying collide—the institution of the voice of the gaucho and that of the written word. The genre collides with its external space. The professor's word challenges with a nonname ("dumb beast") the voice of the minor and of the curandera he refers to, and it gives birth to the narrator of *La vuelta,* who appears for the first time *in order to mediate with the external space.* This narrator is the nobody representative of the author in the interior of the texts. After this point in the text those from outside are introduced (Picardía and the black, the minors of the minor or those of the other families) and, later, the text closes as itself and as a book: as its own book. Here, in the historical closure, the representative of the minor genre is defined by a violent verbal confrontation with the representative of the law of the language of the linguistic unification of the state. *This is the final resistance to a law on the part of the word/voice (of the) "gaucho."* A team or alliance of three is then constituted to confront this resistance and to return to defining the institution of the genre: a number one greater than in *La ida.* On one side are the voices of the absent, quoted curandera and of the minor and the narrator, who quote; on the other is the voice that challenges and corrects. The alliance between those who quote is not founded only in the voice, the register, but also in that which the text itself is going to constitute in place of the truth: proverbs, or *oral testaments.*[5] This is the system of counsels. The quota-

5. See P. Seitel, "Proverbs: A Social Use of Metaphor," *Genre* 2, no. 2 (1969), on proverbs as an attempt to resolve personal conflicts that arise from social contradictions. See also L. M. Lombardi Satriani and M. Meligrana, "Proverbi Giuridici," in *Diritto egemone e diritto popolare,* part 2, which describes the function of the ancients as repositories of knowledge and of the rhythmic and poetic formula as an instrument of transmission. Above all, see Kenneth Burke, *The Philosophy of Literary Form: Studies in Symbolic Action* (1941; reprint, Berkeley: University of California Press, 1973). In the chapter "Literature as Equipment for Living," Burke develops what he calls a new sociological critique with

tion, repetition, and transmission of knowledge in speech, the words for social relations. "As the saying goes, there's always in any herd . . ." (narrator); "Too many fingers in one pie won't work," "because when you're weaving, you'll always find another weaver who is better at it" (singer). The entire fragment is founded in quotation, repetition, and the impersonality of proverbs (alliance of the singer and the narrator), versus the impersonality of the knowledge of how to speak the language (professor): "*cu-ran-de-ras* is the proper name for women who make cures."

But the minor's alliance to confront the representative of the external space is double. On the one hand, with the narrator, it constitutes the alliance of knowledge in saying (proverbs), and on the other it forms an alliance with another genre or institution of knowledge, that of oral medicine, in the voice of its representative, whom he quotes. And he disputes its voice and name with the professor: the voice-word of the curandera ("tabernacle"), and then the word-name ("culandera"). *The professor and the minor debate the word/voice (of the) "curandera."* And this alliance presents not only the definition of the genre in the voice of a female Other from another genre but also that other genre's war of definitions. This is the self-referential moment of the gaucho genre, which defines itself in the voice of another institution, with which it forms an alliance. And therefore it not only defines itself but also traces its strict border, between two kinds of healing. Curandera and professor: on one side the oral institution of the healing of bodies and on the other the written institution of the cure, correction, or education (these three are synonymous in *La vuelta*) of the language. The genre installs itself precisely between the uses of bodies and the uses of words.

Everything revolves around violence and everything is a blow in the wars and alliances between institutions. Words speak of bodily blows and verbal blows: "This one [can't stand the whipping]" (of the tabernacle) on one hand, and on the other "someone standing by the door / [belted out

---

proverbs as a departure point; like literature, proverbs name typical situations associated with social relations; proverbs may serve as consolation, vengeance, mockery, foresight, exhortation. And at times the same proverb may have different meanings or uses depending on who is formulating it in what situation; in short, proverbs *are strategies for not losing*. Burke suggests extending the analysis of proverbs to include the total field of literature, understood as a great proverbial enunciated.

a shout] straight away," and "The stranger had another go / and lashed out at him again." Moreover, the fragment focuses on two impossible cures. It closes with the minor's final blow to the professor: "I didn't think I'd come here / to talk among such [liberati]." Liberal-literate: this is the genre's politicoliterary blow, flung at the double enemy of the external space. The one who strikes the blow calls bad names and aspires to teaching gauchos how to speak, no less. Moreover, he bets, from the door, that he can win with words: "I'll see you, and I win hands down."

Blows and plays on words, with words, and of words. Gambling constitutes another margin of the text of the state. It is not forbidden in the counsels and it is the center of Picardía's story and of the minstrel contest, the verbal challenge with inquiry and test. The game is the metaphor for politics in *La vuelta* and it serves as an instrument of exclusion from the pact: those who lose (like the black in the minstrel contest) remain outside the alliance of laws and justices regarding work. The minor concedes to the other a victory that is ambiguous, as they all are: "I'll ask this *Professor* here / to let me stay in my ignorance— / because when you're weaving, you'll always find / another weaver who is better at it." Once more he situates the genre at a lower margin, that of the social relation of ignorance, but he does not accept the didactic pact.

Internal Exclusions

Blows of bodies and of voices. The center is Vizcacha's body, the whipping, and his death. The center is Vizcacha's evil, his sickness. In reality, the center is Vizcacha's oral testament, the counsels quoted by the minor that immediately precedes the sequence just discussed. Therefore the center is the heretic of the family institution of the verbal pact, because Vizcacha curses. For the professor, what matters is the misspeaking of the minor and the curandera; for the pact, what matters is Vizcacha's cursing, which defines the enemies of the institution. The minor says, "There, the two of us, we went through / the terrible winter nights. / He was cursing the Eternal Father / and the blessed saints as well, / and screaming out for the Devil / to take him off to Hell" (ll. 2487–2492). He blasphemes against the Father, the center of *La vuelta*'s institution of the master/gift. "I said, it'd be better / if I leave him on his own / with his cursing and blaspheming, / and let him go on that way / until Death comes along / and carries off this heretic" (ll. 2505–2510).

Against the bad saying that the professor hurls from the external space, which defines his higher margin, the text turns around (inverting the word order)[6] and uses cursing as a sign of the antilaw. It thus defines its lower margin of internal exclusions.

Vizcacha has the name of an animal (a hare) and *he steals animals.* He represents the prehuman, the prior, from the point of view of species or reason, and harks back to an archaic state of social organization.[7] His testament is that of a knowledge that imitates the instinctive, irrational knowledge of the animal world. Each piece of advice is inspired by this world and says, do as such-and-so animal does. Below Vizcacha is the nonlanguage or "babble" and the animal "howls" and "roars" of the Indians, the other heretics who have the names of animals, curse, and *steal animals.*

The old man is "one of the old sort / and there aren't many of them left now" (ll. 2167–2168): he precedes the institution of the pact as a universal law. The minor, by contrast, represents another type of anteriority; he is the messenger between the fathers who say testaments wrong and steal. Vizcacha the animal gave him the law wrong with his oral testament, and they also gave him the law of the other, written testament wrong: the judge allied with Vizcacha ("Make friends with the Judge" [l. 2319]) lied to him about the age at which he can inherit *the goods* of the testament of the good aunt, *whom he lost:* "She loved me as if I were her son / with real tender-

---

6. [There are several changes in the normal Spanish word order in the just-quoted passage, including "abandonado lo deje" ("I leave him on his own," but literally, "on his own I leave him") and "hasta que venga la muerte" ("until death comes," but literally, "until comes death"). *Trans.*]

7. The laws of language, names, justice, and work are transgressed in tandem in *La vuelta.* Fierro says of the Indian: "For him, it would be just a game / to spit on a crucifix. / I believe God cursed them, / and this is how I solve the mystery— / it's only Indians, and pigs and cats / who'll spill the blood of their own children" (ll. 733–738). And: "Their witch women instruct them / to poison their weapon-tips; / and as they don't even worship God / nothing holds the Indians back— / the very names they're called by / are of animals and wild beasts" (ll. 589–594). The Indians also receive the scourge of God and are decimated by a plague.

ness, / and she named me as the inheritor / of all her property" (ll. 2117–2120). The judge lied to him in order to *steal* his inheritance. Between the oral testament of the old man's curses and the written testament of the goods of the lost aunt, the margins of the pact come to be traced.

Those excluded from the alliance of the state make alliances among themselves, each with his testament. After Vizcacha's death another testament awaits the minor, that of the widow's husband, with which the priest cures his passion. He first goes to a fortune-teller who makes him curse and "robs" him: who tricks him ("'You must put a curse,' he told me, / 'on everybody that you know...'" [ll. 2805–2806]). And finally he goes to the priest who tells him about the testament of the dead husband: she *swore* that she wouldn't marry again, and if she did, "the two of you would go to hell" (l. 2878). Another institution: the threat of damnation that comes from the institution of matrimony cures his passions. And the father-priest, after having cured him, tells the judge that he is *incorrigible:* "that I was an obstinate hard head / and a delinquent youth, / and they should throw me out of the district / because there was no saving me" (ll. 2887–2890). "Maybe it was through this piece of advice . . . they grabbed me suddenly / and sent me out to the frontier" (ll. 2891–2896). The alliances of the heretics become linked through the minor. Beginning with the loss of his aunt, he passes through the judge, Vizcacha, the fortune-teller, and the priest, returning to the judge and from there to military service on the other frontier.

Institutions are placed in crisis through minors because the only moments that question them are those that show the very center of the institution, that which founds it, in process: before the detention that constitutes the border that constitutes them. Minors journey through them and are the very representatives of the process of the institution, when the difference prior to the unification of the pact still exists. This is why abandoned childhood is the center of the reformist literature of *La vuelta.* The usual material of the genre, the voice and the gauchos' proverbial knowledge, is found in the minor's canto, but here without a civilized law for the gauchos. This is the moment prior to the reason of the counsels, occupied by the lack of reason of those who say the law badly.

This also is the precise moment to question the institution of the genre with the representative of the enemy literary institution in the exterior space, which is that of learned language.

The Body of the Crime

Vizcacha is the most hopeless case.[8] According to the oracular word of the curandera, he has received a definitive blow: the lash of the "tabernacle." The word "tabernacle" cannot be corrected by "tubercule," because it is the scourge of God that takes the place of the word under dispute. "Tabernacle" is *the place* of the Old Testament Ark, that of Jehovah. Vizcacha is punished in body, *in the arm that steals* (and after death, also in the hand: a dog eats it). The justice of the God of the tabernacle is *the justice of retaliation,* which also ruled in the *oral justice* of the gauchos. "Tabernacle" is an *uncorrectable,* untranslatable word. It represents the sacralized justice of a god who castigates heretics: animal names, the theft of animals, or relations between men and animals. If it is replaced by "tubercule," as the professor insists, it will come to the vegetable world, to the pope,[9] to the *representative* of the institution of the other testament, the New one. The archaic word of the curandera's voice supports other beliefs, knowledges, justices. Changing the system of beliefs means breaking down the old apparatus of prohibitions and replacing it with a new one: it means changing the statute of transgression and crime. This transformation, which is that of the pact itself, cannot be effected by a simple translation or correction of language from the voice of the learned word. The

---

8. Vizcacha "educated" the minor through blows, and the minor, in order to return them, *doesn't tell:* "One evening, he came across / a whole lot of broken-down mares. / After he'd got a few of them down / he was busy cutting their manes— / I saw the owner coming, / but I didn't open my mouth" (ll. 2223–2228). The owner hits Vizcacha, but the old man is not cured. He also curses and spits in the barbeque so that no one can eat it: "The one who cured him of that habit / of spitting on the meat / was a mulatto, a deserter, / who went about with him as his friend. / A devil of a one for fighting— / *Barullo* [confusion, disorder] was what they called him" (ll. 2565–2570). The mulatto "aimed a stab of the knife at him / that another man fended off" (ll. 2581–2582). Here the cure comes from below: this is the only mention of a deserter in *La vuelta.* A deserter, a mulatto, with a knife. Here the two old types of gaucho are linked, or the two meanings of "bad gaucho," and an episode is repeated in the text, which is the introduction of a third party in order to avoid direct confrontation. The central function of the didactic text of the pact is that of confronting confrontations.

9. [In Spanish, the word *papa,* when masculine, means "pope"; when feminine, it means "potato." *Trans.*]

new pact doesn't translate the old one; rather, it constitutes another universe *using the same words.*

We have arrived at an uncorrectable voice, which has a double façade (body and space of the law), and at the same time at another impossible correction. "Tabernacle" supports the old gaucho universe and its justice, which must be sacrificed and abandoned: exclusion is what the pact requires. Institutions constitute themselves through a brutal force of cruelty. And in the very place of the sacrifice a sacred sign is erected and the institution is sealed.

The set of relations that allows the correction of the minor to be read could be one of the metaphors for the relation between state and motherland in the genre. The bad testaments and their representatives are included in order to be excluded by their own justice; the testament of goods has been lost. Between the two is the set of events that precede the pact with the real father and his testament.

Who Educates

A Review

Chapter One

One of the specific contexts of the gaucho genre is constituted by a net, that of legalities: on one hand is the so-called delinquent peasant (the "vagrant" gaucho: not a property owner and without fixed work or domicile, the well-known equation dispossessed = delinquent) and on the other hand, the existence of a double system of justice that differentiates between city and country: the law of vagrants and its corollary, the law of levies, reigned above all in the countryside. This duality is connected, in turn, with the existence of a written, state law that in the country confronts the customary, traditional, oral code: the juridical order of rules and prescriptions that founds the peasant community.

The gaucho's "delinquency" is only the effect of a discrepancy between the two juridical orders and between the differential applications of one of these, and it responds to the necessity of use, of laborers for the ranchers and of soldiers for the army.

The revolution and the war begin the practice of the gaucho's demarginalization. The gaucho's use by the army, with coercion, produces a new social sign: the gaucho patriot who fights in the armies of the revolution and gives his voice to the genre in Hidalgo. It's the grand gesture of the sublimation of the delinquent and at the same time the first gesture of division: the gaucho who deserts and falls back into illegality is excluded in Hidalgo, but he appears in various shades in Pérez, Ascasubi, and Hernández. The two meanings of "gaucho" (the legal and the illegal; the "good" and the "bad") become superimposed and divided and form one of the axes that articulate the set of the genre.

The revolution introduces a fundamental fact: the principle of freedom and equality before the law, which gives meaning to the struggle: the writer of the genre (the first, Hidalgo) proclaims these principles and his patriotic word is linked with the voice of the patriotic gaucho. These are the two new protagonists, the ideologue of the revolution and the soldier of the war, those who unite their words in the genre. (The alliance of words and cultures—of the one who "sings" and the one who writes—appears as the first functioning logic of gauchesque poetry.)

But the principle of equality before the law and the integration of the gaucho as a citizen enter into conflict with the differential codes and juridical orders (and even with the very existence of the army). Through and in this conflict or contradiction a figure is introduced into the genre, that of *the one who knows* and educates, who has specific functions. (And beginning with this apparition the genre deploys its other great logic: that of the debate. The gauchesque texts argue among themselves over the representative of knowledge.)

The net of legalities, the chain of uses, and the alliance of words converge in the didactic scene of the genre.

Chapter Two

In Hidalgo's first dialogue, "Interesting Patriotic Dialogue" (1821), the ideologue and the representation of the learned one and his functions appear for the first time with the name of Jacinto Chano, overseer, old man, "book-larned" one, and sage. "Everyone knows / that Chano, the old singer, / is a man of reason / wherever he goes / and that a sentence of his / is like one from Solomon." Contreras tells him this, and also says, "I'm turning over my weapons to you / because you know more than I do." Chano incarnates written, abstract thought, or "reason," and Contreras, direct experience and orality. The dialogue describes a negative situation: the division between provinces, between country and city, the difference between the treatment given to the gaucho and the city dweller, the rich and the poor: *the difference before the law.* Contreras says, "Well, I've always heard tell / that before the law / I'm equal to all men." He continues, "if a gaucho steals some spurs . . . [and] they treat him / as a bandit and bad guy, and send him / with some trouble to a prison / [Then] the law is carried out, / and that makes me happy: / for whatever you do against it, that's what you pay for." But, Chano says, they don't do anything to the "fat cat." The complaint of inequality before the law is followed by the basic idea that stealing is a crime that must be punished: the overseer Chano tells the peon Contreras that stealing is what makes the difference between the good gaucho and the bad. *The sequence,* a didactic-illuminist scene, could be constructed in the following way:

a) The legitimation of the word of the one who knows: he writes, he is just, he is old, and he is an overseer. This function of mediator and superior in the relations of work in the countryside refers to a conjuncture of peace: the war is over. Now the gaucho is needed for another type of obligation, duty, or use.

b) Complaint—*lament*—over injustice and inequality in the application of the law (popular, folkloric—*oral*—theme).

c) Inculcation of the *written law:* no stealing. It must be noted that in the customary code of the gaucho private property does not exist.

d) The difference between the good gaucho, who may be incorporated into the pact of the genre, and the bad is established.

In the sequence, the discourse toward power (no more division and inequality), the discourse of the gaucho and his protest (no more difference before the law), and the discourse toward the gaucho (no more stealing) are connected. This combination among numerous enunciative postures links a "lawless" orality (without land, without writing) with the "legal" (legitimized) place of the word of the one who knows, and it constitutes one of the founding nuclei of the genre and of literature for the people: the recitation of the law or the representation of its inexorable triumph in the verbal register or with the intonation of the voice of those whom it is necessary to inculcate.

Chapter One

One year earlier another voice confronts Hidalgo's position and traces a schema that breaks away from authors and texts and constitutes another of the multiple nuclei and variants of the genre: an alliance with another type of learned one and law; a political alliance of the opposite sign. This alliance is that of the gaucho with the priest, in function of an anti-illuminist sermon: this is how it appears in Fray Francisco de Paula Castañeda's "Romance" of 1820.[10] The text polemicizes against the revolutionary and rationalist learned figure (and against his possible alliance with the rural masses), and with this the figure of the priest emerges in the genre; he seems to represent the learned one in and of the peasant culture with more "naturalness" than Hidalgo's figure because the priest is a traditional intellectual with numerous functions, among them that of mediating between peasant society and the power of the local administration,[11] as may be clearly seen in the minor's canto in *La vuelta*. In Hidalgo there's another kind of mediator—the captain—and the relation is with the nation.

Castañeda's gaucho sings against the city, students, and infidels. And from the outset he reiterates *the two marks* of the genre that are necessary for constituting its register as literary: he says that "a gaucho is the one who sings" and that he is "a patriot." But "if for some reason / the motherland does not accommodate me / it's because of that lack of devotion / that's already becoming a fashion." For the motherland but against the city, the site of the illuminist and Rousseauian ideology: "I already know that in the city / some lazy youths / are mocking piety / disguised as students." Here there is no reference to the unjust law or the differential justice, and the word of the priest is cited by the gaucho: the one who knows is not present with his voice. The debate is over who educates and who can advise the gauchos. And this debate, which is already installed in the texts themselves, is linked with the dispute over the relations between city and

10. In *El despertador Teofilantrópico Místico-político,* no. 6, Buenos Aires, May 28, 1820. The text is reprinted in Rivera, *La primitiva literatura gauchesca.*

11. See Antonio Gramsci, "Para una historia de los intelectuales," in *Los intelectuales y la organización de la cultura* (Buenos Aires: Nueva Visión, 1972).

country, another one of the genre's lines (*and another chapter, chapter Three:* the gaucho's visit to the city to attend the political celebrations of May 25). What Castañeda wants is to transform the gaucho into an "old Christian" ("This philosophy stuff / is not something that comes into my house / because this old Christian / carries the substance in his soul") and submit him to the ideological tutelage of the priest, the father: "to speak of the poor fathers / is another barbarity / since they have such authority / over us: / they must reprimand us, / and also break us in, / and it's for our own good / that they humble us."

Castañeda's text is absolutely pure from the point of view of the genre: it doesn't narrate events and only makes the gaucho "sing" in a position that returns him to his private peasant sphere, far from the military and political spheres: "I respect my priest . . . I fulfill my devotions";[12] among these duties are included the obligations of Easter Week, burying his wife if she dies, and taking care of the flock. The final figure is that of the priests as shepherds and the gauchos as sheep who allow themselves to be quieted. This no longer pertains to the didactic-illuminist scene, with its specific hierarchy, but to a paternalism of another order, with another learning and another law; the romance form opposes that of the dialogue (and, again, the one who knows is absent, cited or evoked through indirect discourse, without a voice) and accords with its traditional tone.

Another priest wrote the first text in gaucho dialogue: Juan Baltazar Maciel, professor of theology in Córdoba and Commissioner of the Holy Office between 1771 and 1787, an erudite man much concerned with education. His text is from 1777: "A Gaucho Sings the Triumphs of the Excellent Viceroy Don Pedro de Cevallos in the Peasant Style," and it opens thus: "Here I begin my song / under these tala trees." But the alternative figure of the one who knows and the debate of the new learned revolutionaries and the traditionals over the education of the masses are only in-

---

12. In Pedro Feliciano Sáenz de Cavia's "Salutación gauchi-zumbona" (1821) (which appeared in the periodical *Las cuatro cosas o el Antifanático*, no. 1, Buenos Aires, March 1821, and is reprinted in Rivera, *La primitiva literatura gauchesca*) there is a direct attack on Castañeda. The text is written in gaucho dialect but in prose, and the narrator is en route to the city, to his patron, a professor "in both laws" who advises him to sell the ranch and become a journalist with two protectors (a politician and a poet), in order to "finish off" Castañeda.

corporated into the genre beginning with Castañeda. This dispute, with various signs, is one of the political marks of Argentine culture.

Chapter Four

La vuelta de Martín Fierro is the great didactic text of Argentine literature: a space of diverse knowledges and masters ("fathers," "aunts"), and of various instructions and counsels (from how to treat Indians and how to cross the desert to how to cheat at gambling or how to pass the night under the stars). God is also a master: "In the holy heights above / lives the master of all / who teaches every animal / to find its own nourishment; / [and he offers food / to every rational being]" (ll. 463–468).[13] But at the same time it is a space of conversion and correction: all the speakers have been in some kind of disciplinary apparatus (exile, prison, army), and they all narrate their past with a final promise of correction. And these scenes and spaces are always constructed on basic binary oppositions: "good" and "bad" counsels and instruction, good and bad fathers and aunts; the text seeks autonomization, equilibrium, and closure.

The culmination of knowledge may be found in the minstrel contest: the duel with knives has been transformed into a verbal duel, and it constitutes a true trial (or test), a requirement of the final class session of counsels to sons. The one who wins is legitimized in his knowledge and may teach. Fierro wins out over the black because the latter doesn't know the tasks of the countryside: *he doesn't know how to say them* and therefore lacks a specific knowledge for the gauchos. Fierro, by contrast, is the popular hero of *La ida* and is now old; he knows because he has suffered and moreover is the father of the ones he educates. (The pluralization toward one's own kind in *La ida,* the fact that, in order to constitute a principle of

---

13. Every didactic program in the interior of the genre, and each figure of the educator, relies on a concrete philosophy: the presence of Rousseau can be detected in Hidalgo, with "Merit is what decides" (in the first dialogue, l. 127). Here in Hernández it's Masonic philosophy, not only through the allusion to the "high master" but also through numerous references—in the 33 cantos (Hernández had reached the highest level in the Obediencia a la ley No. 13 lodge, in 1879), the "pen nib," the Older Son's path of perfection, the symbolism of letters and numbers. See B. Canal-Feijóo, *De las "aguas profundas" en el* Martín Fierro (Buenos Aires: Fondo Nacional de las Artes, 1973), in which the symbols of Masonry in *La vuelta* are analyzed. [Bracketed translation is mine. *Trans.*]

association, Fierro unites with Cruz, his equal, is here replaced by a family plurality: the two generations represent the natural relation of the transference of experience.)

The black loses the minstrel contest because his master was a friar: "and whatever I know, I learned it / because I was taught by a Friar" (ll. 4005– 4006). Here, in the middle of the debate and the test of the minstrel contest, *La vuelta* is connected with the debate of the genre. The other priests of the text also represent the included/excluded: the one who "cures" the Second Son of his love for the widow with his sermon tells the judge to throw the Second Son out of the army; the Witch who steals on the frontier with Picardía is always reading and "studying / to become a friar" (ll. 3755–3756).

But the debate is not only over the alternative Fierro or black (and priesthood or work in the countryside); it also unfolds indefinitely, even into the voice of the final narrator, directed above and outside: "but the gauchos ought to have houses / and a School and a Church and their rights" (ll. 4827–4828). Fierro's exact antithesis is Vizcacha, who gives "an education" (l. 2258) to the Second Son: he is the old gaucho who, degraded, follows the traditional code. His antisocial utilitarianism, the absence of morality in his counsels (empiricism ignores morality),[14] his adaptation of the laws of power, his feigned weakness, and, above all, his cynicism, are marked in the text by a complete negativity. Moreover, in his counsels and in the instructions of the fortune-teller who pretends to cure the minor's love the use of the *vos* appears. *They don't know how to speak.*

And the antitheses of Vizcacha and of Fierro and the black (and the priest) are separated by the frontier episode of the maverick or outsider who interrupts the minor's narrative to correct his diction: it isn't about this kind of education either. In *La vuelta,* then, a series, the most precise and diversified of the genre,[15] appears to close the polemic surrounding

14. See the observations of A. Jolles, *Formes simples* (Paris: Seuil, 1972), 126, on the amorality of popular proverbs as purely empirical enunciations.

15. This diversification of negative and positive masters and the enunciations of the final narrator asking for "a school and a church" announce, in their modernity and in the impersonality of those institutions, the definitive installation of the state and its organization, and they are radically opposed to the concentration of functions, as they appear in Luis Pérez's *Biografía de Rosas.* In this volume Rosas is not only an educator but also a

the question of who educates: two learned ones (the priest and the "liberati") and two oral educators (Vizcacha and Fierro). Observe their disposition: Vizcacha's counsels—maverick or liberati—black or priest—Fierro's counsels.

The minstrel contest not only defines the duel that authorizes Fierro as a master but also contains, *in the black's mouth,* the criticism of inequality in the application of the law: "the law is made for everyone / but it only rules the poor" (ll. 4233–4234), and "the law's like a knife, it doesn't hurt / the one who handles it" (ll. 4245–4246). And, finally, "There are plenty of learned Professors / and I don't doubt they know a lot; / I'm just a poor rough Negro / and don't understand much of this— / but every day I can see their law is like / a funnel, with a big end and a small" (ll. 4253–4258).

In Hidalgo as in Hernández—at the two extremes—the educative scene in the voice of the one who educates follows the complaint over inequality. Fierro's counsels inculcate the law: do not steal, do not kill, do not drink; work, be prudent, be moderate. Fierro clearly establishes what constitutes a crime and establishes the definitive division between legal and illegal ("good" and "bad") gaucho. *The sequence as a form is that which speaks:* the relations of continuity and succession are fundamental in popular literature. All signification plays in the contiguous enunciateds for different publics and the contiguous enunciateds that form a sequence; signification accumulates not in effects of ambiguity but rather in series

---

model of accomplishments in the countryside, honest, Christian, giving advice for founding a ranch and for correcting vices and relieving the unfortunate wretch (assassin): "He is noble and generous, / And with an honest heart, / But when he witnesses treason, / Woe to the one who played with him. / He abhors the thief, / Gives no quarter to the rascal; / But he always looks kindly / On the wretched peasant. / He knows well how to tell / When a man commits a crime; / And if the deed is unpremeditated, / He supports him in a conflict." And further down: "And this is how his luck has been / The making of a bad man / Into a good family man and father / And an honest citizen." As can be seen from these excerpts, Rosas is an outstanding incarnation of the function of the one who educates in the genre, insofar as he establishes the law and differentiates the "good" gaucho from the "bad." But the text also introduces the debate: "Of the *sages* of the Earth / He had no good opinion; / These have surrounded us / With their cursed theories: / And if not, just wait / And you'll see them one day. / These are not good men, / They presume too much. / God willing! I'm mistaken, / and I've got that wrong" (emphasis in original). In Rodriguez Molas, *Luis Pérez y* La Biografía de Rosas *escrita en verso en 1830.*

that mimic syllogisms, enthymemes, conditions, causes, and effects. In the construction and destruction of the nexus among enunciateds (scenes, situations, cantos, words, actions), what is at play is precisely reading: Hernández is the only one who read Hidalgo's sequence in its totality and meaning.[16]

The solution proposed by the genre for ending peasant "delinquency" *and simultaneously (and therefore)* for ending inequality in the application of the law is the inculcation of the "civilized" written law in the gauchos; that is, the abandonment of their traditional code (which doesn't prohibit either stealing or killing in a duel if one has been offended; in *La vuelta* the true criminals are criminals according to both codes: the Indians and Vizcacha kill women or children). In this sense, *La vuelta* would be *La ida*'s complementary text; together they would form, once again, a sequence: from *La ida*'s denunciation of injustice in the application of the law of levies-vagrants to the gauchos (which produces desertion and abandonment of "civilization": the law transforms the good into bad) to *La vuelta*, the didactic text of the enunciation of the law in order to end inequality if the popular code is abandoned. Only from the point of view of this reading are these two complementary texts, enunciated at different political conjunctures. The alliance would then tend toward a double integration: the rural masses pacified under a liberal law, and the power and the state as protector of these masses.

But the efficacy of an educative practice can only be achieved if the one

---

16. Ascasubi did not read Hidalgo's sequence; in *Paulino Lucero* one can find the complaint over difference before the law and the injustices to the gaucho on one hand (in "Diálogo entre Jacinto Amores y Simón Peñalva, describiendo el primero de las fiestas cívicas en Montevideo por la Jura de la Constitución en 1833" [Buenos Aires: Estrada, 1945], 22) and, on the other hand, the figure of the priest, always cited by a gaucho, in "Los misterios del Paraná o la descripción del combate naval de la Vuelta de Obligado" (1845), but the message of the priest is political and partisan rather than legal-didactic: he exhorts abandoning Rosas's cause and paraphrases the *Comercio del Plata*. It's logical that in Ascasubi there are no didactic scenes: as can be seen in *Santos Vega*, which is said to be written by a Cordoban friar, gauchos *are born* good or bad and therefore are ineducable. In this moralizing text (and herein lies the difference between this and didactic-juridical texts) one of the twins is an assassin and a thief and the other an honest worker. A priest also appears here, the adoptive brother of the twins, as do the other representatives of power, but not the protest over injustice and difference before the law.

who educates and his discourse once more create the alliance between the voice and the written word, the first logic of the genre. The voice of the one who educates cannot be external and it cannot represent the Other (the professor, the priest allied with power); rather, it must emerge from the very interior of the popular countryside, and, above all, from a mode that is the form in which traditional knowledge and the experience of resistance to power are enunciated and transmitted: that is, the counsels and proverbs of the old man. It can emerge only in the oral form, which is the form of social wisdom and of the regulation of relations with other men. Fierro's counsels, sayings, and proverbs are at the same time traditional and new, and as such they achieve the transmission of learned law into the heart of the popular code. In the closure of the genre, they install what they define: the verbal conjunction and with it the production of new cultural forms.

The Reading of the Motherland

The folkloricization of the classic and its incorporation into the national culture and language corrected the genre's text of the state's law. The incurable old man, Vizcacha, represented the bad father and his counsels were the old testament of the animal thief, which had to be rejected and sacrificed. Here there is no use of the body for work. At the other extreme, there's the gift of reason that Fierro's counsels constitute, the new testament of the law of work. But the citations, repetitions, and transmissions mixed what had been separated, incorporated what had been excluded: they created a montage between the lower margin of the *vos* and the higher margin of the almost learned language of the lord of the rings. *They constructed another alliance on top of the alliance,* in which "Make friends with the Judge" (l. 2319) (Vizcacha) was connected, for example, with "Brothers should stand by each other" (l. 4691) (Fierro), and "if you're born with a fat belly, / you'll never change by squeezing it in" (ll. 2419–2420), or "cows that change their pasture / are late at calving time" (ll. 2341–2342) (Vizcacha) with "A man must work / in order to earn his bread" (ll. 4655–4656), or "there's no shame in being poor / but there is in being a thief" (ll. 4731–4732) (Fierro).

Here is where the voice of the writer of the genre is erased and those of its readers and listeners are heard: the voice of history, which in its chain of uses, following the very law of the alliance that founded the genre and the motherland, appropriated what it needed, in its very form.

The Word/Voice (of) "Picardía" and the Literature of the Future

Picardía possesses the two uncorrectable features that are necessary for the final chapter of the treatise: he can't say the prayers dictated by his aunts properly (the rascally mulatta tempts him), and he can't correct his name (the bad name cannot be erased). He is the final card of the genre in its historical period and the border of the narrative system of the text of the state, before the minstrel contest and the counsels of Fierro and the narrator. He is the card with the most past in the literature of the "mother of the motherland" [Spain] and with the most future in the literature of the motherland: Picardía is at the margins, on the first page of *Don Segundo Sombra,* thinking about the enigma of his name.

In the new code of names and crimes of Fierro the father's counsels, "picardía" is defined from outside as different, by its lack of discretion: "A man is born with the astuteness / that has to serve him as a guide. / Without it he'd go under; / but in my experience, / in some people it turns to discretion / and in others, dirty tricks" (ll. 4673–4678). *And in others, dirty tricks.* Picardía is the Other of the family of the pact, the third or the minor of the minor: an illegal-legal, an Other by his name. The subjects thus defined cannot assume the generic being that marks them because they would assume the totality of the symbolic system that differentiates them in and through their being. To be Other, to be defined by a lack and to be guilty are one and the same movement. And the movement that constitutes the Other and condemns him through his being in his name also divides him into two parts: Others always have to do with good and bad.

Picardía recounts the final oral biography of the genre. It follows not only the schema of the picaresque but also the schema (which also appears in the picaresque) of autobiographies written at the request of the confessor, such as that of Saint Teresa. The majority of these autobiographies emerge from a conversion that marks the rupture between "the prior man" and "the new man." The final card of Picardía appears in the genre with the representation of the peaceful state and it will reappear, in the future, in the future novel, to signal the state's breaks, reformulations, and historic changes. This is the card of the patriotic gaucho of the state: the avatars of his relation with politics (and with the master or father of the motherland), could also scan the history of the motherland, *from within literature*. To construct the apparatus for measuring "Picardía" is another utopia or future novel.

The Trickery of Inocencia or the Innocence of Picardía?

Picardía says: "I lost my mother before I knew
                  enough to weep for her" (ll. 2945–2946).

And also: "and even though it's to my shame
            there's something I must warn you of—
            as my mother's name was *Inocencia,*
            Picardía was what they called me" (ll. 2961–2964).

Picardía is the son of Cruz, the ally in *La ida,* and of Inocencia, his woman, who now takes this name. In *La vuelta, La ida*'s names undergo the same process that the entire text and genre must undergo: they are institutionalized or transformed into metaphors. In the older brother's canto, Fierro is that which can't be bent (l. 1928) and Cruz is the cross that Fierro put on his desert tomb among the heretics, the cross of the Lord (l. 2049). Picardía is the son of Cruz's Inocencia, or of the innocence of the cross, and also the space of the quotation of *La ida* in *La vuelta.* In *La ida,* Cruz's drama (his woman had relations with the commandant: she had put the army in her house) excludes the mention of the son. Cruz's drama was a double drama, of loss and of knowledge. Only before dying in *La vuelta does Cruz recognize Picardía,* but he has not named him: he didn't know if Picardía was his own *or the Other's.* He leaves him to Fierro as an inheritance: "He entrusted a young son to me / that he'd left back home — / 'He's been left all on his own, / poor boy,' he said to me" (ll. 909–912). "'There were just the two of us in the world / as he's already lost his mother'" (ll. 915–916).

Cruz's Inocencia maintains a double meaning, juridical and political: the gaucho is innocent, not guilty (central thesis of *La ida*), and he's the one who doesn't know (central thesis of *La vuelta*'s didactic literature). These double meanings accumulate and are inverted in Picardía, who has lost his innocence in both meanings of the word, and says so *with shame.*

He is a scoundrel who is ashamed, oscillating between good and bad. His laws are loss and division.

"Trickery" and "shame" are double-sided words, with two opposed meanings, like "gaucho patriot," and they seal the genre's alliances with the condition of the loss of one of these meanings. Note the place of shame in the counsels; it occupies the central sextina (the 16th out of 31), and says:

> A man loses a lot of things
> and sometimes finds them again,
> but it's my duty to inform you,
> and you'll do well to remember it,
> if once your sense of shame gets lost
> it will never again be found. (Ll. 4685–4690)

Therefore, in the 22nd and 23rd sextinas:

> Do your best not to lose
> either time or your [shame];
> as you're men with power to think
> use your judgment when you act—
> and keep in mind that there's no vice
> which ends as it began.

> The carrion bird with its hooked beak
> has a taste for robbery,
> but a man with powers of reason
> will never steal a cent—
> because there's no shame in being poor
> but there is in being a thief. (Ll. 4721–4732)

"Shame" implies two possible subject positions, active and passive. It is the painful feeling of loss of dignity through a fault committed by oneself, or through humiliation or insult suffered from another. A "man of shame" is a man of honor, of courage: the center of the courageous gauchos' code. To lose one's shame, therefore, is to commit the crime of cowardice. But in the new code of the counsels, it is to commit theft. The center of the old law is also the center of the new institution of the genre: the shameless gaucho is delinquent according to both laws. *The same words with a different meaning constitute the place of the alliance with the condition of a mark of loss.*

"Picardía" [trickery] is a word with two meanings, *divided in its interior,* like the voices of the patriot gauchos in the genre's emergence. It oscillates between the definition of the differential law and the name that the genre gave it. It represents both simultaneously and simultaneously does not represent them. It is always a yes-no: the place of political alliance. For the first time in history the genre installs a pure political alliance with the voice of the gaucho: it is not military, economic, juridical, or familial. Or rather, it is semieconomic, semijuridical, and semifamilial.

Because Picardía's law is that of division and loss, his profession is gambling.

The Rules of the Game

Picardía lost his innocence in both senses of the word. And therefore he interweaves all the codes in a vertiginous net of losses and gains because *he gambles with all the political institutions of the genre.* He can say it all: he speaks from a lower margin, he is the son of the Other. The following all meet in his space, in the word/voice (of) "Picardía":

- the gaucho's old code of courage (that of his father Cruz, *who loses* in both senses of the word);
- the differential law of vagrants and levies, *which loses him and makes him win* simultaneously with the story of the rations or divisions;
- the new code of the worker, which is *the promise that wins* for the future: another of the genre's political institutions;
- and also the patriotic law of political freedom and political equality before the law, which defined the genre from its emergence. This law is represented in Picardía by the law of the game *in which he wins* with "resources."

He gambles, then, with the losses and gains of the genre's net of political codes.

In the political game of the vote, Picardía verbally confronts electoral illegality (the fraud or trick of the judge *for winning* the elections) with the laws of the game: freedom and equality. "'I don't care who orders— /

I'll vote for whoever I like. // If it's at a gambling table / or an election stand, / I'm equal with everybody— / I respect those who respect me, / but no one's going to interfere / with my voting paper or my cards" (ll. 3365–3372).

The judge's flatterer tells him: "'Anarchist— / you've got to vote for the list / which the Committee orders you!'" (ll. 3358–3360). And later *the commandant of the army defines anarchism as trickery:*

> "Here's another trouble-maker
> who spends his time at the country store
> making speeches night and day
> and turning people into Anarchists,
> You're going in the contingent—
> that's what you get for that kind of trick." (Ll. 3445–3450)

And after the confrontation the police fall on him, and Picardía does not confront them with Cruz's law of courage: "And though it was all a dirty trick / I decided to give in, / and I didn't resist them, because that day / would have meant the end of me" (ll. 3375–3378).

The particularity of the political game of the codes "in trickery" is that they represent the counterstructure of *La ida* within *La vuelta,* and *also* the counterstructure of *La vuelta*'s state. The canto of Picardía's life includes quotations of the decisive moments of *La ida* (Fierro's not voting and the law of vagrants, which together send him to the border and lose him; Cruz's drama with the commandant and the moment of his desertion to the law of courage, and also the figure of the toady that Fierro and Cruz each killed), but *turned around,* without crimes: with trickery. It also includes in its interior the decisive moments of *La vuelta* (the season in the hell of the border and of exile, and the return with counsels or knowledge), but turned around: with trickery.

In a theatrical sense, Picardía represents the game of the political as counterstructure of the state in the interior of the state of the genre, its included-excluded place. Gambling is the simulacrum and substitute of war in the peaceful state; its goal is the elimination of the adversary, on whom it depends. Picardía evaluates the relations of force (and his counsels consist more than anything else of this) and refers to the positions of the gambler in relation to his adversary. The first hypothesis of the game is that chance does not exist: "Whoever relies on luck / is making a huge mistake" (ll. 3109–3110). Gambling is a *tekne,* an art, and a knowledge: "I know how to do it with art" (l. 3190), and "The one who doesn't know, doesn't win" (l. 3157).[17] Gambling is the desacralizing activity par excellence; its knot resides in the opposition between the game and the sacred.

It is also ambivalent from the beginning. According to Saint Thomas, the two roots and meanings of "game" are *ludus* (training, exercise through combat or study: "The training I'd done was at playing cards, / and gambling was my career" [ll. 3097–3098], and *jocus* (play of words, the gratuitous game par excellence, which Picardía plays, unwillingly, on the praying aunts: "she was a devil, the colored girl, / and it was her who was tempting me so" [ll. 3029–3030], and also, willingly, on the toady). Picardía uses all the meanings of the game to represent politics as a game and the game as politics and to exclude, between losses and wins, the political enemies of Hernández and of the gauchos: praying aunts (this knowledge of how to speak is not the one that educates), gringo cry babies, toadies, country storekeepers, judges and commandants, bad masters. Those who are allied with Picardía in the game are also enemies of the gauchos. He is first allied with the landlord of the inn, the typical commercial bandit of the gaucho's visit to the city. Later, on the border, in the story of the rations (in which Picardía repeats toward a lower level the illegal game or theft of *halves* that he receives from above), he is allied with a delicate friar-in-training who can read: "everyone there detested him / and they called him The Witch" (ll. 3763–3764). And around the fire the gauchos used to say: "What with Picardía and The Witch / the rations are in good hands!" (ll. 3779–3780).

La vuelta systematically disrupts any possible political alliance among the gauchos themselves; hence Picardía's political alliances in order to win. This is also the significance of Cruz's death. Fierro and the captive separate after crossing the desert together; the family itself separates after the pact; the sons form an alliance with only their father, and Picardía's alliances for winning are with nongauchos, with those the gauchos hate. The pair of equals, the emblem of the alliance in *La ida,* is transformed into the pair

---

17. [I have retranslated these four lines to highlight the features of the original that Ludmer's reading draws on. *Trans.*]

of polar opposites (good and bad: Fierro and Vizcacha, with their respective counsels), or, in Picardía's tricks, into good-bad, into negative alliances with those from above (a landlord, a witch: a learned person) for the purpose of stealing from those from below. Only when he gambles alone, and with the political codes of the vote and the renunciation of the code of courage to confront the armed law, does Picardía truly play for Hernández. This is the place of the gaucho patriot in the didactic alliance of the closure of the genre. The *yes, but* (the adversative construction that defines Picardía's name in the counsels) marks the division between that which may be read as the voice of the gaucho and the learned word of Hernández. This is as true in *La ida* as in *La vuelta*. Picardía is entirely a *yes, but*.

These are also the moments in which two political options open: that of above or that of below. The final narrator of *La vuelta* says (with a double adversative), after asking for protection for the gaucho:

> "And some day this accursed mess
> will be brought to an end:
> I don't see it as an easy job,
> because the racket's made worse
> by the people who act like carrion birds
> and stand over the carcass and scream.
>
> *But* God will make it possible
> for these things to be put right—
> *though* it's important to remember,
> to make a good job of it,
> that when a fire's for heating
> it must always come from underneath." (Ll. 4829–4840)

Picardía is the genre's last fiesta; the only place in which challenge and lament have been directly replaced with laughter and tears. And "with trickery": when he laughs the others cry, and vice versa. *And he laughs and cries at the same time.* "With trickery," then, means: with division (good-bad), with losses and wins, with laughter-tears, with yes-no, or with-without. And all this simultaneously: Picardía's card has three faces.

In Picardía's final return (because he is *La ida* in *La vuelta*) the system of the genre forms a knot, *as a counterstructure:* division, good-bad, and the alliance with the master. It contains the whole design of the genre (its logic, and also the logic of the debate) as in a microuniverse, and, *simultaneously,* time with its three faces.

Picardía's Motherland

"Our Province is a mother / who does not look after her sons" (ll. 3715–3716), and "if you don't take care of your countrymen / you're not a true patriot" (ll. 3723–3724).

The genre has made a complete turn in its history, and the gaucho patriot Picardía's motherland of death and shadow is once again (as in Sarmiento and at the same time in the opposite meaning to that of Sarmiento) the small motherland, the natal land, *that has been lost.* Picardía is an exile from work: he first worked with a bad master who beat him, did not give him "even an old blanket or two" (ll. 2969–2970) and moreover made him pay for the lambs that got lost. He therefore deserts and goes to another province: "and I went off towards Santa Fe / with a troupe of acrobats" (ll. 2981–2982). From then on he comes to represent the counterwork or the work of idleness, gambling, and politics.

Picardía loses his natal political motherland, in which he gambled with the universal values of freedom and equality (and therefore this motherland is the mother of the land, death, and shadow), and wins the entire space of the four winds of the father's motherland of the state, with the brotherhood of the counsels as first law.

The Life of the Writers of the Genre and the Future Novel

Picardía could also metaphorically represent the written lives of the writers of the genre. He carries a stain in his birth (the stain of the difference of the motherland), he has passed through exile and the loss of the motherland, he is the son of a traitor and hero, and he enters the master's house as a dependent.

Picardía's two fathers reappear in Ricardo Güiraldes's *Don Segundo Sombra* (1926), the didactic novel of the signs of the genre's motherland. The radical depoliticization of the text inverted the places of the masters and the names of the fathers. The second master or *don segundo* not only gives "Picardía" (the gaucho who flees from the praying aunts and is shameless), with his voice, the knowledge of work and prudence but also the soul and the old law of freedom and courage of the gaucho, *without the differential law.* The novel gives "Picardía" (*but without a name: without a politics*) a heard voice and written word so that he can recount his life with the master before transforming himself into the third master and closing another cycle of the genre. He completely inverts the political meaning of *La vuelta* and recounts an exemplary education of a kind never heard in the genre. His other father, the "true" one, is the boss who leaves him the other inheritance—his name, writing, land deeds—and transforms him into a master with the precondition of his own death or loss. And also with the condition of the loss of the second master with which the other margin of the text is closed: "I left, like the one who bleeds to death." And the voice of the gaucho and learned writing are clearly separated. This is the perfect unique alliance in the same subject (who is moreover the writer himself), divided between the gaucho master and the master of the other testament. The economic, juridical, familial, and didactic alliance of *La vuelta* meets, in the depoliticized signs of the motherland of the second master (a fantasm, a shadow, an idea), its purest expression prior to the first crack in the state in 1930.

The Times of the Genre: The Past of Picardía's Present and the Once and Future Barbarism of the Motherland

The women ("the poor sisters, / the mothers and the wives"), when the gauchos are carried off to the frontier:

> A lot of them went to the Judge
> for him to help them out of this fix.
> He gave them the run-around—and just to show
> how innocent he was,
> he told them, "You must be patient,
> because there's nothing that I can do."

> So there they remained, imploring
> this figure of authority,
> and, after a fair amount
> of talking, the Judge said,
> "I'm washing my feet, like Pilate—
> this is the Commandant's affair." (Ll. 3499–3510)

Index

Josefina Ludmer is Professor of Latin
American Literature in the Department of
Spanish and Portugese at Yale University.

Library of Congress Cataloging-in Publication Data
Ludmer, Josefina.
[El Genero Gauchesco. English]
The gaucho genre : a treatise on the motherland /
Josefina Ludmer; translated by Molly Weigel.
p. cm.   Includes index.
ISBN 0-8223-2830-5 (cloth : alk. paper)
ISBN 0-8223-2844-5 (pbk. : alk. paper)
1. Argentine literature—19th century—History and
criticism. 2. Argentine literature—20th century—History
and criticism. 3. Gauchos in literature. I. Title.
PQ7652 .L813 2002   860.9′352636—dc21   2001007044